THE EVERYTHING® Leadership Book

Dear Reader,

Both of us have worked under, over, and with many people over the years. Some of the external circumstances have been exciting and challenging, and some were routine, but the conditions themselves were never what drove our satisfaction. The most important factor in fulfillment has been working with real leaders—people who had a vision of something worth accomplishing and who wanted to work with others to make it happen.

There are supervisors, bosses, managers, coworkers, and associates aplenty in the world, but few people are leaders. Yet those rare individuals hold the world together. They are the ones who see that life is more than title or self-interest or even casual nihilism. By setting out to support principles that are greater, these people help bring meaning to life and show a way that others can use to take a step into a larger world. This book is for all those who want to become leaders, no matter where they are or what they are doing. We wish you good luck and success in your dream.

Eric Yaverbaum

Erik Sherman

Welcome to the EVERYTHING Series!

These handy, accessible books give you all you need to tackle a difficult project, gain a new hobby, comprehend a fascinating topic, prepare for an exam, or even brush up on something you learned back in school but have since forgotten.

You can choose to read an *Everything*® book from cover to cover or just pick out the information you want from our four useful boxes: e-questions, e-facts, e-alerts, e-ssentials. We give you everything you need to know on the subject, but throw in a lot of fun stuff along the way, too.

We now have more than 400 *Everything*® books in print, spanning such wide-ranging categories as weddings, pregnancy, cooking, music instruction, foreign language, crafts, pets, New Age, and so much more. When you're done reading them all, you can finally say you know *Everything*®!

QUESTIONS?
Answers to
common questions

FACTS
Important snippets
of information

ALERTS!
Urgent
warnings

ESSENTIALS
Quick
handy tips

DIRECTOR OF INNOVATION Paula Munier

EDITORIAL DIRECTOR Laura M. Daly

EXECUTIVE EDITOR, SERIES BOOKS Brielle K. Matson

ASSOCIATE COPY CHIEF Sheila Zwiebel

ACQUISITIONS EDITOR Lisa Laing

DEVELOPMENT EDITOR Elizabeth Kassab

PRODUCTION EDITOR Casey Ebert

Visit the entire Everything® series at *www.everything.com*

THE EVERYTHING®
LEADERSHIP
BOOK
2nd Edition

Motivate and inspire yourself and others to succeed
at home, at work, and in your community

Eric Yaverbaum and Erik Sherman

avon, massachusetts

An Everything® Series Book.
Everything® and everything.com® are registered trademarks of F+W Publications, Inc.

Published by Adams Media, an F+W Publications Company
57 Littlefield Street, Avon, MA 02322 U.S.A.
www.adamsmedia.com

ISBN 10: 1-59869-632-7
ISBN 13: 978-1-59869-632-5

Printed in the United States of America.

J   I   H   G   F   E   D   C   B   A

Library of Congress Cataloging-in-Publication Data
available from the publisher.

This publication is designed to provide accurate and authoritative information with regard to the subject matter covered. It is sold with the understanding that the publisher is not engaged in rendering legal, accounting, or other professional advice. If legal advice or other expert assistance is required, the services of a competent professional person should be sought.

—From a *Declaration of Principles* jointly adopted by a Committee of the American Bar Association and a Committee of Publishers and Associations

Many of the designations used by manufacturers and sellers to distinguish their products are claimed as trademarks. Where those designations appear in this book and Adams Media was aware of a trademark claim, the designations have been printed with initial capital letters.

This book is available at quantity discounts for bulk purchases.
For information, please call 1-800-289-0963.

Dedication

EY: To Harry and Gayle Yaverbaum and Bernie and Noreen Nisker—
your grandchildren and all you have taught me about life are priceless.
And to my best friend since I was a kid myself, my wife Suri.

ES: To my family, who have taught me how little importance
"authority" has and how much "influence" does.

Contents

Acknowledgments

I owe so much to my decade-long association with the Young Presidents Organization and the hundreds of CEOs whose wisdom and friendship has been both enriching and fulfilling. It was all of you who started me on the path to my fascination, education, and interest in leadership around the world.

I have run and led public relations agencies for over two decades. Nonetheless, it has been the CEOs of my many clients, in conjunction with those who have spent quality time with me in writing my previous book on leadership, who have given me a real-world education on what it takes to lead effectively. I am grateful to so many for the honor of being invited into "the C-Suite"—and into their living rooms, their lives, and their minds.

Thanks go to the next generation in my family, who inspire me every day to be the best leader I can be: Cole, Jace, Remy, Logan, Max, Mitchell, Adam, Seth, Jeffrey, Yehoshua, Micha, Nechama, Yisroel, Samuel, Alexandra, Jenna, Brandon, Nadav, Peleg, Gilad, Sebastian, and—forever in my heart and mind—Wiley.

Thanks also go to my most cherished lifelong friends and the most graciously blunt advisors a man could ever have, my sisters Dana and Lori.

—Eric Yaverbaum

Thanks to our editor, Lisa Laing, for her patience during what was a challenging and interesting project.

—Erik Sherman

Top Ten Ways
You Can Be a Leader

1. You can learn to lead, even if you aren't a natural-born leader.

2. Use your personality traits to your advantage to make your leadership more effective.

3. To rally people to your cause, connect them to something greater than themselves as well as to their own sense of meaning.

4. By setting the right types of goals, you and the others working with you can energize your activities and achieve success.

5. Use interactive coaching to help people see their own weaknesses and overcome them.

6. One of the best ways of leading is to let others lead.

7. Change and conflict can be intimidating, but they are the two factors that make possible what you'd like to achieve.

8. You don't have to wait for permission to lead if you learn how to work with others within the organization.

9. Ethics are not just nice to have. They are an essential part of keeping on track with your goals.

10. Leadership is a process of constantly learning what you next need to move ahead.

Introduction

▶ LEADERSHIP IS AN ODD THING. Almost everyone thinks he knows what it is. Unfortunately, we all have suffered from bad examples in history, in mass media, and, most sadly, in everyday life. Yet there are also wonderful examples of leadership throughout time, whether of religious figures who preached their understanding of truth, people who stood up to tyranny at great personal cost, explorers and intellectual luminaries who opened new worlds, or everyday people working hard to ensure that someone would always do what was necessary for the world.

Leadership is a critical topic, particularly during times when too many people are willing to let others undertake the thinking and the doing. If the world is nothing more than a collection of petty self-interests, then it is ultimately a roiling cauldron of chaos. But there are interests that transcend the personal.

The world won't get anywhere without someone leading the way, and that's what this book is about: how you, today, right where you are, can expand your leadership abilities and skills. It doesn't matter in what part of your life you want to accomplish something bigger than yourself. It could be at work, with a volunteer group whose mission you applaud, or even in getting something important done in your city or town. You can be a leader in your family, in your neighborhood, or in your country. If you have the desire, you can start or continue on your journey to leadership.

Because leadership is a path, this book doesn't offer a laundry list of check-it-off points. You won't memorize the rules to leadership.

Memorization can help for a limited time, but when circumstances change, you may find yourself stuck. Instead, you'll concentrate on important areas of knowledge and skill that you can then intelligently apply. If you understand the requirements of leadership, you can apply your efforts to varying circumstances.

You'll start by considering the leadership styles and traits that can help you in your quest. You'll move to establishing a vision, which is probably the most critical part of leadership. Without connecting your efforts and those around you to something greater, things won't go very far. You'll come to grasp the need for motivating others (and yourself), communicating with everyone involved, and driving progress through goal setting. Building a team, coaching those working with you, and learning to keep people interested, involved, and working together are the ways to harness the power of a group.

The book also addresses some specific leadership issues, such as the differences in leadership between corporations and nonprofits, how to best recover from mistakes, and how to lead when you aren't technically in charge of anything. The book closes with a section on ethics; in today's society, we could all stand a reminder of what it means to take a stand for what you believe is right.

All this might sound like as much fun as hitching yourself to a plow and working the back forty acres, but don't worry. Though the topic is serious, you can still have a lot of fun being a leader. There are few things as enjoyable as taking charge to get things done and finding that people listen and work with you. Before you know it, you might be like the guy who was a pretty good trumpet player. He worked his way through high school and college. When a job wasn't quickly forthcoming on graduation, he started his own band while he wanted to find something suitable. Years later he was passing a mirror, took a glace at it, and said, "Good Lord, I'm a trumpet player!" Work hard: The mirror is closer than you think.

CHAPTER 1

Lead On

Deep down, everyone knows that things don't happen by themselves. A world without leaders would be a world without striving, without progress, without achievement—and without much fun. People led the efforts to build the Great Pyramid of Giza and the Taj Mahal, to cross oceans, to find a cure for polio, to cover the Sistine Chapel's ceiling in glorious murals, to create the Boston Symphony Orchestra.

We All Have to Lead

Whenever humanity achieves anything, it is leaders who drive the hard work. Not only do leaders help ensure that all the big things get done, they make sure all the little things happen as well. A skyscraper needs not only architects but workers to take responsibility for cleaning up the work site night after night. A Michelin-rated three-star restaurant has its executive chef and the person charged with washing pots and pans so they are spotless and ready to use again.

Some people yearn to lead millions and accomplish great things. Some have leadership thrust upon them when they are asked to work with others to get a task done at work. But whether eager or unwilling, if the leader is going to be successful, he or she needs to lead at some point.

Born to Leadership?

There is a pervasive myth that all real leaders are natural born: Either you've got it or you don't. Some people, through charisma and a sort of personal magic, are doubtlessly able to get just about anyone to do almost anything. But on its own, that isn't being a leader. Under a selfish person of this sort, nothing substantial gets done, and as history has shown, a great deal of damage can occur.

Some people grow up with the expectation that they are to lead in the future. Members of royalty or family dynasties are examples, but for every strong leader like Queen Elizabeth I, you'll find a Louis XVI, whose profligate ways hastened the French Revolution. Talk about an anti-leader.

Then there are those who spend time learning the ways of power, cultivating their tans and good hair, and who think that being hired to manage a group or company makes them leaders. Sorry, but that is only evidence of good genes, a stylist, and enough time on their hands to sit under a tanning lamp.

Thrust into Leadership

This is the long way of saying that there are numerous misconceptions about leadership. You don't need to exude animal magnetism, come from a storied background, or impeccably follow a list of external characteristics. Leadership is the act of gaining cooperation from people in order to accomplish something. If you can do that, you can lead.

Sure, there are personality traits and talents that can make the work easier. People as naturally charismatic as John F. Kennedy or Ronald Reagan find it easy to get supporters on their sides. Yet others who don't have that automatic command have found themselves capable leaders when they needed or wanted to be.

If you doubt whether some people really do have leadership thrust upon them and aren't looking for glory, consider the Old Testament. Moses had no interest in leading the people of Israel, but circumstances were such that he did. But then again, if you hear the voice of God calling from a burning bush, it's difficult to live your life out in quiet obscurity, pretending that it never happened.

Learning to Lead

If you want to—or need to—lead badly enough, you can learn what you need. If you couldn't, then no book could help. Here are the factors that form the foundation of leadership:

- Something needs to be done.
- No one person can do the task.
- Others are interested in helping get the task done.
- You take responsibility for accomplishing the task.
- You harness the combined efforts for success.

The first two are the circumstances that create the need for leadership. The third and fourth are the ones that let leadership work. It's the fifth—where you actually exercise leadership—that is the subject of this book. You could depend on luck or inherent talent, but the surest way to lead is to learn the necessary skills.

The Leadership Attitude

To understand leadership, let alone exercise it, you need the right attitude. There are a lot of bad examples of what it means to be a leader, and so to some degree everyone grows up with wrong ideas. The only solution is to discover where you might be headed in the wrong direction—because if you're going that way, you can't expect people to follow you to the right one.

Leader, Not Boss

Being a leader is a subtle thing. Because of the way institutions work, many people associate leadership with being in charge. A boss is someone who has authority over others, a power that is granted by a formal relationship within an organization. Supervisors can give orders, and if they lack leadership skills but have some luck, the people in their charge might even listen. Then again, they may not. In reality, it's almost impossible to force most people to do what they don't want to do.

That is why leadership is so powerful and necessary. Those who know how to lead don't force others to help them achieve goals. They persuade, inspire, coax—and motivate. Leaders are successful because those who follow actually want to.

Focus on a Goal

The biggest difference between a leader and a boss is motivation. What the leader wants is to achieve a goal or a set of objectives. Ego is not part of the equation; those who would follow don't feel that they make efforts for someone else's glorification.

By focusing on goals, the leader also makes it possible to track the success of the venture. With a clear agenda, the group can see if it is approaching its goals.

Giving Yourself Permission

For similar reasons, being persuasive, popular, or charismatic isn't the same as being a leader—and a good thing, too. Few people have that sort of animal magnetism, and yet many who don't still want and need the ability to lead, no matter where they find themselves.

When you understand that a leader isn't the same as a boss, you also start to free yourself from a debilitating attitude. When only the boss is allowed to lead, what does every other person in an organization or society do? They wait for something to happen, for the boss to decide. While waiting, they accomplish nothing toward that common goal.

But when you know that anyone at any level can lead, you've given yourself permission. No longer do you have to wait, frustrated and angry that nothing happens. By taking responsibility for a goal, leaders also take charge in their own lives. In the process of helping a group strive toward a common goal, leaders actually do become bosses—of themselves.

Leading at Work

The most obvious place where you might find yourself needing to lead is at work. If you have people who work for you, you need to get them to do their jobs. You might have to get other departments to buy into your plans or talk your boss (everyone has at least one) into accepting your recommendations. That means gaining active cooperation.

Spreading Leadership Around

Leadership can't be relegated to managers, either. Many aren't good leaders, and even the best managers can't oversee all the things that need to be done. If no one below the managerial level is willing to lead, nothing gets done. Small tasks in and of themselves may seem insignificant, but add them up over a long enough period of time, and inattention can turn to financial disaster for the entire company.

ALERT!

Counting on your official authority is dangerous in business. Although you technically can give orders to employees working for you, everyone knows that the same employees can become uncooperative enough to discredit your work and even cost you that position. When working with your peers and superiors, issuing orders isn't possible. To get along in business, you must learn how to lead.

Look at the U.S. steel industry. In the 1960s and 1970s, seemingly every-one at these corporations assumed that times would always be good and that they would never have to buckle down and work hard. The money was too good, and although the work was hard, things were going along as well as they always had.

Well, almost. During that same time, upstart companies—first in Japan, and then throughout the rest of the world—focused on leadership in technology, effort, and business models. The U.S. steel market began to weaken. Steel managers blamed labor, labor blamed the managers, and both blamed that damned foreign competition. A major domestic industry was crushed because it wouldn't take the direction it needed. More simply put, there was no leadership on any level.

Asian Achievement

Contrast that with the Japanese automobile industry. Decades ago, ana-lysts and major industry players considered it a joke. The cars were poorly built and lacked style. So Japanese manufacturers like Toyota decided to make a change. Japanese managers brought over quality-control expert W. Edwards Deming, who taught them new ways to design and build.

FACT

Leadership hasn't made only Japanese firms. Korean conglomerate LG worked hard to crack the U.S. market in appliances and consumer elec-tronics. Success required a concerted effort over fifteen years, with con-tributions from engineering, finance, marketing, and customer service. Now the company has one of the best-recognized brands in this country, all because leadership brought the company together.

Year after year, company leaders pushed to get better at what they did. They inspired workers, who picked up the cause as their own. Then an amazing thing happened: Everyone became a leader. Those who worked on assembly lines would suggest how to do things better where they were. Engineers pushed the boundaries of quality design. Managers listened while setting the overall direction. These days, Japanese companies continue to lead an entire industry in quality, features, and financial success.

There are some remarkable aspects of the ascendancy of the Japanese automobile industry. One is that it was clearly an effort that required leaders at every level. Another is how adaptable the concept of leadership is. Not only did it work in the Japanese home offices and factories, but it worked in every location to which it was exported. Compounding the irony is that some of the leading facilities were established in the United States.

Leading in Society

Leadership may be typically associated with business, but leading is necessary in all parts of life. Nonprofit organizations offer a broad view of the various needs for leadership. Each nonprofit has a mission, and that means people have to lead to reach the goals.

Social Leading Everywhere

Beyond the realm of nonprofits, there is a whole world of schools and parent-teacher organizations, neighborhood associations, social clubs, religious and civic groups, or support groups. Each one exists for a reason—to further a cause, promote the welfare of certain people, or see to the needs of a church or synagogue. To support those underlying purposes, any organization has a host of tasks that must be done, from contacting members about the next meeting to coordinating a fund-raiser.

FACT

The International Swimmers Hall of Fame in Ft. Lauderdale, Florida, faced enormous financial difficulties, and hall of fame honorees like Mark Spitz sent letters in 2004 indicating their lack of confidence in the institution. Executive recruiter and swimming enthusiast Dennis Carey was brought in as CEO. His plan was so compelling that he was able to put together a new board, including Spitz as chair. That's leadership.

Leadership can happen in an executive office or other high-ranking position. It can also come, as in business, from people willing to roll up their sleeves and take full responsibility for getting a job done. Although it's important for socially oriented organizations to have the right top leadership, it's just as important to have leadership throughout: the person who makes sure the community theatre has a set for its next production, someone to put together the volunteer cooking schedule for the kids' baseball association, someone to arrange for the blood drive at the community center.

All People Leading

In fact, it's not just the people who are in charge of an effort who are the leaders. Working with others to do what must be done isn't restricted to those who keep the volunteer lists. Everyone who decides to take action becomes a leader. This is because those people aren't just following orders; instead, they're making their own decisions based on what they see is right.

It might be that a need is organic and not the regular focus of some organization. In such cases, it takes leaders in the community to step forward and do what must be done. For example, when Hurricane Katrina devastated the Southeast, tens of thousands of people all around the country were moved to pitch in and organize their own relief efforts with neighbors, people at work and school, and others in their social networks.

The people who made this help possible didn't wait for someone to give them permission. Seeing what was necessary, they did something and accepted the responsibility they saw was needed. You could say that another definition of leadership is the process of turning an idea into action with other people. In fact, it's this grassroots-up form of leadership that is perhaps the most important to communities. Even when there is not an established organization to address a local situation, these leaders see the need, create a plan of action, recruit help, and get something positive done. That is even true for those who aren't taking up a given cause but are taking the initiative to act in ways they know are right. Setting a good example when gaining attention is not the intent is one of the most fundamental and true ways of leading. Not only are there opportunities to lead in everyday life, you can also gain experience today and practice skills that will help you lead in other contexts as well.

People Skills

Skills for leading are vital; you can't be a leader without them. The first type of skill is working with people. Because leadership always involves others, you must learn how to effectively coexist and pursue goals with them. They fall into three categories:

- Communication
- Motivation
- Coaching

Leadership cannot exist without communication. If people can't communicate with each other, they certainly cannot work together and ensure that, as a group, they accomplish their goal.

Communicating Well to Lead

To reach a goal, a group needs a shared intent, common meaning, and coordination. The better you can communicate, the better you can help people work together, and the more effectively you can collectively reach the goal.

The first part of communication is learning to speak and write clearly. If you want people to follow you, they have to know who you are, what you represent, what you can do, and where you want everyone to go.

ALERT!

Communication also means fostering interactions among all the people with whom you work. If people aren't getting along, then they will work badly together, which endangers your goals. Sometimes communication turns into mediation. You have to be aware of when communication breaks down among others and take action before the cracks become insurmountable fissures.

It's actually much easier than most people think. Later in the book, you'll learn a lot about how to get your meaning across to others and how to be persuasive. But that is only one part of communication. You must also develop your listening skills. People you work with should always feel that they can come to you with ideas, suggestions, and problems and that you'll be interested, patient, and willing to hear what they have to say. Finally, you must learn to involve the people on your team in meaningful ways, giving them the power and opportunity to make a difference and working to recognize and retain them.

Stoking the Motivational Fires

Things don't happen of their own accord, and that includes the way people undertake tasks. Excitement helps, but the initial rush of enthusiasm wanes as they start to experience how difficult success will be. Some people are able to keep themselves forging ahead, but most can't, and that's where motivation comes in.

It can be hard enough to motivate yourself, never mind ensuring that other people get down to business—and stay there. Simply telling or ordering people to do what they should doesn't help. All that does is create resentment that will actually make it more difficult for a team to achieve its goals.

To really motivate people—that is, get them to approach a goal in a creative way—you have to combine various approaches. That may include such traditional methods as rewards and public recognition of accomplishments of team members, but motivation also extends to helping people find new ways of approaching their tasks and helping them find value for themselves in what they are doing. It's creating an environment that calls forth the best of people, so that they thrive and use all their talents and energy. Motivation isn't giving speeches so much as it is subtly encouraging others in a host of ways to be more than they think they are.

Coach for Success

Coaching is closely related to motivation. It's the process of working with others and giving them the support they need in what they're trying to do. Although many associate coaching with a supervisory role, the process is closer to how it's used in sports. When it comes to player development, the coach can see someone's performance in a way the player can't. Combined with a knowledge of how to achieve good performance, that insight lets the coach offer feedback. Players take the suggestions and implement them to improve their performance.

The coach nurtures the team, all with the intent of getting it to win. In an organization, a leader coaches the team on how to better meet its goals. In this way, coaching can become a communication tool that makes life easier and more satisfying for everyone involved. At its best, coaching can build stronger relationships between leaders and other team members with a minimal amount of conflict.

Organizational Skills

Good intentions and noble purposes mean nothing in utter chaos. Staying on top of what you are doing requires a good amount of organization. When you're also depending on others, having organizational skills will spell the difference between success and failure—and perhaps whether you reach for the aspirin bottle at the end of the day.

Managing Your Time

Organization starts with time management. Leaders become responsible not only for their own activities but for the collective actions of the entire group. (And you thought your usual to-do list was getting long!) Time management for the endeavor as a whole becomes a major issue.

The fundamental principle is learning to create priorities. There are never enough people, hours, or funds to do everything you would like in the time frame called for. The question becomes whether you are getting the most important things done. If you are, you have a better chance, overall, of keeping things on track. If you aren't, then it's like sitting at your desk, trying to accomplish something while immediately answering every phone call and e-mail that come in.

After you have your priorities, you need to learn how to use your time most effectively. Accurate scheduling is critical. You have to learn how to track what is going on, make sure that certain things happen in the proper order, and know who is doing what. This will ensure that people are not duplicating efforts and that critical items have the help they require.

ALERT!

An old prank is to push a potato into a car's exhaust. When the driver tries to start the car, it starts to turn over and then shuts down because the potato keeps the gases from leaving the car. Because the gases can't escape, the pistons can't push them out of the cylinders, and the entire engine stops. That's what disorganization does to the engine of group effort.

Delegating Duties

Once you have time organized, you'll need to organize everything else. As the old saying goes, "A place for everything and everything in its place." Although that may seem boringly clerical, it's of particular importance to leaders. Now you're responsible for your own things as well as those of the entire undertaking—not just those in your work space, but those of all the other team members. Organization is like building a house: Disturb one floor of the house, and it can affect every floor. Disorganization on any level becomes the chokepoint for activity.

To keep yourself from being the chokepoint, you'll need to improve your delegation skills. If you micromanage, you're not leading; you're trying to do everything yourself. You can't properly motivate others because you make your own level of participation and control more important than your goals.

Project Management

Once you've developed your time management and organizational systems, the tough part starts. Now you have to maintain what you've spent so much energy setting up. This book offers advice on how to use time management and project planning intelligently, building flexibility into everyone's schedules so that when—not if—things go wrong, you'll have the ability to recover and put things aright. You'll also have the flexibility to look ahead, not being satisfied with things as they are now, but ready to modify your plans and even change directions when necessary. The idea of time management and organization isn't to be rigid, but to have enough control that you can always advance the company, organization, or cause as new opportunities permit. Do what you need to do, delegate other things, and then consider how else you can improve the overall effort or organization.

As you organize, you also must be sure to maintain the right principles in what your team does. You must consider the organization's requirements and also reach them within the appropriate ethical, regulatory, and legal limits. In other words, it's not just where you end up that counts, but how you get there. Consider the "leaders" of such companies as Enron, World-Com, and Tyco. Although they worked with employees to achieve a goal, the goals were really focused on the leaders, and their resulting disregard for proper behavior brought those businesses to the edge of ruin. In the quest to achieve, you can't forget to take the high road.

Personal Traits and Skills

The final set area for a leader to learn is personal traits and skills. The traits portion may sound odd. After all, how can you learn something that is considered inborn? Actually, many traits are learned. Consider some of the classic traits associated with leadership:

- Vision
- Courage
- Loyalty
- Self-discipline
- Strong work ethic
- Creativity
- Ability to learn from mistakes
- Willingness to stand for something

Other than possibly vision, none of these is inherent in a person's character. Some of these characteristics will come more easily than others, but through diligent effort, you can check off literally all of them. You don't need them all to lead, but the more you have, the more effective you can be.

Top Characteristics

Some leadership traits are more important than others. Self-discipline, for example, is key to leadership—and everything else in the world. Without it, you can't accomplish anything. After all, how can you manage others if you haven't figured out how to manage yourself?

A work ethic goes hand in glove with self-discipline. A willingness to learn from mistakes is worth more than its weight in Warren Buffett because leadership must constantly adapt to the changing nature of reality. Add loyalty to goals, principles, and other team members, and you have a good start on a supportive set of traits.

QUESTION?

How can I develop leadership traits?
This is a topic not generally taught even in the finest business schools. But there are clues that can lead you down the right path. One of the best ways to approach developing these characteristics is to use an old actors' trick. Behave as though you are, and you will become what you seek.

A leader must also have the flexibility to handle change. Learning to accept and work with change helps you ultimately to learn from it. It teaches you to keep aiming for your goals, even when facing delays and detours. It also helps you change your own behavior when you are the one that is slowing progress—and that will happen.

Looking to Others

You'll need to learn how to identify talent and willingness. Because a leader must work with others, it helps to find team members that can significantly contribute to the group effort, and you are the designated talent scout. You'll also have to learn to handle the problems that always come when people work together. Then you'll need to learn how to keep learning—always expanding on your skills and capabilities.

It may sound like a lot, but it's not. Step by step, you'll move toward leadership and keep improving on what you can do. There's no degree at the end of this book, no graduation ceremony. But your leadership abilities and skills will keep increasing as you practice more, until one day people will ask you how they can learn to lead.

CHAPTER 2

Leadership Styles

Alexander the Great. Joan of Arc. Socrates. Queen Elizabeth I. Abraham Lincoln. Sojourner Truth. Bill Russell. Aung San Suu Kyi. These men and women came from different times and backgrounds and different things were important to them. Yet all have been leaders in their own ways and for their own causes. This chapter takes a look at some popular theories of leadership and how you can use them to further your own leadership goals.

Popular Leadership Models

No two situations or people are alike, and no two leaders can be exactly the same. All leaders have to find their own way, but there is no reason to stumble about blindly. Academics and management consultants have studied leadership. The first step to finding your own leadership style is to look at the development of the following schools of thought about leadership:

- Great man
- Trait
- Behavioral
- Contingency
- Transactional
- Transformational

Each of these schools includes many individual theories of management, but it is sufficient to focus on the general concepts. By doing so, you will find some useful tools for developing leadership.

ESSENTIAL

The University of Exeter's Centre for Leadership Studies has an extensive treatise on the evolution of leadership theory. It includes the schools of thought discussed in this chapter as well as many specific academic theories. For a free copy and to see other resources, go online to *www.leadership-studies.com*.

Great Man

According to the great man theory, people are born to leadership. Members of royalty, military commanders, and captains of industry throughout history and into much of the twentieth century were the natural heirs to authority and rule. That picture was generally of a white male of Western European descent.

In the present, it is easy to laugh at the smug naïveté that dismissed most of the world's population as candidates for leadership, but don't start chuckling yet. There is an enormous residue of expectation that is culturally conditioned into most of us. It's easy—and foolish—to turn your back on this intellectual and emotional heritage, which can affect your own expectations of yourself and your relationships with others.

Rejecting the great man theory is dangerous on another ground. Not only do many people subscribe to this belief, making it more difficult for many to enter leadership roles, but it had some basis in fact in the sense that some people have personalities that lend themselves to leadership. That includes personal traits, habits, and knowledge. Studying these people—regardless of whether they fall into the historic definition of leader material—can offer lessons on what you need to achieve to advance your own leadership capabilities.

Trait

The trait theory of leadership derived from the great man theory. It suggests that you can identify a potential leader by examining the personality traits of the person and matching them to the characteristics "real" leaders possess.

ALERT!

Part of being a leader is working with what is around you. Be aware that many people still hold to the trait school even if they don't realize it, and they may not see you as leadership material if you don't fit their particular view of a leader. You can still lead; it just takes additional care and planning.

That might sound arbitrary, but it's surprising how much general agreement you can find among people on the topic. Over twenty years, two researchers, James Kouzes and Barry Posner, interviewed 75,000 people, asking them what top ten characteristics they'd need to see in someone to willingly follow the person. Here are the characteristics, from most to least popular:

- Honest
- Forward-looking

- Competent
- Inspiring
- Intelligent
- Fair-minded
- Broad-minded
- Supportive
- Straightforward
- Dependable
- Cooperative
- Determined
- Imaginative
- Ambitious
- Courageous
- Caring
- Mature
- Loyal
- Self-controlled
- Independent

It's a daunting list, and there are factors other than personal traits involved in leadership. However, leadership is personal, and you don't have to be born with each of these traits. In fact, you can actually develop characteristics in yourself through work and intention.

Behavioral

In the behavioral school, leaders are not born, nor are they required to possess a proper collection of traits. Instead, leadership is a matter of proper behavior. The evolution of this school of thought is important because it represents the first time people began to see leading as something that could be learned. Experts observed people who were able to act as leaders and studied how they handled human relationships and the behaviors that led to failure.

Behavioral theories are generally founded on categories of behavior and leadership types. The thinking can result in the fallacy that simple imitation of outward behavior is enough to establish leadership.

Over-reliance on a behavioral view can result in a surface interpretation of leadership, one reason you can find so many carbon-copy executives roaming the halls of corporations. People go through the motions rather than truly becoming leaders. The difficulty is to take behavior and internalize it so that the expression is genuine.

Contingency

In the contingency theory, the study of leadership took another step toward a modern view. Every other school to this point assumed that there was only one type of leader and that all people would need to use the same approach in every situation. But nothing in the world is so rigid and unchanging.

A leadership style that works for a given person in a particular context isn't universal. The proper approach to leading depends on the goal, the people on the team, and the relationship of the leader to everyone else. It's a more flexible and realistic concept.

Transactional

Transactional leadership models treat the process of leading as a cross between a social and business transaction. There are specific hierarchies and structures in which some people are leaders and others are followers. A leader and follower agree to a contract. The latter is responsible for following orders to do a job, and the former provides rewards for proper execution of responsibilities.

The transactional model should not be taken to a rigid extreme, but the concept has an appealing clarity. Ultimately, people must know what they need to accomplish and what others expect from them. Without this, communication will always be flawed.

The difficulty in transactional leadership is that the concept doesn't apply well to all circumstances or cultures. For example, job-performance-and-reward model doesn't pertain to volunteer efforts, where the reward is usually something other than what the leader can directly provide.

Transformational

The transformational school is popular today. It is based on vision. A leader is an inspiring figure who works with followers to achieve a goal. In the process, everyone helps each other to reach greater levels of achievement. Trust is an essential bond, and those who follow voluntarily buy into the goals. Transformational leadership has become a fundamental tool, particularly in the concept of getting others to buy into necessary changes in the workplace.

One reason this model is a true development is its goal emphasis. The relationship between the leader and other members of the team isn't of primary importance. Such roles and duties exist because there is an outside something that all wish to reach, and so they take their places and undertake their own necessary tasks. For the first time, those studying leadership began to see it as necessarily being in relation to something greater. Transformational leadership depends on a greater context or meaning, which is something all people desire.

Yet desirability and popularity are not effortless. Building trust and getting cooperation are far more difficult than giving orders and monitoring process. In transformational leadership, the leader must continue to be an inspiring presence. The leader leads by example and is responsible for motivating others.

Driving the Pragmatic Hybrid

Models are a blessing and a curse to those who want to learn. In this case, it seems that because of their inherent strengths and weaknesses, quantity is necessary to reach quality.

Model Strengths

On the positive side, models offer the critical ingredient of an intellectual framework. Whether you are studying carpentry or calculus, to become proficient, you need to master various skills and then weave them together. Using a handsaw quickly is useless if your cuts are inaccurate; mathematical integration is impossible if you haven't mastered the concept of the derivative.

Learning skills one at a time, though, can lead to isolated knowledge. To weave fabric, you need a loom to keep lines of yarn taut as you pass various threads back and forth to create the pattern. The loom is the framework that holds the work together as you perform it.

A model suggests the interplay of the various aspects. In carpentry, the model may be a set of guiding principles that shows how a building goes up from foundation to roof and from outside to inside. Calculus teachers might offer geometric representations of derivatives as tangents to lines and integrals as adding little boxes of area or volume. If the model is strong, you will find yourself more readily grasping ideas and putting them into action because the model lets you see the essential of what you need to do.

FACT

A civil engineer designing a bridge looks to mathematical descriptions of the parts and their relations to each other. That framework, or model, lets the engineer calculate how much stress various parts of the structure bear, the inherent strength of the materials, and whether the final construction is likely to stand or do an imitation of the London Bridge of nursery rhyme fame—go boom.

More ethereal skills also need a framework. In leadership, you need to bring intellectual, emotional, and physical abilities into play to accomplish anything. Without a model, you stumble about, trying to make the parts work together, possibly scuttling your goal in the process because of the weight of accumulated mistakes. There would just be too much stress, in all meanings of the word.

Model Weaknesses

For all their strengths, models also have their weaknesses. The principle one is that a model is a simplification of reality. If the world were really so uncomplicated that you could describe it in a few paragraphs, life would be much easier. Any model, no matter how good, is still quite a distance from the real thing.

FACT

In a way, thinking about models in terms of pros and cons expresses the essence of the problem. It takes a real pro to use models widely, and it's all too easy for a model to con you into thinking that you face reality and not an approximation of it.

Leadership in a Bottle

Once you grasp these essential problems of models, you can understand the danger that the development of leadership models presents. Each model focuses on a given aspect of leadership. No single one by itself covers everything you would need to know. Nevertheless, different models are popular at different times. Teachers, from formal academics to role models in action, have their own favorites. Institutions may have biases toward one school of thought or another.

Depending on their experiences, individuals may have learned that one particular model or another is "the" answer to grasping leadership. That may be fine if you have the right mix of people, model, organization, goal, and culture. But what if the particular combination at hand isn't a fit for the reality? You might find that your efforts came to nothing—or even that they made things worse.

The result is like a replica of a sailing ship in a bottle. It may look like the real thing, but it's not going anywhere in the near future. What you must do is find ways to break out of these boundaries—to think outside the glass, if you will. One of the best ways to do so is to combine all of the above models.

Holistic Leadership

No model offers a complete answer to the problem of leadership. For example, the trait school attributes everything to personal traits, but it acknowledges neither the possibility of acquiring traits nor the need for different traits to meet differing situations. Transactional leaders can miss opportunities to improve the organization when they insist on team members holding closely to their assigned roles and not venturing out to make observations and suggestions that might open new possibilities.

The business world is filled with the stories of organizations that withered under a change in management. Sometimes the new chief executives had a history of success and assumed that what they had done before would work again. In reality, the companies had different cultures. Employees reacted differently, and the formula for success became a prescription for disaster.

Additionally, the models don't actually teach how to lead. Instead, they attempt to explain the concerns and dynamics that leaders face and how successful leaders deal with them. But by intelligently using the models, you can anticipate what you will face and find ways to lead under many different circumstances and conditions. It's a matter of taking a few steps to create a personal management style:

- Matching style to self
- Matching style to other people
- Matching style to organization
- Matching style to situation

That doesn't mean you should develop a single approach to leading. Instead, you should aim to understand the principles of management and see how you might have to express them differently depending on when, where, and whom you lead.

Matching Style to Self

Those who know and enjoy golf get a tremendous pleasure from watching Tiger Woods swing the club. Louis Armstrong had a riveting and unique style of playing the trumpet, even as a young man, and no one could have mistaken his playing for that of Miles Davis. Listen to almost any composition by Mozart and you can tell who wrote it.

Painters, musicians, composers, carpenters, architects, cooks, barbers—in any endeavor, accomplished people have some degree of personal style.

Leading with Style

Those who are good at what they do, who lead in whatever form it takes, adapt the techniques they've learned and available materials to perform the tasks at hand in a way that is distinctly their own. Heredities, upbringings, backgrounds, inclinations, personalities, and tastes all influence how they do what they do. They all have personal styles.

FACT

The essence of parody is to take a few strong elements of someone's style and to exaggerate them. Even distorted, though, you can pick out the inspiration. Ernest Hemingway had such a distinctive voice that it's become the subject of an annual parody contest.

Style has a number of meanings, and one is a conscious approach to life choices. Eavesdrop on teenagers, and you'll often find them expressing such a style in their speech, dress, and behavior. Though often arbitrary and an imitation of patterns set by large corporations trying to sell their wares, this style is an early attempt to find a personal way to interact with the world. The expression may be off, but the impulse is vital.

You're Always There

As the old saying notes, no matter where you go, you always bring yourself along. No matter what the situation, the goal, or the other people involved, the one constant when you are a leader is *you*. Your heritage, psychology, strengths, and weaknesses will meet any challenges or demands. As you grasp the essence of leadership, your self will always come though. You will have a personal style because, given human nature, there is absolutely no way that you can't have one.

The song "Company Way" from the show *How to Succeed in Business Without Really Trying* is a must-hear. It is a parody of the drive to become the perfect employee who thinks, feels, and acts only as the company requires. As is true of any good parody, it can be uncomfortably accurate.

It is sometimes, though not always, helpful to follow company guidelines and stay within the corporate structure. Chances are good that you've seen or known people who have tried to forgo their own style and adopt one imposed from the powers that be. These clones become the cookie-cutter managers, the manufactured citizens who talk and act in given ways because they are looking for acceptance and a minimum of personal responsibility. But in suppressing themselves, they reduce or eliminate their true ability to contribute.

If you want to be a good leader, you must find how your personal idiosyncrasies will affect your efforts. The only place to start is with some self-knowledge of a practical sort. Evaluate how your achievements are affected by what you do and who you are.

Taking a Personal Inventory

Now is the time to go through the leadership assessment chart in Appendix A and answer the questions as accurately as you can. Although there are points and an overall result, the total at the end won't give you "the answer."

The whole point of completing the chart is to give yourself the time and even the excuse to take stock in an honest manner. No one else cares about how you do, and you are the only one who will have any real stake in changing how you act. So relentlessly look for the truth. It is the only way to gain from the exercise and start moving in the right direction.

Use this as a tool for active reflection. You will get a score at the end, but it won't be an easy answer. The same score can mean different things for different people. Two people might need to do similar amounts of work but in different areas. Or they might have similar needs but require different approaches because of their varying circumstances. The more you know about how you approach leadership, the more you'll know about what tools and approaches will best fit your strengths and where you need to improve your efforts.

Matching Style to Other People

The essence of leadership is always personal relationships. To lead, you must, by definition, work with others to achieve the goal you've set. Undertaking a quest by yourself might be considered heroic, but if you aren't inviting others to come and help, the interpersonal dynamic is missing, meaning there is no room for leadership.

Lead the Individual

At its core, human nature is immutable. Individuals certainly find unique ways of balancing and expressing the drives and concerns we all have.

A situation that affects one person in a certain way will cause a different reaction in a neighbor. You can't assume that a given approach to any leadership will be effective with every person. Just as you need to better understand yourself, you need to better understand the people you want to lead and your relationships with them.

Those who study human learning have long determined that people learn in different ways. Some work best visually, some through hearing information, and others through physical interaction. At a bare minimum, that means a leader needs to find the best way to present goals and motivate individuals.

Individuals, Not Groups

No two people are completely alike, and there is no such thing as the average person. If there are no average people, there is no way to conveniently group them and treat them in a singular way. That means it's impossible to have impersonal, mechanical relationships with the people you lead.

As you move upward through the ranks of a hierarchy, being a leader becomes ever more difficult because of the increased distance from the others involved. That's why large organizations have formal mechanisms. But the big mistake is to confuse those tools with the process of leadership. In each case, they depend on a chain of personal connections from the leader down to everyone else. Leadership may become more removed, but it always stays personal. You can have no relationship when you don't recognize that you work with human beings. Recognition of that only comes when you see their view as well as your own.

To lead, you need to understand the relationships you have with others, and that means to look at those people individually. Don't get preoccupied with personalities, which in a sense are insignificant. Actions are more important.

Look at Actions

The truest form of communication is action—important, since leadership is ultimately about getting things done. When you consider the approaches to leadership that might work with others, focus on what is happening, not what you feel about each person. You might think that a certain person's attitude is a bit too casual, for instance, but if the same individual is greatly advancing your group's goals, something is going right. Likewise, the perceptions others have of your actions are just as important as your perceptions of theirs.

Getting a Personal Evaluation

Taking stock of yourself is important, but it can be tricky. As human beings, we are deceptive creatures, both to others and to ourselves. Market researchers often ask people how they'd react under given circumstances, such as whether they would buy a new type of product and how much they would pay. At the same time, marketers are aware that such data is among the least reliable. People often answer in a way that reflects how they would like to think of themselves and how they think others will perceive them.

Because leadership only happens in the presence of proper relationships with others, you will need to understand what drives those interactions. Make copies of the reflective leadership evaluation tool found in Appendix B. Ask your coworkers to fill them out. The more you understand how people perceive your actions in an impersonal way, the better you can evaluate how your leadership approach is working.

Most people find it difficult to be blunt with those they don't know well. That is true even for individuals who pride themselves on being direct. By using a formal method of feedback, you reduce (though, unfortunately, never completely eliminate) the conditions that might call for surly proof of independence or a bootblack's deference.

Matching Style to Organization

Any organization is like a big person. Organizations have personalities, strengths, and weaknesses. They come in all ages, tastes, and sizes. Each one has its own set of expectations and idiosyncrasies. As with individuals, there is no single form of leadership, and you'll have to adjust your style to work within the context of the organization's culture.

Culture in this case means much the same as it does in society. An organization promotes certain types of behaviors and discourages others. It has its own way of communicating, planning, structuring activities, and accomplishing things. One other thing the organization has is an almost irresistible force.

Inertia

The force comes in a number of forms, but the most formidable is psychological and operational inertia. Consider the existence of organizations, and it becomes clear why there is inertia—and why it's necessary.

If you have N people, the maximum number of two-person relationships within that group can be expressed mathematically as follows:

$$\frac{N \times (N - 1)}{2}$$

Now add an additional person and you have additional possibilities for two-person relationships. As the group gets larger, the number of people and the interactions among them increase. In a short amount of time, you have an incredibly complex interrelated set of relationships. If you could introduce unchecked change to the system at any relationship, the entire organization could come apart because there would be no stability. Different groups could head off in opposite directions, which eliminates the possibility of progress.

FACT

Inertia in physics is technically the inherent characteristic of resisting change. An object can be moving or sitting still. Either way, you'll have a difficult time changing its course.

The entity must have a certain amount of inertia to ensure that work continues in the same direction. Of course, that direction may be right or wrong, and the work might be good or flawed. But what do you want? It's a bureaucracy, and it's doing the best it can.

Leadership As Navigation

Inertia is like the currents of the Mississippi River. It's a force that ebbs and flows, and if you aren't careful, it can drive your craft in directions you hadn't intended to follow. Captains on the Mississippi, as on any large body of water, must learn the currents, know the capabilities of their vessels, and understand how to steer. They can't change the currents, but they can learn to work with them to minimize the interference and even to use it.

A leader must do the same thing in an organization. Inertia is a force, and some leadership tools and techniques might work better with the inertia in one organization than in another. For example, if you have a large number of inexperienced people, more coaching will be necessary. People who have been under stress for an extended period of time might need more in the way of recognition and reward to help them remember that there is something for them to attain. You might have to encourage experimentation if the organization has been overly controlling or push on the discipline front if people are creative but not applying enough diligence to get things done. The important thing is to look for the characteristics of the organization—just as you'd look for the characteristics of yourself or of your team members—and match your approach accordingly.

Matching Style to Situation

Leadership style involves one more variable. Situations can change even when the leader, people, and organization stay the same. As external conditions change, so will the reactions of leader, people, and organization. Take a block of dry ice from a cooler and place it into a sink of water and it will suddenly explode into dense clouds of fog. Why? The conditions changed.

People and organizations change slowly, but circumstances can move on a dime, particularly when it's least convenient. Leaders must be able to make adjustments quickly and efficiently.

An important part of leadership is keeping a close eye on conditions and the reactions of others. When the current situation is in flux and your leadership needs to change, you'll see early warnings of it in the actions of your team. What seemed stable and settled suddenly starts to go awry. Progress toward goals gets sluggish. People become disenchanted, and communication starts breaking down. You'll hear the metaphoric squeaks and groans of a machine you thought was in fine tune.

As a leader, you have one option: reinvention. Real leaders know that solutions have a natural lifetime. You grow and sustain them, but eventually they show their age. Then you have to start developing a new solution again. Don't think of it as frustration but as a natural process. The reinvention process actually starts from the beginning of your attempts to be a leader because you'll find that you need to assess your own traits and to reinvent who you are.

CHAPTER 3

Personal Traits of Leaders

Years ago there was a television commercial with a line that went roughly like this: "I'm not really a doctor; I just play one on TV." Amusing as this is—at least before you'd heard it hundreds of times—it shows a rampant problem in this country. People often associate leadership with a certain appearance. This chapter is about how to move beyond appearance to the real substance that will help you in your quest to become a leader.

The Leadership Trait Trail

We talk of people "looking presidential" or "having the presence of a CEO." As a result, many who are interested in leadership try to cultivate the outward look of a leader by posing. Unfortunately, this isn't enough.

When it comes to leadership, most important is what you do and how you do it. Your actions come from the most important tool you have in leadership: yourself. If you want to lead, you must marshal your personal traits, as they are what people see.

Acting Like an Archetype

Everyone has an image of what it means to be a leader. The popular view generally includes a number of characteristics idealized in formulaic Hollywood movies and political campaigns:

- Charisma
- Decisiveness
- Persuasiveness
- Single-mindedness
- Vision
- Drive

Just because a view is popular does not make it true or accurate. Many preconceived notions about people's roles come from archetypes, or collective cultural models, that have been around longer than recorded history. Scholars, great thinkers, and scientists such as Joseph Campbell, Bruno Bettelheim, and Carl Jung have explored how we internalize such myths and use them as examples of what we are supposed to do.

FACT

Popular opinion has scored a number of amazingly wrong concepts. From the world being flat to the meteorological prowess of Pennsylvania-based rodents (otherwise known as groundhogs), people have subscribed en masse to a number of questionable concepts throughout the ages. Concentrate on what you want to achieve and don't get distracted.

Society's understanding of these archetypes often goes astray. Instead of grasping the essence of these roles and how they relate to our own existence, we grasp the superficial aspects and head off in the wrong direction.

True Leadership Traits

When you observe and talk about leadership to people who have implemented change, a different set of character traits generally come to mind:

- Commitment
- Loyalty
- Self-discipline
- Strong work ethic
- Creativity
- Ability to learn from mistakes
- Principles
- Passion for something greater
- Trust
- Honesty
- Tenacity
- Openness
- Patience
- Responsibility
- Courage
- Confidence

A leader can incorporate elements from the list of archetypical or realistic traits—or a leader might have characteristics from both lists. But there is an inherent difference between the two. The archetypical traits are the ones that you either have or you don't. The realistic traits are those that most people can actually learn and improve upon.

That's crucial. If the basic stuff of leadership were impossible to learn, you'd have to give up. Only a tiny percentage of leaders are naturals. The others didn't appear like Athena, fully formed from Zeus's head. They must have come from somewhere.

FACT

The stereotypical leader whose characteristics come mostly from the archetypical group can be a problem. Without realistic traits to balance him, the leader can become inhuman, with disastrous results. Genghis Kahn was courageous, and Hitler was persuasive, but neither was a leader you'd want as your own.

And that they did—from their own efforts. They may have started with some of what they needed, but it took effort over time to learn the characteristics and behavior they needed to lead. That's exactly what you can do. There are two important steps. One is to know how to make the changes you need, and the other is to know what changes you'll have to make.

Where the Heck Are You?

The first step is to get a sense of what you'll need to encourage in yourself. You might have a good sense of that, but it will be helpful to review your results from using the leadership assessment chart in Appendix A. The important thing is to look at the results honestly although not brutally. Beating yourself up does no good and only reinforces the status quo. It becomes an excuse. "Oh, I beat myself up really well today," says the subconscious, "so everything must be okay now." However, nothing has changed.

You want real change, not finger-wagging. The question is how to move. For all the time you've spent in school, one subject you probably never approached was how to achieve self-change. It's not something you can get out of a book, but there are places that teach the skills you need. Those establishments are called acting schools.

Acting the Part

Being able to cry on command isn't a prerequisite. But something that actors have to master is the ability to create characters. They must be able to establish sets of emotions, thoughts, postures, and reactions that express a created role. Some things, such as thoughts expressed in lines from the script or in movements, are within conscious control. Others, like emotions or attitudes, aren't.

You can learn from acting techniques. When actors want to create a feeling or characteristic in themselves, they are taught to act on stage as though they already have it, and the sense will come. You need to do much the same thing.

There is a type of acting, all too prevalent, which is really play-acting. You can see this when a politician tries to portray herself as the ideal candidate for the office she is running for. If you focus on you more than on what you have to do, you're play-acting, and it isn't doing you any good.

For example, say you find yourself lacking in creativity. How do you bring a greater sense of creativity? Start facing the world as you would if you were more creative. When faced with a problem, for example, instead of taking the first solution that comes to mind, think of two or three others first. Before assuming that you know how two facts connect, sit down with a piece of paper and brainstorm other ways they are connected, no matter how contrived or silly they sound. Read biographies of people known for their creativity, paying particular attention to how they approach their activities, and adapt their ways to what you do.

You can do this for virtually any characteristic outside of the physiological. (You're not going to develop better hair by acting as though you had it.) Nevertheless, you might find that you gain confidence by approaching life in the way you would if you possessed it—and that would likely prove more satisfying, anyway.

Grouping Traits

It is sometimes best to address the characteristics you want to change or improve one at a time. But often you can save time by grouping the traits. Your psychology isn't separate from the rest of you, and the parts of it interact. Why not use that fact to develop different aspects of yourself simultaneously?

FACT

If you've ever used weight equipment at a gym, you know that you don't exercise one single muscle at a time. Such a specific approach would take forever, and it wouldn't be successful; your muscles are designed to work in groups. The same goes for your psychology. Traits relate to one another, and employing one successfully generally means you'll use others.

Look again at the leadership assessment chart from Appendix A. All of the questions fall into categories, but we can make an even tidier summary, as you're really considering four areas of your life:

- Spiritual
- Intellectual
- Emotional
- Physical

In each of these areas, your traits do not act alone; they use other aspects of your personality as accomplices. Because they are connected, what affects one affects them all. Instead of having to address each part of yourself in isolation, you can often group things together and make progress on multiple fronts at the same time.

Spiritual Traits

We'll start at the metaphoric top. The following traits could be classified as spiritual:

- Vision
- Principles
- Passion
- Openness
- Commitment

Instead of thinking that we're getting ready to join hands around the campfire to sing "Kumbaya," look at this in a more grounded way. Vision is the ability to imagine possibilities that most people don't recognize until a leader articulates them. Being principled means being willing to put yourself in the service of that which is bigger than you. Passion is a drive, in the form of action, to support something; openness is being receptive to other things; and commitment is enlisting in the service of something other than yourself. All of these traits are about a connection to something outside yourself and your readiness to put yourself in its service.

ALERT!

There is a danger in the concept of putting yourself in the service of something else—the potential to lose yourself in that other. You can only be of help when you exist and can bring your own goals to hand. If not, then you'll find yourself used up and empty.

Some people will see this "something" as a deity. For others, it may be Beauty, Art, Truth, or some other idealized concept. Some are drawn by business success and others by social activism. No matter what, it needs to be something.

Robert Browning once wrote, "Ah, but a man's reach should exceed his grasp, or what's a heaven for?" People are genuinely attracted to those who move in reasoned, affirmative, innovative, or intrepid directions. They want to go somewhere, which means that you, as the person inspired to lead them, need someplace to go and a reason to go there.

Goals and the Spiritual

Whatever the guiding principle, it provides a context for you and, by extension, your team. All of you want to help in this greater context, which means you'll want to achieve things to support your guiding principle. You'll have goals—the very common goals outlined in Chapter 1. Without a principle, you have no real goals, and without a goal, there is no team or leader.

Trying to lead without a goal is like trying to find your way through the woods without a destination. You can load up with equipment like a fine compass, a GPS system, maps, and specialized measuring devices to your heart's content. Yet even if you can pinpoint your position within a few feet, what will it matter? If you aren't going anywhere, your location isn't important.

When you do have a principle that is important to you, leadership isn't about you; it's about something else. When you are more important than the principle, then what you do becomes ego fulfillment and the entire undertaking turns into an elaborate con game.

You cannot lead without a goal because there is no place to go and no one who wants to get there. A group following a leader who has no goal greater than ego and show is a cult of personality. The aim of the leader and others on the team has to be greater than any one individual. With a goal, there is a reason for people to work together and a reason for some individuals to lead the effort.

Choosing the Right Principle

As you can see, the term *spiritual* is being used loosely. The way you take it really doesn't matter. You might be religious; you might be driven by the philosophy of ideas, as Socrates and Plato were; or you might be driven by business competition (and, as of late, by philanthropic principles), as Bill Gates is. People may agree with you or not. Others might hold the same driving motivation, or they may despise it and view you as a skunk or a dupe. It doesn't matter. What really matters for a leader is that the "spirit" be something greater and personally compelling.

If the principle and related goal result in something real and positive, there's something true in them and that's so much the better. However, you don't have to be grandiose. No matter what goal is governing your actions at any moment—and it doesn't always have to be the same one every time you are leading—so long as you find it honest and worthwhile, then you are making that connection to something higher.

There are people who will think you a sap for holding onto something greater. They will call you sentimental. Let them. To open up and be of service to something larger than yourself is a wonderful and ennobling experience. It's also what makes leadership necessary and possible in the first place.

QUESTION?

Does my goal matter?

It does, at least in terms of its scope or size. A goal can be so trivial in nature that success is never a question. Such a purpose won't call forth the best in your ability to lead because you'll have finished practically before you've even started. The bigger the challenge, the better a leader you'll have to become.

Although the goal can be of various sizes, what it cannot be is something trivial. If it is, the possibility exists for everything to degenerate back into an ego trip. Additionally, such an effort would be so small that you wouldn't need to grow your own capabilities.

Intellectual Traits

Intellect is vital to a leader. You don't have to be bookish, use large words, or walk around armed with a pocket protector. All the same, it is impossible to be a consistently effective leader without applying your mind.

Before anything else, leadership is all about getting things done. To get things done, you can't run about willy-nilly. That means putting your mind to do things in a way that will be effective. Feeling and instinct are fine and necessary, but they aren't replacements for planning and managing your approach to the goal in question.

The emergence of leadership occurs when someone becomes intolerant of the status quo and commits to making a change. You don't make a change if you cannot correctly analyze what is wrong in the first place, what would make things better, and how to get from where you are to where you want to go.

Leaders are also able to present a dual vision of the future, one that stimulates, excites, and motivates their followers and requires both intellect and emotion—not one without the other. Look again at some important intellectual traits:

- Honesty
- Confidence
- Decisiveness
- Persuasiveness
- Creativity

Some of these may seem emotional, but they are really intellectual. Honesty means to look at a situation and be able to tell the truth to yourself and others. That is an intellectual capacity because you have to discern between fact and fiction and make a choice between the two. Confidence? It's having done your homework and having a strong sense that you're doing what is right—that is, doing what supports the principle and goal. Decisiveness can be inborn, but it can also be the result of having a thorough plan and knowing what you must do next. Some people have the gift of a silver tongue, and others learn persuasiveness by having thoroughly mastered it. Creativity in leadership means approaching problems in a new way—thinking outside the box. Thinking means intellect.

FACT

In many types of project management—whether programming, engineering, consulting, or manufacturing—a rule of thumb is that 80 to 90 percent of the time should go to planning. The less time for planning, the greater a chance that things will go wrong and the total amount of time necessary for the project will balloon.

Notice that there is no requirement that a leader must be a Rhodes Scholar, member of MENSA, holder of advanced degrees, Nobel Prize winner, or winner of a mind-bending television game show. What you do need is a sincere understanding of goals and an approach that is systematic, clear, and flexible. Instead of *brainy,* think common sense merged with pragmatism and a healthy dose of imagination.

Emotional Traits

In the ditty "Heart" from *Damn Yankees* there's a line that goes, "You've gotta have heart!" Truer words the aspiring leader never heard. If spirit inspires and guides a leader and intellect is the steady hand at the tiller, emotion is the wind filling the sails. If you don't have the heart, you won't even start.

The emotion you specifically need to encourage and develop is that which has a positive impact on what you are trying to achieve. Here are some of the traits that can make a difference:

- Drive
- Tenacity
- Loyalty
- Empathy
- Trust
- Courage

As with the other types of traits, these relate to what a leader must do. Without the drive—the desire to see the goal done—it will be difficult to make any progress. Similarly, tenacity keeps you at the difficult tasks when the going gets tough. Loyalty is a bond among you and all the people with whom you are working. Empathy lets you better understand where your team members are emotionally and how you can support their efforts. Without trust, people can never really bond and work well together. Without courage—not simply the lack of fear, but the willingness to keep going even in the face of it—no one can accomplish anything of note.

At the same time, expressing emotion cannot mean carrying your heart on your sleeve. You need the ability to proceed toward your goal without experiencing emotional trauma at the hint of a setback. When people spend significant amounts of time baring their feelings for all around, it can be dishonest if the real motivation is to curry attention and become the center for a personal drama.

It is a peculiarity of our culture that people in charge are expected to be cold and steely, able to proceed in an almost inhuman fashion no matter what the circumstances. That's not leadership; it's being an android, and it's unhealthy for you and for the people with whom you work.

When people normally consider feelings, they do so in isolation and focus completely on themselves. After all, what are emotions but human experience? The difference in focusing on leadership is that the feelings in question are not a sole issue of experience. Leaders must harness these emotions and use them as a way to further advance their goals and principles. When you spend your time reacting, you aren't acting and you aren't achieving.

If intelligence for a leader is about putting your mind to doing things effectively, then emotion for a leader is about putting your heart—in a smart way—to the tasks at hand. Use those feelings to fuel what you need to do and to connect you to the others who are going with you. Develop an emotional intelligence. The more you do, the more you will recognize it in others. When you begin to realize how important and useful emotional intelligence is, you'll know that it's rare and valuable.

Physical Traits

As we said at the beginning of this chapter, leadership has nothing to do with looks. Really. Nothing. So why are we talking about physical traits? Because the other types are important, but they mean nothing until you get off your duff and into movement—not literally, but metaphorically. Physical traits, at least the way we define them, are those that help you actually get the important things done:

- Self-discipline
- Strong work ethic
- Ability to learn from mistakes
- Responsibility
- Patience

Self-discipline is obviously critical to a leader. There will be many times that you and others will get tired and discouraged. You will also experience the times that true leadership requires you to do things that are difficult for you—even if that means something like delegating responsibility to others. A strong work ethic is self-explanatory. Learning from mistakes is taking stock of what you have actually done and making any necessary corrections. A sense of responsibility will keep you on track. You'll also learn patience—there's no such thing as instant gratification for a leader.

Strengths and Weaknesses

Another way of looking at traits is to see them as strengths and weaknesses. Instead of using the typical "good" and "bad" approach that you might see in Sunday school, think of strengths and weaknesses as they relate to leadership. A strength is anything that helps advance efforts toward your goal and supports your guiding principle, and a weakness is anything that hinders what you are trying to accomplish.

For a good example of how something can be good and bad, depending on who is making the judgment, consider individuality. It's prized in the United States as a foundation of our society, and we celebrate those who cut their own paths. Yet the same behavior in parts of Asia might be considered inexcusably rude.

A New Approach to Value

The concepts of good and bad are a mix of morality, cultural mores, and presumptions. For example, many women have been taught early on to accept whatever they were given and not to demand anything. Many men were brought up learning not to ask for help and not to pay attention to their emotions. Society held up those values as desirable—that is, as good.

However, neither value is particularly helpful for leaders; in fact, it is their opposites that are actually of value. What you must do is see your traits in the light of their usefulness. Passion, creativity, and self-discipline are not ends in themselves, but they are important in relation to your goals.

Don't Rely on Strengths

People normally assume that working from their strengths is the best thing to do. It can be—at the right times and in the right place. However, there's such a thing as relying too much on strength. You tend to do all things and solve all problems the same way because you approach everything from those same strengths.

An analogy would be a person building a house who was comfortable with a circular saw but not a jig saw. That circular saw is just the thing for cutting wood in framing the building, but it lacks the flexibility to make an intricate cut to fit a piece of trim against plaster molding. What the builder then needs is a jig saw, which can make sharp turns. The would-be carpenter had better gain a new skill to get that part of the job done.

Don't be satisfied with the strengths you've always had. Keep expanding your horizons. Sometimes you can do that with your selection of team members, but also look for opportunities to grow your own abilities.

Don't Ignore Weaknesses

Just as strengths are not straightforward, neither are weaknesses. Most people ignore their weaknesses when they focus on their strengths. This is a bad idea for two reasons.

One reason to keep an eye on your weaknesses is to keep them from gaining control when you aren't looking. That's the problem with a weakness; it keeps tripping you up. If you knew when and how it was going to act, you could do something about that, but you don't.

Another reason is that you can actually strengthen your areas of weakness. Think of a new skill you picked up. Was it easy? Probably not. Unless you were a born natural, you had to spend time learning and practicing. Guess what—you indulged in the process of strengthening what was a weakness. Do that regularly. You develop more muscle to get things done, and you also create a better understanding of others who may share the same problem. That will only make for an improved team.

CHAPTER 4

Building the Vision

You can know all there is about leadership styles and the traits of leaders, but that alone doesn't mean a thing. Why? Because it's all about you—how you act, what you have going for you, how you'll try to get people to work toward goals. Who cares? We live in a society where relatively few people find themselves driven by duty or demand. Much of the emphasis in life is what people and organizations can do for you. As a leader, you need to get beyond that—and you need to get beyond yourself. That requires vision.

Working for Something Greater

Listen to people around you and you'll hear understandable yet disturbing concerns. Many refuse to engage in the political process because they're sure they can't make a difference. At work, they look out for themselves: Corporations don't show workers any loyalty, so why should they get what they don't give? Even many sports fans come to wonder if there is anything to their favorite games other than employment for millionaires.

The Shrinking World

People feel tiny and insignificant, so they focus on finding a little peace and a little comfort and staying out of the way of trouble. Much of what you will notice in the world is of agonizing smallness. Your neighbors rarely connect with anything greater than themselves, which is why they sometimes hold on so fervently to anything that strikes them at first glimpse. The popular political figure looks around to adoring ovations. Actors and musicians find themselves asked about everything from social theory to quantum mechanics. People are desperate for something more than what they see.

If despair and disillusion were all there was to life, existence would be pretty grim. That's why you'll find people who devote time to causes they find important, work extraordinarily hard to accomplish projects, or throw themselves into painting or gardening or some other activity merely for the love of it. Ordinary people even have the potential to be true heroes.

Hope for People

People need hope, and they need to feel that there is meaning in what they do. One problem that teams run into is that the tasks facing their members become routine. You knock door-to-door, canvassing a neighborhood, or you work on an assembly line. If you do anything often enough that the activity becomes rote, it is a chore and ultimately seems unimportant.

Contrast that with someone who sees the importance, in context, of the task to the team. At that point, the activity is anything but rote. Every action, no matter how mundane, connects to big goals of the team. Every success of the team becomes possible because of all the tasks that the team members do.

FACT

The word champion is an apt description of a contributing team member. By definition, it means someone who takes up a cause. You're looking for a team of people who will take on a challenge, not a group that always waits until it's told what to do.

Meaning transforms individuals from cynics and skeptics to champions. The person running into the blazing building to save a child, the worker who spends all night to perfect an important project, the volunteer who coordinates a reading tutoring program for adults—no one who achieves anything of value does so by accident.

Hope for a Team

If people work with a sense of drudgery, they are nowhere near as effective as if they worked with purpose. You only have to think about your own life and experiences to know the difference between the two states and the results you get from each. If people in the first category are on your team, you can forget about high achievement.

On the other hand, when people do their part with joy and intensity, then the team similarly benefits. How could it not if all the team members work with passion? The difference is that in the second case, the team members know how the work they do fits into a greater effort. They work with vision. Leaders who want to harness that power need to develop, instill, and make use of vision.

The Nature of Vision

Some terms are charged with so many associations and so much baggage that using them can get in the way. Vision has been overused so much that it approaches the realm of words like proactive and branding. Unfortunately, vision also happens to be descriptive of what you need.

Vision Is Connection

We've discussed how people work best when they can see how their activities fit into a larger scheme. In other words, they need to feel connected to something bigger. That's one view of what vision really is. That "something bigger" can be a personal ideal or principle, or it can be a larger context that people acknowledge as important. This chapter focuses on the larger context in terms of what the team and, to a broader extent, the organization want to accomplish.

Many people think Thomas Edison invented the light bulb. He didn't. Instead, he had a big vision of a world powered by electricity, and the incandescent bulb was one of the most potentially dramatic changes. So he led his company, including researchers and technicians, to create a viable commercial bulb.

That's where a leader comes in. Vision is the connection between what someone does and the "big picture" that requires the action. It's the ability to see these connections and frame them in such ways that others can see them. Vision is seeing in your mind's eye how the parts work together to achieve something larger.

Operating with that grasp of context and how things work within it is critical. Without that, your group will never achieve a thing because no one will see a reason for doing so. With such vision, on the other hand, you can move mountains—figuratively and literally.

Vision and Synergy

Ever hear of the word *synergy*? Many people freely use the term without knowing its true (and intriguing) meaning: an interaction of people or forces that creates something greater than its sum. In other words, you get something from nothing. The different forces or entities interact in ways that are invisible to the casual observer. Nevertheless, they exist and have a potent impact.

FACT

Chemical reactions are an excellent way to think of synergy. You mix a number of substances together in a container, reach in with tongs, grasp a small bit of something, and pull. Suddenly you are extruding a line of nylon—something that was in no way present before.

Vision is like a catalyst. It's a substance that doesn't take part in a reaction between other materials, but whose very presence makes the reaction possible. When vision is present, people can come together and reinforce each other's efforts, creating synergy and a result that would otherwise not be possible.

Vision and Visionaries

To try something new, you actually have to think about *doing* something new, and you need the nerve to ignore all the naysayers. You need that idea of where you want to go if you are to head anywhere at all. Are you founding a corporation or working on solving a big problem that will win you a Nobel Prize? Wonderful! Good luck, and more power to you.

Such efforts are relatively infrequent. Yes, we do have examples like Bill Gates and Aung San Suu Kyi—people who have such powerful views of where they want to go that others are swept up and carried away. While those are great examples of leadership, there are many other ways of being a leader. You can't force yourself to suddenly be creative in specific ways or see what others don't. Leading is a more fundamental and universal phenomenon. As a leader, it is your responsibility to help others see the vision of what you want to accomplish.

Out-of-This-World Vision

The early story of General Motors's Saturn division illustrates this concept of vision. Saturn was originally an experiment in automobile design and management styles. Employees got to transfer to the new division because they shared an enthusiasm for the new idea and way of working.

Part of this new idea was the ability for any employee on the assembly line to stop production on the line if there was a defect or problem found with the process or a specific part. By allowing individual employees to stop the assembly line, Saturn was able to ensure that the problem would be found early on in the manufacturing process, saving thousands of dollars.

FACT

A standard criticism of companies floundering in the marketplace is that they lack direction. The leaders don't have a clear strategy, and generally people don't seem to know where they are heading. In short, there is no vision governing corporate operations.

The exciting aspect of allowing employees to stop the assembly line is the power it puts in their hands. They feel totally committed and connected to the Saturn process. The positive impact on employees is immeasurable, but the positive impact on the Saturn division is clear—in saved time, reduced quality issues, and fewer recalls and defects. Employees understood the vision because leaders put the power to reach objectives literally in their hands.

Vision Is Communicated Direction

For a leader, vision is all about helping others see that bigger picture and begin to make those connections to a larger effort. As a leader, you need to focus on being the effective communicator of direction to your team.

Knowing Where You're Going

Is there any doubt whether an organization with clearly defined goals and objectives has a greater chance of achieving them than one operating in a muddle? It only takes one experience working with a befuddled group to wipe the doubt from your mind. The single biggest contributor to a lack of team vision is that the leaders haven't thoroughly sought to understand where the group is going and what it takes to get there.

The fatal mistake many make is thinking that because they say they want to do something, they must have vision. Nothing is further from the truth. Talking about a direction is no more than stating a desire. Before helping others find their way, leaders must have developed their own vision of a group's goals. The process is rigorous and demanding. Unless effort is put in at the beginning, there will be no results at the end.

Communication Makes Things Possible

Leaders can have a fully developed vision of where they need an organization to go and still get nothing from it if they can't communicate their vision to everyone else. When you do communicate a vision effectively, amazing things are possible. Just as having a vision is more than simply saying you want something, communicating a vision means more than just telling someone what you see.

ESSENTIAL

Explaining vision is like explaining the experience of eating a peach. Your words may be well chosen and your imagery may be strong, but ultimately all you have is a person hearing about how good a peach is and wondering why you don't just give them some fruit.

Communicating vision is the process of working with others so they can create and implement a vision. That way, instead of depending on an intellectual grasp of an idea that will fade or just become some kind of curiosity, you pass along an experience that sticks with your team. Then, as circumstances change, the team members can refresh and expand their vision as necessary. You see the effect and effectiveness of the communication in what happens with the team members. You're on the right track if they become more enthused and involved. People are stimulated and excited in an environment that rewards learning and renews commitment.

No Communication? No Vision

When the leader doesn't effectively help people establish vision, then the exact opposite of "stimulated and excited" happens. Team members cannot know what they need to achieve or how to get there because they don't know where the team or organization is going. Why? Because no one bothered to tell them.

As a leader, you need to give the people on your team more than a road map. They need a tangible sense of the path—a 3D relief map, if you will. You want them to feel the rises and dips and see the goal as a palpable place.

Without such a map, the team will do nothing—at best. At worst, members will start setting their own objectives, which could easily go off in directions you don't want. But they don't want to stand around waiting for someone to tell them what to do. So don't make them wait. Build a vision and communicate it.

The Vision Process

Creating vision is really a process of building understanding. You don't come up with the "magic phrasing" that brings things alive for team members. Instead, you move through a series of steps:

- Review the organization's principles.
- Examine the specific goal.
- Determine how the goal supports the principle.
- Break the goal down.
- Help team members build their own vision.
- Be receptive to vision from below.

Fundamental to all these steps is the ability to ask the right types of questions.

Questioning and Vision

Vision is different from typical decision-making. You don't commission a survey. You don't sit around a table with a group and pick mission statements out of the air. You don't concentrate on the paper trail to keep your posterior out of a sling. What you do is try to understand the essence of an organization and its goals and then see how what you do relates and where it fits in.

The Need for Questions

Why are so many statements, rallying cries, and marching orders so excruciatingly dull and predictable? Because some group of people sits around a table and comes up with something that "sounds good." That's a huge mistake. The result becomes corporate group-think and group-speak, even if you're talking about a nonprofit organization. Unfortunately, many people learn such managerial blandishments as a form of proper expression.

If you want a good example of what happens when groups make statements and don't ask questions, take a look at the average organization's mission statement. Inevitably they are ballooned by platitudes and rarely reflect how the entity actually operates.

Such pronouncements generally embody the assumptions and biases of the people at the table. Surprise upon surprise, they may have nothing to do with anyone or anything else in the world. That's no basis for getting others to take part in what you want to accomplish.

Starting with a statement is an almost-guaranteed way to torpedo whatever you want to achieve, even before you start. Since vision is about the connections between what people do and the greater intent, you need to understand the nuances of the venture and have a grasp of what team members are doing. That means getting past your dearly held assumptions and premature conclusions for long enough to see what is happening and establish context. Any time you want to learn something about reality, work from questions, not statements.

Open-Ended Questions

In both interviewing and negotiations, the standard advice is always to ask open-ended questions. There are two reasons for this. One is that when you ask close-ended questions, you let people answer with a monosyllabic yes or no. These are answers in name only because they don't tell you anything more than an elementary fact.

But relationships are never simple, and to build them, you need to understand the intricacies. That's why you need open-ended questions. You want the nuances, and that means being open to hearing those things you didn't know you were asking about.

Open-Ended Trick

Creating open-ended questions is harder than you might think. Don't feel bad—even professional journalists often flub this assignment. The problem is that you assume the range of things you want to know from a question, but you don't parse out the actual words like a grammar geek to literally notice what you actually said. For example, if you wanted to know how a team member was doing on a project, you might ask, "Are you going to be done soon?"

Ah, poor questioner. You're thinking, "I want to know when this is going to be done." But you asked if it will be done soon, leaving open the yes/no door, and you extended the opening by not defining what you considered "soon." You could try breaking down your questions first. In the context of vision, that is usually possible and helpful. But if you're stuck, here is a trick. Instead of starting a question with a verb, use one of the great interrogatives taught in every introductory journalism class:

- Who?
- What?
- Which?
- Where?
- When?
- Why?
- How?

Let's look at the previous example: Are you going to be done soon? You're interested in the time frame, so recast the sentence with the "when" interrogative at the beginning: "When will you be done?" Or you could ask variations: "What progress have you made?"

Close-Ended Loaded Questions

On the surface, stating a question so that it's open-ended sounds easy and is mainly an issue of avoiding close-ended ones. After all, a close-ended question is one that allows a binary answer: yes or no, black or white, right or wrong, good or bad, chocolate or vanilla. An open-ended question, on the other hand, allows a range of answers.

Structuring a question well is nevertheless more difficult than you might think. A big problem is asking a loaded question. The format is not technically binary, but the wording sets such conditions on the answer that you've drastically narrowed how someone in her right mind would answer.

ALERT!

Be careful. It is terribly easy to ask what seems to be an open-ended question but that really forces a specific type of answer, even with an interrogative. Look at the classic "When did you stop beating your wife?" Starting with "when," this question would seem innocent enough, but it has an agenda worthy of a joint session of Congress.

As an example, let's say you are in a corporate setting and say to someone on your team, "Is the project going okay?" Just what do you expect the person to say? "No, we're completely underwater and only a miracle can help us"? You'll probably hear, "Fine." By the time you hear a more complete answer, it will be too late.

You got the simple answer because you telegraphed what you wanted to hear. Had you wanted a real answer, you would have lowered the judgment-value component of the question and asked, "Where are things with the project?" The team member cannot be tempted to toss off a quick "Fine," because you were not asking a loaded question.

The Vision Hierarchy

If a team is building a car, not everyone does the same thing. Some work on the drive train, others install the air conditioning and radio, and yet others add the upholstery. The overall intent of assembling the car has many parts. The vision has to be extensive enough to support everything the team needs to do. The thing to do is start at the top and work down. At each step, use your questioning skills when considering your answers. You want to encourage yourself to think in an open-ended way.

The Organization's Vision

The team is trying to support what the organization wants to do, which is why you need to start at the top with where the organization is going. That means first looking at the organization's principles. Any vision will have to begin with that as the foundation or your efforts will be wasted.

ALERT!

Trying to set a vision without relating it closely to that of the organization is like being in a silent slapstick comedy centered upon a moving hook-and-ladder truck of a fire department. The cab starts going one way, while the back of the truck, separately steered, swings off in another.

Identify the principle or principles with which your group's efforts should most closely align. This will help you refine what your group should be doing because it lets you focus your efforts to best advance the interests of the organization. This step sets the destination on the map when you are taking a trip. You can further extend this by considering the structure of the organization. It may be that your group is contained within another, which is part of yet a third, and so on.

Use Active Imagination

When you have a strong sense of what the organization stands for and what it is trying to accomplish at every level, you have the groundwork to understand how your group fits in to the whole. The group's objective is to support the organization's principles and intents.

One of the most important responsibilities of a leader is to see practical ways that he and the team can further the principles and intents. At times, it will be clear what your team should be doing. For example, if you are in charge of the marketing department at a corporation preparing to release a new product, you know you need to develop an appropriate campaign. If a community group is planning an outdoor cookout, you need to make arrangements for food, grills, volunteer cooks, and so on.

But there will be many times when what you ought to do isn't so obvious. These situations require active imagination. We all know how to daydream. What you want to do is have a directed daydream and consider what supportive things your group might do. Don't censor what comes to mind; note all your ideas for later consideration. Those ideas will spark goals that bring you closer to supporting your organization's principles.

Examine the Specific Goal

Now it's time to take apart the group's goal. Understand its parts, intents, requirements, expectations, assumptions—in short, anything and everything that explains where the group is supposed to go, how it can get there, what the barriers might be, and what resources and techniques you have for overcoming those barriers.

Goal Supports Principles

You've built a principle ladder from your group upward to the top of the organization and have examined your group goal. At every stage, you should see the ways in which your planned actions fit in with some aspect of that goal. If there is a divergence at any point, your group's efforts will fail because they won't connect all the way back to the top.

At each stage, you should also be able to directly relate your group's goal to a bigger goal of the organization. Your efforts are to reinforce, as completely as possibly, what the organization is trying to achieve and to create harmony between your group's efforts and those of the rest of the organization. That makes synergy on a grand scale possible.

Break the Goal Down

A group goal can still be too general. Often one will split into multiple parts handled by different people. Each of those parts needs an explicitly understood connection to the group goal's aims and to all the principles up the line. Once that is accomplished, you've established criteria by which group members can examine their efforts and determine whether the group's goals remain on track.

Help Team Member Vision

What you did in understanding principles, breaking down goals and connecting them with top principles and related goals at every level of the organization, was an example of building vision—your own vision. By using open-ended questions and examining what you wanted the group to achieve in a larger context, you established a vision of what the group's efforts meant.

Need for Personal Vision

In creating your own vision of the group's efforts, you reinforced a number of factors for your own work. One is purpose. When you don't know why you do what you do, it seems purposeless. However, when you can see a chain of connections leading from you to much larger efforts, you can more easily put energy into your efforts. Also, by putting things into context, you can proceed more reliably. You have a range of checks and balances—your understanding of the part you and your group play in a larger context. You can see if things start going off track because you see the direction in which you should be going.

For the same reasons, the members of your team also need a personal vision. It may be more restricted; depending on the structure and size of your team, people may be more involved with smaller and more focused responsibilities. But the same quality of personal vision must exist, or your fellow team members will lose a sense of relevance and will not be able to help keep the correct course through their efforts.

Helping Build Personal Vision

Although you can explain your own vision and the vision of people up the line in the organization, you can't actually *give* people a vision. They have to create it for themselves. Nevertheless, what you can do is help them find their own vision. Go through the same open-ended questioning you did with yourself in examining the organization's principles and its goals at every level. In this case, however, you ask the questions of team members and not yourself.

Don't give the people you question the answers you want. You want them to develop their own responses, which might suggest additional questions that you'll ask. When you work this way, you allow people to make the same mental effort that you did. The process of answering the same questions (even if they didn't ask themselves) creates a personal vision for them.

You can ask the questions in groups, in one-on-one meetings, through memos, or any combination of these methods. As you do, you help develop the process of vision for everyone, and when you succeed, that turns into enormous opportunities for synergy. The group can actually create something together that is more than any of the members could have done alone.

Vision from Below

The problem with a traditional hierarchy is that everything gets passed down the line. When things move only from top to bottom, they reinforce old concepts of managing people. The organization never gets the synergy and help that comes from all the team members being completely engaged. To remedy this, you need to include a return path for everything, including vision.

ALERT!

Always pushing ideas and concepts down and never letting any bubble up is like constantly breathing in and never out. Toxins build up in the organizational bloodstream, doing great damage, and all you have to show for it is a lot of hot air.

Vision is a companion to direction—the connection between what needs to be done and why it needs to be done. But as anyone who has spent time in a hierarchical organization can tell you, when direction comes only from above, it quickly becomes ineffective. Experience on the front lines can provide critical information and clues about whether an organization's direction is working or if some collective is headed serenely and resolutely into a brick wall.

Scheduled Feedback

Make time on a regular basis to hear feedback from team members. Using open-ended questions, ask about their experiences and how they see their accomplishments interacting with the principles and bigger objectives. Stress that this is not a secret form of performance evaluation, and bring up your own concerns about where things might be going off track. If there are problems that people can see developing, it's better to know them now and to take steps while it's still be possible rather than to bury your head in the sand.

Unscheduled Feedback

Sometimes the most important information will come when you're least expecting it. Be sensitive to what people say around you, both directly through words and indirectly in body language and action. When you see signs that what people are being asked to do is not meshing well with the overall direction of the group and organization, ask about it.

When asking questions, you keep in mind that this is a learning process for all and not an interrogation. People will open up to the former while hiding from the latter.

Building the Upward Ladder

The bigger and more complex your team or group, the more isolated you can become from the people who compose it. In such cases, you need to create mechanisms to ensure that communication can occur from the bottom to the top of the organization. In those answering directly to you, instill a discipline of ensuring personal vision and its transmission upwards. Regularly hear what these people are learning, and make the lessons learned available to all. That's taking the information that percolates up and disseminating it out and down again, so it helps enrich everyone's experience.

CHAPTER 5

Communication

Without communication, no leader can succeed. Whether the attempt is to inspire, exhort, or inform, working with others always requires everyone involved to exchange ideas, experiences, concerns, problems, and solutions. Some people seem born with the ability to speak or write, but anyone and everyone can learn to communicate better. In this chapter, we'll look at the basic requirements of communication and many ideas and tips on how to better facilitate conversations of all types.

Communication: The Essence of Leadership

One of the great examples of leadership in technology was the NASA moon landing in 1969. Not only did brainy people from many disciplines pull off something astounding, they did so together. Untold thousands of systems had to work together. Efforts to monitor the progress of the flight involved facilities literally around the globe. While the astronauts were the popular heroes, the mission was only possible because people communicated.

The public nature of everything that NASA did at that time underscored both the quality of the agency's communications and the nerve to stay focused even in extreme circumstances. It teaches a lesson: In the most challenging situations, focusing on the basics of communication can be an anchor to your goal.

Leadership and communication in the space race shone especially bright during the Apollo 13 mission. A malfunction put the three astronauts on the flight into jeopardy. Only through the cooperation of everyone in space and on the ground was the trio able to return home safely. Communication is the lifeblood of leadership. A leader who wants a group to achieve a goal will have to communicate.

Leaders Need Communication

Leadership doesn't exist without relationships, and communication is key to any interaction. When you truly communicate, you create dialogue and reach shared meaning. Without that shared meaning, people literally go off in their own directions and you're lucky if you accomplish anything. Miss the communication, and you have the organizational equivalent of that old movie gag where two people are unknowingly pulling on the same object, only in opposite directions. Each fights the progress the other makes, and both go nowhere fast.

Many organizations have failed from a lack of communication. That might mean a lack of clear direction, missed coordination across levels, mixed signals, or poor dialogue with partners or stakeholders. Improving communication creates better performance, which in turn further boosts communication. The two people look back and see each other, at which point they can decide on a common direction and both pull that way.

The Nature of Good Communication

Good communication is focused and bidirectional. Those who just talk and don't listen aren't communicating; they're dictating. If you want to be an effective leader, you must nurture and encourage various types of communications:

- Leaders convey plans and directions.
- Team members tell leaders what they require to do their jobs so the leaders can provide it.
- All team members directly coordinate their activities with each other.
- Leaders monitor progress toward goals by talking to team members and listening to what they have to say.

The better you can communicate with others, and the more you can get everyone else to talk, the better a leader you can be. Luckily, proper communication doesn't require advanced oratory skills or long training in writing.

Communication Essentials

You communicate effectively when you and the other person have both absorbed and understood what has been said. That is a three-stage process:

1. Send a message in a clear and straightforward manner.
2. Let the other person accept the message.
3. Be sure that the person has received and understood the message.

You can learn to use your communication skills to cultivate relationships throughout your organization. If you communicate your desire to lead

THE EVERYTHING LEADERSHIP BOOK

or to try new things, leadership opportunities will present themselves over and over again—and you'll be able to succeed in them.

FACT

Abraham Lincoln, one of the greatest leaders in American history, was tall, gangly, and had a high-pitched voice. Although he might not have met many people's ideal of an attractive man, his ability to communicate through humor helped establish his career.

Only three rules—that seems simple enough, and it is. As always, though, the devil is in the details, and those devilish particulars lie in the foundation of communicating.

Say It with Meaning

When you communicate without a reason, you spew empty words. Sometimes it's fun to chat about nothing. But small talk is unfocused and won't get you closer to your goal. Real communication is about creating shared meaning. By definition, meaning has to be about something; it's not an empty exercise.

Meaning and Goals

The goal is central to the leader, so it makes sense that goal-orientation is central to communication. If your communications are not ultimately serving your goal in one way or the other, then they are unnecessary. That still leaves plenty of room to take care of everyone's needs.

ESSENTIAL

Think of a time at a party or social occasion where you were making small talk. Now contrast that to a time when you were trying to communicate something important. There is a tangible difference. As a leader, you need more of the second and less of the first.

Goals become a great litmus test for your communication. If you can't find a connection between what you want to say, your goal, and all the things that support it, chances are that you can find something more constructive and useful to convey.

Goals and Intent

When you have a goal, you have a reason to do something. You now operate with intent. The intent becomes your navigator. It tells you whether you are proceeding in the right direction—exactly what you need to avoid misunderstandings in communication. After all, if you're not sure where you're going in a conversation, how is the other person ever going to know?

When you know why you want to communicate and what your communication must achieve—the meaning and goal—you'll have a better sense of how to express yourself. There isn't a single type of intent in communication. At different times, you will find yourself trying to achieve a number of things: inform, motivate, persuade, elicit, and explore.

Depending on your intent, elements like your choice of words, the rhythm of the language, and delivery will differ. Your effort to create a dialogue will be pragmatic because you will communicate in the way that best upholds the goal and serves the intent.

Elements of Communication

To understand how to communicate, you need to grasp three basic elements that must support your purpose:

- Your audience
- What you want to say
- The medium of communication

The better you understand each of these areas, the more effectively you will be able to communicate. The surest route to getting something across is to pay attention to these communication basics. Charisma, poise, and persuasiveness can help, but without a foundation, the message falls apart.

Reach Your Audience

When you know what you want to achieve through your communication, you might think that the next step would be to hone your content. Instead, you must first consider the audience.

When professional writers take on an assignment, one of the first questions they ask is the nature of the audience. They know that the points they will make and the tone and vocabulary they use will depend completely on the answer.

You'd talk to a group of business executives differently than the way you'd address a grade school class. Every audience, no matter what the size, has its own needs, preconceptions, and expectations. To reach your audience, you have to speak the right language.

Finding the Audience Need

You've started your approach to communication by considering the goal and what you need to achieve. But you can't forget the need of the people on the receiving end. They have their own relationships to the goal, their own responsibilities, and their own lives as well. They are independent and aren't bound to follow your lead, even if you directly employ them.

Communication in companies often breaks down at this point. The dangerous attitude is "We hired them, so they have to do what we want." What a foolish assumption! Resentful underlings have scuttled more strategies than any set of fierce competitors, all because they weren't treated as human beings and they received no consideration for what they needed.

This mistaken approach consists of talking *at* people and assuming that they have nothing to say. Communication is always a two-way process. When you won't hear someone, that person won't hear you.

The answer is to speak the language of the people on your team. Don't use a pandering approach, like using specific slang to better fit in. Talking so that a group of people hears you means acknowledging them and addressing their concerns. Although you want to achieve something through your communications, put yourself into the shoes of the audience members and let their needs come first. To really get into those shoes and to learn to better hear others, it helps to understand how people listen.

FACT

Management experts know that employees often have the best idea of what is really happening in the company. They are the people who face the problems, customers, and organizational shortcomings.

Types of Listeners

People listen in many different ways, and the way someone listens determines how much of a message actually gets through. Mismatch the type of communication with the listening style, and up to 70 percent of what a person hears or reads can be lost.

When you better understand how people listen, you start to modify how you communicate so that others will get an even larger percentage of the message. There are five basic types of listening:

- **Appreciating:** Listeners become completely involved and pay close attention; if not totally engaged, they may miss a point.
- **Empathizing:** Listeners try to match their experience to what they are hearing but can become so wrapped up in one aspect of the information that they can miss something equally important.
- **Comprehending:** Those who listen through comprehending try to organize and make sense of the messages being sent and to understand the relationships among ideas; they often miss unspoken communication or the subtext of a message.
- **Discerning:** These listeners want complete and accurate information and will sift and weigh each bit of information for accuracy, validity, and content. If the speed of processing the information doesn't keep pace with the delivery, they may miss things.

- **Evaluating:** Evaluators put information into a larger context and will accept or reject messages based on personal beliefs. They will miss anything that doesn't fit into their belief systems.

The better you can understand these types, the greater your chance of delivering your messages. The real challenge is to teach others—and yourself—to use multiple methods to improve listening as much as possible.

Talk to Yourself

The biggest single failure in communication is lack of planning and thought. You can have the smoothest delivery and most captivating style, a willing audience, and any communication medium you want. All those are fleeting. Eventually, people leave your presence, and they are no longer paying attention to the medium. They finish reading the e-mail or memo or your speech comes to an end. What will stay are ideas and words that speak to them, and those don't come from thin air.

President Lincoln spent hours before a trip to Pennsylvania writing a speech only a few hundred words long. Although news reports at the time derided the talk, the planning and intent must have been good; students have been memorizing the Gettysburg Address ever since.

To communicate, you must first know what you want to say and how you want to say it. Before selecting your words, consider what they will need to convey. There will be times that you must communicate in an impromptu situation, which is why you must spend time considering what subjects might come up and how you will approach them. When deciding what to say, you'll need to keep in mind the subject of your message, the structure of how you will say it, and the setting in which you will present it.

Subject

Your subject is the focus of your communication. It's the container that gives shape and context to your words. A subject includes the supporting arguments and evidence you want to present to motivate or convince your audience.

The easiest way to start, particularly for critical writing and speaking, is to jot down your thoughts on the topic in a notebook over a few days. Always keep the notebook with you so that when your subconscious pipes up, you can capture the material. Wait until later and you might as well wait forever; chances are good that you'll lose the train of thought.

Structure

If the subject is the focus of what you are going to communicate, and your audience helps you understand how to express it, structure is the scaffolding that lets everything happen. In well-structured communication, things start naturally and move through a series of points to a conclusion that should seem inevitable by the time you reach it.

Don't go overboard when thinking about structure. Take the points you have written down and arrange them in a natural-sounding progression. Forget about rhetorical flourishes. Just cover what you need to and put down what you want to say as simply as you can.

Setting

The way you express yourself depends on the situation in which the communication takes place. One thing to consider is the nature of the audience and the type of language that it is most likely to be able to hear. A group of engineers might disdain the type of wording that would help motivate a sales team. Choose the wrong vocabulary, and the listening will stop.

The specifics of your communication also depend on the emotional context. Let's say you have two weekly staff meetings. The first covers a performance shortcoming, while the second is about a recent success. The tone of your language will differ significantly from one to the other.

Types of Communication

After considering the intent, the audience, and what you need to say, your next focus should be on the actual form you'll use to deliver a message. Leaders generally communicate by the following four means:

- In person
- In writing
- Graphically
- Via broadcast

Each medium has its own requirements, strengths, and weaknesses. Each also needs a particular approach if you want to make it work for you.

In-Person Communication

Delivering a message in person is the most powerful form of communication, and it's also the most natural. From the day we are born, we all communicate. Babies cry when they want a nap or food or a clean diaper. A smile or grimace say enormous amounts.

Over the years, we pick up language and a range of nonverbal skills to add specificity and nuance to what we say. Messages get more complex as we convey ideas, desires, and interests, combining the intellectual and the emotional in ways no other form of communication can achieve.

ALERT!

Nonverbal communication is not only a powerful tool but a potential danger. If you are ambivalent about something, your body language can send messages contradictory to the words you use, muddying what you are saying.

A leader might find it necessary to use in-person communication in ways ranging from highly personal and informal one-to-one conversations to scripted speeches delivered to any number of people. The constraints are similar. Normal speaking runs around 125 words a minute, which means you have a hard limit on how much information you can fit in.

You also have to be careful about the complexity of what you say. When people listen to information, they can't easily go back and pick up the thread of the message if it gets tangled. That's a greater problem in large groups and formal situations, where listeners don't have the interactivity of a conversation that might allow the other person to ask questions and grasp what you are saying. In a speech, simplicity of language and structure become paramount.

Written Communication

When you put words to paper or the electronic equivalent, you can spend time reviewing the message and honing its execution. People use different vocabularies when writing and speaking, and you probably phrase thoughts differently in both.

Do some reading about how to write well. George Orwell wrote a marvelous essay, "Politics and the English Language," that also offers excellent instruction in how to effectively use language. Another recommendation is *The Elements of Style*, by William Strunk and E. B. White.

The desire to impress the reader is a potential danger in writing. When writing, it's easy to fall victim to elaborate vocabulary and overly complex structure that can lose the reader. You also should consider how the words appear on the page. Avoid block after block of dense text, which is physically difficult to read. For memos, consider using something more than single spacing. Add headings to help direct the reader through the document, and incorporate visual aids where appropriate.

Problems of Electronic Communication

All forms of communication have their own idiosyncrasies, but there are some particularly thorny ones in electronic forms. Electronic communication often effectively combines the worst aspects of writing and speech.

The written word misses the emotional cues that we use when talking. Traditionally this hasn't been a problem because the process of writing has been a reflective one. Someone gives thought, writes a draft, checks it, and possibly rewrites it before someone reads the results. People don't tend to blurt something out in writing as they might in speech because they have too much time to reconsider.

But electronic communication—e-mails, instant messaging, and online discussion forums—are more casual and instantaneous in nature. People tend to use the informality of speech, dash off something without reviewing it, and then hit the send button.

Always give your e-mails a second read before sending them. How would that message seem to you? Are there potential areas of misunderstanding? Take a little extra time now to avoid having to spend a lot of energy later cleaning up an unnecessary mess.

Graphical Communication

A picture can be worth a thousand words, and graphics can show the relationships among sets of information in a more effective way than pages of explanation. Use images to help communicate your points, both in writing and speaking. Don't add graphics just for the sake of having them any more than you'd add to a memo an extra hundred words that said nothing.

Be wary, too, because graphics can also create false impressions. For example, changing the scale of the X and Y axes of a sales graph can change the way a curve looks, creating a different emotional impression of how well an effort has gone. Be scrupulous. You don't want to do something that others might perceive as dishonest, undermining your position as a leader. If a graph seems to you to convey a different impression than the numbers do, others will have the same reaction as well.

Promoting Good Communication

Good communication encourages creative interaction among all members of your team. Your communication strategy should support, encourage, and reinforce your goals, and should do so within the culture of the organization. To do that, you need to develop healthy habits and encourage them among everyone else.

Be Positive

In today's world, culture reinforces cynicism. Certainly when something is wrong, you need to directly address it and change things for the better. Rose-colored glasses are actually negative because they cause you to ignore that which needs change. But cynicism isn't corrective. Instead, it is an attitude that things are wrong because life is like that. Cynicism becomes an excuse to do nothing but sit at the sidelines, disdainfully watching life go by.

To combat cynicism, work to be positive in your communication. Focus on improving situations instead of simply pointing out what is wrong. Work with others. Get their ideas and help on how to make things better. Avoid criticism where you can. If you don't have something positive to say, something that can help improve things, then say nothing.

Have Fun

Let your communication be upbeat and enthusiastic whenever possible. The more your audience enjoys listening to you, the more they will retain. Again, this has to be genuine and not the relentless cheerfulness that often passes as being positive.

FACT

For a humorous view of the relentlessly positive, you might read the classic *Candide* by the French writer Voltaire. This work was a satire on the philosophical concept that we live in the best of all possible worlds and so everything that happens must be for the best. Characters twist themselves into knots trying to rationalize the various disasters that befall them.

Fun and enthusiasm come from action, so take some. Be bold and courageous, and then when you communicate what you do, your gusto will be catching.

Be Open

Communication is a two-way activity, so you need to be receptive to what others have to say. Whenever possible, ask open-ended questions that allow the person you are speaking with to talk with you. Once you have asked the question, truly listen to the answer.

When you become engaged in conversation with another person, allow him or her to complete the full thought before you respond. Listen to the total idea or statement; don't jump on one word or phrase. Hear the person out and then offer your responses.

Allow yourself to recognize the importance of this topic or information to the speaker. Even if you think it is unimportant, demonstrate to the person that you value and respect her contribution.

Creating a Communication Strategy

You have many tools for better communication, and that's good. Now you need to put them into place through a communication strategy through specific vehicles. Depending on the leadership role you fulfill and your unique group, your choice of which to use, and how to use them, will differ. There are a number of largely one-way forms of communication that can keep everyone in sync.

Memos

For many organizations, particularly corporations, memos are almost as prevalent as air—but they are frequently misused. A memo should focus on one specific topic; otherwise, you run the risk of people forgetting the first points by the time they've reached the end.

Write memos simply and only when you have a significant amount to say on an important topic, or when for legal or regulatory reasons you need to clearly document something. The more memos flying about the environment, the less important they seem.

To help retain the effectiveness of memos, only include people on the routing list who need the information then. If there are other people in the organization who should also be kept informed, you might create a less frequent status report.

Reports

A report is a longer, more structured document than a memo. It focuses on a topic in depth. These take more time and thought and shouldn't be done on impulse. Incorporate graphics and headings to improve readability. If you do write a report, plan on giving people enough time to consider the information, and have a meeting to address the topic if necessary.

This is also a type of communication that benefits from a smart-looking presentation. Psychologically, people give greater credence to something that looks impressive, so use that to help get your point across.

Short Messages

A short message that you send as an e-mail, an enclosure in a pay envelope, via voice mail, or as an instant message offers an informal way to communicate routine information. Match the specific mechanism to the habits of the recipients and the timeliness of the information.

A critical and urgent message needs quick delivery, which rules out a pay enclosure. For speedy delivery, e-mail might work, although some people might only check their inboxes once or twice a day. Mass voice mail over a corporate telephone system is fine unless important recipients are traveling and have limited access, in which case you'll need to duplicate the message over cell phones.

FACT

For important but less time-sensitive communications, you could also use an old-fashioned letter. Given the changing nature of telecommunications, people have come to depend on e-mail and telephone and are less accustomed to receiving letters. This is a format that will have more impact and, as a result, drive your message home more certainly.

Newsletters

Newsletters are tricky. Many organizations overuse them. Think of your own e-mail inbox; you may have a number of electronic newsletters that come in every week that you no longer bother to read. Employees might be more likely to at least look through a corporate newsletter than donors are to read one from a nonprofit.

Newsletters require information that people find useful and that they will want to read. Even more than meetings, a newsletter has to be about your audience and its needs if you have any hope that they will read what you want them to. Plan on a mix of topics, articles, and information graphics that satisfy the reader while delivering your critical messages as well. Be sure the front of the newsletter clearly states the benefit to the audience.

Communicating Across Levels

One of the most difficult things to do in communication is to ensure the flow of information across all levels of an organization and over the boundaries between the organization and other groups.

As a leader, success in reaching your goals means that you must encourage, support, and embrace communication with, to, and from everyone below and above you in your organization's hierarchy.

Communicating with Your Key Players

It is critical that you work with other leaders within the organization so that all of you are communicating the same message. This group of leaders is the one that develops communication strategies and policy statements. When all of you reinforce the same set of messages, you are far more likely to succeed. Now that the entire team shares a common language, the whole organization will be able to work toward the same well-defined goal.

Key players must have real dialogue with each other so that they can freely share their views. All should feel that they have contributed to decisions, and all should agree to support a decision in action and word, even if the decision is not what a specific team member wanted.

Communicating Up and Down the Line

When you talk only to your peers, you are cut off from the organization. When that happens, you can do nothing. Talking to your immediate team is also not enough. You must strive to build a communications channel up and down the entire organization. Concentrate on communication principles and promote them so that the same principles work at all levels.

FACT

Stress to those who report directly to you the importance of maintaining open communication and create structures so that crucial things move easily up and down the organization. Then the lessons learned and vital information can reach you and others who need it.

When you manage to have clear communication throughout the organization, you build the psychological equivalent of a resonance chamber, like a pipe in an organ. The tone—your message—reverberates and strengthens, reinforcing your goals.

Communicating with the Outside World

It doesn't matter what your organization does or wants. Eventually, you must deal with the outside world. This is the ultimate challenge in communication. As a leader, it is your job to set the example for others to learn from. Communicating with those outside your organization is merely an extension of the same good practices that work inside.

You will deal with customers, supporters, agencies, people who have a need, and others who want something. They will all have goals and interests that may or may not mesh with yours. So while communication is always important, it becomes vital when the organization must turn its face outward to the rest of the world.

When your organization listens to those from the outside using a disciplined and principled approach to communication, it will succeed. When your organization listens to what it only *thinks* others are saying, it is gambling. The successful business is able to clearly understand the needs and expectations of the customer and find the best ways to make the customer happy.

CHAPTER 6

Setting Goals

Being a leader means guiding a group in pursuit of a common goal. If you don't have a goal, you can't do much leading. In fact, it turns out that setting some high-level goals is not enough. You must also learn to work with the objectives of others and use goals in everything your team does. Once you set goals, you must follow through to make sure your team meets them as efficiently as possible.

Nothing Happens Without Goals

Ask any expert, any consultant, any accomplished person, for advice on how to achieve something. Chances are that the first thing you will hear is that you need a goal. If you think about it, this makes perfect sense. What is a goal, after all, if not the place you want to go? Achievement is arriving at your goal, no matter where or what it is.

All accomplishments, great or small, have started with a goal. The Great Pyramid at Giza did not start growing out of the desert because a group of people had nothing better to do that decade. Attila the Hun overran much of Europe because he wanted to rule the known world, not because he took a wrong turn at what would become Cologne.

FACT

Goals don't necessarily have to be big at the start to ultimately end up large. Sometimes one goal—like developing a new approach to running a food establishment—can lead to other possibilities and other goals. Take McDonald's, which has sold so many hamburgers that it can't keep up with adding the zeros to its signs to indicate the number of happy customers served.

However, there's nothing to say that a goal must be grandiose. People attend college, build structures, cook holiday meals, read books, and give the dog a bath. In each of these and countless other scenarios, people have goals. They may not be glamorous or newsworthy, but they are all goals people want to accomplish.

Goal Requirements

It's a mistake to assume that everything people do in life results from a goal. People commonly want things, and they undertake many activities, but it is relatively unusual to find someone truly acting from a goal. No matter what its scale, a real goal differs from simply wanting something. It incorporates specific properties and requirements. Fail to meet any of these, and you no longer have a goal that will let you lead.

Goals Are Practical

You've doubtless heard the old saying that if wishes were horses, beggars would ride. But without significant changes in life circumstances, a mendicant will not have money to keep and feed a stallion, let alone purchase one. Wanting a horse in a daydream sense is completely impractical. However, with some changes—such as establishing a regular income, saving, and amassing capital—the beggar could one day ride.

A desire without a plan for implementation is a pipe dream—something nice if it would happen, but clearly the stuff of wishful accident. On the other hand, a goal is always practical, which means it needs a plan for implementation. Instead of inspiring dreams, a goal promotes the action of pursuit. That's not to say you can easily achieve your goal, but success is always a possibility.

Goals Order Activities

A goal is important because it becomes a point of ordering your activities. Look to your own experience in traveling by car. If you're lost in an unfamiliar place, you'll either look at a map or stop people and ask them for directions. In either case, you try to pinpoint where you are and see the path from there to the particular place you want to reach. Your destination might be the nearest entrance to the highway, or it could be the new house of some old friends who just moved. No matter the specifics, you do have the goal of reaching a particular spot. When you know a direction, you can go somewhere. When you don't have a place you want to go, you're driving around aimlessly.

The goal orders the activities. It may be a matter of scheduling. You cut the lawn on the weekend because you want to get it done—a goal—and you've determined when you can do it. A corporation might change the emphasis of its activities because it wants to boost its stock price. Doing that requires enough profit to satisfy the estimates of analysts, who will then suggest the stock to their clients, many of whom will buy the stock, causing the price to rise. Running shy of that level of profit, corporate management focuses its activities on business that can quickly close. Parents want a safe place for local children to play, and so they look for space, raise money, and build a playground.

Goals Allow Measurement

Any parent has heard the plaintive wail of "Are we there yet?" drifting up from the back seat. The answer is generally an expression of time, based on the distance left to reach the destination. Without that goal, there is no way to answer the question. First of all, there would literally be no "there" that ended the auto trip, meaning there would be no answer.

A factory might measure its output in glockenspiels per day, but the number would be meaningless in itself. Data only takes on meaning when considered in relation to a stated level of production that supports the company's marketing and financial goals.

Progress means how closely you have approached your destination or goal. It is only in relationship to a goal that measurement makes any sense because that goal orders your activities and gives the ultimate reference point.

Goals Are Always Practical

You can only achieve when you have a goal. Not all goals are equal. Some are easier; some are harder. Some are complex; others are relatively simple. You couldn't compare the do-it-yourselfer's desire to build a new deck with Martin Luther's intent to reform the Catholic Church as it existed in the sixteenth century. One problem is solved with tools and materials, while the other required a mighty effort to shake off centuries of habit and the interests of powerful clergy members.

Nevertheless, the two are identical in the sense that they are completely practical. In either case, a person plans (or planned) on reaching a goal. A goal that is empty or intended only to rally the troops is worthless and should be consigned to the waste can. Since it is not real, it cannot drive real action and will be useless to a leader.

Goals Are for Groups

Goals are just as indispensable for groups as they are for individuals. In fact, a clear goal is even more important for a group. If people are going to work together, they need a common framework so that their efforts reinforce each other and don't pull in opposite directions. The leader—you—helps to direct the group's activities in light of the goal and to measure its overall effectiveness in reaching that destination.

Actually, you could argue that the goal is even more vital for a group because there are so many different places that mistakes could happen and efforts can go awry. Think about the massive amounts of coordination that must happen to have a planned lunch ready by noon for a grade school. People have to take budgets and nutritional requirements into account to decide what goes on the menu, purchase the necessary food and equipment, and hire the proper staff—and that's even before you get into the logistics of serving food. Each day, the staff needs to start cutting vegetables and bread in the morning and have everything cooked and in place in warming trays before the first students line up.

QUESTION?

Can every activity help me to learn better leadership?
Absolutely. The reason that the school meal sounds like directing an army is because it essentially is. Real activities all follow the same principles. Learn to apply those principles in small endeavors, and you'll build the leadership muscle for larger ones.

Because a set of activities that a group undertakes is more complex than that of an individual, goals become more complex. In fact, leaders must learn to use a family of goals and not just a single one.

Goal Complexity

On a grand scale, goals are simple things that exist on their own. But as the scale of the goal increases, so does its complexity. Instead of a single goal for all members of a team, you have multiple goals, each with its own needs and degree of importance. In addition, all members have many interests in their lives, not just the single-minded pursuit of whatever the group is trying to achieve.

In no time at all, life gets complicated. You need to deal with the complexity of goals, and that means understanding goal hierarchy in all its forms. The first step is to look at goal complexity.

Goal Towers

Forget about sitting back and leading your team to greatness for one and only one goal; that situation never exists. Goals aren't monolithic because they don't happen in one step. A goal rests on everything that must occur for it to happen. Instead of seeing a goal as a position off in the distance with continuous progress that must happen before it can arrive, think of your goal as a structure—a tower. At the very top of the structure is the goal. Under that ultimate goal can be any number of stages. Each stage comprises some number of columns that represent sub-goals. Sometimes, when a goal comprises several steps, a column consists of multiple pieces stacked one atop the other, as shown in **FIGURE 6-1**.

FIGURE 6-1:

The Goal Tower

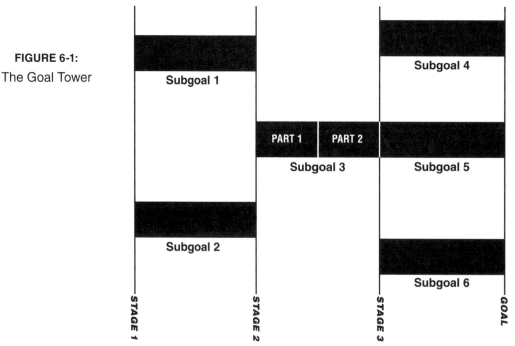

Let's return to the idea of cooking a meal—not at a school, this time, but in your home for some friends. Here are just some of the steps that must occur:

1. Research recipes.
2. Buy ingredients.
3. Do preparatory work.
4. Decorate the surroundings.
5. Cook various dishes, starting each so they are ready at the same time.
6. Serve the meal.

Someone practiced in entertaining doesn't labor over the division of steps, but she does perform each and every one. Each part breaks down into other elements. For example, preparatory work might involve cleaning the food, chopping vegetables, and making a stock for a soup—and that's just to cook dinner for friends.

If you ever think your goal is simple, it means that you aren't giving it enough thought. Take some time and plot out all the steps that must happen before your team can achieve the goal. Each step becomes an intermediary goal.

The more complex the goal, the more parts it has. Each part is a goal in itself, with its own set of contributing elements. Suddenly single-mindedness goes out the window. To lead a team to make an overall goal, you now have to accomplish a whole group of objectives.

You reach the goal one stage at a time. You can't skip any because the goal is a structure, like a building. Remove one part and the entire tower collapses. Next comes another source of conflict: other goals.

Competing Goals

Achievement would be much easier if you had nothing to do but focus on one task. Unfortunately, the world rarely waits until you are ready for it. Aside from the complexity of what they want to achieve, leaders must deal with a range of goals that may all be necessary. Priorities can conflict, either in terms of what the goals try to achieve or in the resources they demand.

FACT

The Civil Rights movement of the 1950s and 1960s certainly faced such challenges. There were a range of potential legal challenges, groups interested in direct nonviolent action in one place and another. Leaders of the movement had to work together to determine the courses of action that would bring them closer to what they ultimately wanted: equal rights.

Instead of one goal for the team, or even goals with multiple parts, you often face many potential goals. Rather than the goal tower, you've got the goal office park. You must know which of the goals you will be visiting and how you can support all of them without leaving anything undone.

All entities—whether they be neighborhood associations, nonprofits, or global corporations—must at one point or another determine the relative importance of goals in the face of their fundamental principles. What does the organization or group stand for? Which goals are most important? How can the organization effectively strive toward the principles it holds true? When leaders can answer those questions with some uniformity, they can better invest resources and minimize the conflict of egos and personal agendas. Leaders who are responsible for multiple goals must weigh the options and focus on what most effectively supports the organization's mission.

Communication is also vital in this context. There will be many times in your growth as a leader when people will assume they can continuously ask you to do more without providing you with additional resources. You face the dilemma of opposing the extra work and being branded an obstructionist or taking it on and eventually failing at part of it by causing undue stress on your team. Generally, you must chart the course of doing what you can. Before things become unmanageable, you must let those above you know in a positive way. Back up your stance with as much hard data as you can muster, and ask for help in determining your priorities. When done judiciously (and not as a case of crying wolf), you bring the point home and gain tacit acceptance of the need for limitations.

Competing with the Personal

Furthermore, you find competing goals outside of the organization as well. People have their own lives, and other things are more important to them than the goals of the organization or its leaders. It's absurd to expect people, whether volunteers or paid employees, to embrace team goals at the complete expense of their own. If that happens, leaders face either a high turnover, making success far more difficult, or a warping of personalities and sublimated resentment and anger. This generates subconscious resistance, if not out-and-out antagonism and sabotage.

For that matter, your own goals and principles might or might not mesh with those of the organization at any given time. A leader must be prepared to make some degree of personal sacrifice, but it isn't boundless. For example, you might decide that one goal of an organization is incompatible with your personal morality. Under such circumstances, you have a painful decision to make.

ALERT!

A common problem for organizations actually is when personal career goals come into conflict with overall goals. Instead of focusing on the needs of the organization, high-level managers think first of advancing their own careers and departments. In operational research terms, the consequence is called suboptimization: What is best for the whole is not necessarily best for the part.

An effective solution to the problem of personal goal conflict is to erase the dichotomy. Be human with your team members. Learn about their interests and drives, and then think creatively. How can group goals reinforce those of team members and help them achieve more of what they want? Let's say your team members are away from home too much. You can consider cutting down travel, or even offering a day of telecommuting with no meetings, so time is more productive and team members can knock off at a reasonable hour without facing a commute. If someone is taking classes at night, is there any part of a volunteer project that might benefit from experience in that particular area?

Goal Construction

Once you've got a sense of the theory and issues of goal structure, you can start using them. That doesn't mean you pick a goal and hit the ground running. Instead, you want to incorporate a more systematic approach, realizing that a goal is more than a word. Build something that will work.

Establish the Full Goal

Your first step is to get a sense of the goal's terrain. You know what you want to achieve, but you need to understand exactly what the goal entails. Asking some questions is a good way to start exploring a goal. Here are some you might start with:

- What steps must happen before achieving the goal?
- What must happen for each of the above steps to occur?
- Do you face any constraints on how you pursue the goal?
- How do all the parts and their components interrelate?
- Do any depend on the completion of others, even if they're not apparently directly related?
- Why focus on this specific goal?
- Must you work with other teams to achieve the goal?
- How will your team's strengths and weaknesses affect pursuit of the goal?
- Are there any time constraints?
- Will you face any conflicts with other goals?

This list isn't definitive—no preformed set of questions could be. What it should do is give you some ideas of what you might ask when trying to get a solid grasp of a goal and what it would take for your team to achieve it. As leader, you are responsible for ensuring that your team achieves the goal. The more thought you invest at the outset, the greater the chance that you'll meet with success.

Establish All Steps

When you have a sense of what the goal entails, list every single step along the journey. Don't leave out a thing. Write them down on a piece of paper, on a time management schedule, or even in project management software—so you can see everything the goal ultimately requires. Also leave room for other information that you'll add shortly.

Set Time Limits

It is possible to have an open-ended goal. We are all governed by the combination of time's relentless journey and the never-ending demands of others. Unless pushed, we all will tend to pay attention to what calls most loudly. That almost never includes a task that isn't due.

It may seem artificial, but you always need to attach deadlines to your tasks. Start with the overall goal and assign a completion date. Next, associate each of the steps along the way with an estimate of the time you'll need to complete it. That lets you work backward from the goal due date to figure out when every stage must begin and end. This should go into a calendar.

Determine Necessary Resources

Every part of your goal will need resources: people, time, and money. You need to know what each step will require, including who on your team is responsible for any given activity, the people the team will work with, and whether you need to arrange for specialty items or help.

Resources aren't just what your team possesses. You might need things from others—possibly money or physical goods. Check with them far in advance, because you don't know what other requests they might receive or whether they'll have their own needs for those resources.

The big mistake in determining resources is to forget routine things whose availability you take for granted. If you need resources that you share with others, reserve them in advance so you don't have to scramble at the last minute. Remember to check that you don't have resource conflicts with other goals, or even with the personal lives of your team.

Make the Goal Happen

Eventually you must move beyond thinking and get into doing. But when you've properly laid the groundwork, achieving a goal becomes far easier. If you've prepared, you can make a few final checks and then proceed, taking the whole team along with you.

Set Down the Plan

Once you've got some idea of what the achieving the goal will really take, you can begin planning. By writing down all the information for the previous sections, you should have everything you need to develop a comprehensive plan. You know what must happen and when, what it will cost, and who is necessary at what times.

Put this plan into a coherent form. You can use paper, a calendar, project management software, or any other tool you're comfortable using. The critical thing is to spot problems before they begin and catch conflicts in advance.

If you've never before used project management software, consider giving it a try. You can graphically see how parts of your plan interact and, with many packages, get color-coded alerts that show you when the interaction of the time and dependency requirements you've specified are doomed from the start.

Being so formal in your approach may make you feel as though you're a candidate for some geek achievement reality television show. Don't let it shake or deter you. There is no loss of your old fun-loving self or of any spontaneity. All you are doing is anticipating problems and taking steps so you don't have to deal with them. That leaves you with far more time to act on whim than if you constantly had to clean up after problems.

Look for Problems

Everything is laid out; it's a perfect time to uncover trouble. Look for conflicts, areas where you lack resources, inadequate time at a critical part of the goal, or any other issue that could derail your efforts. Unfortunately, in much of life, many call such efforts negative, but stumbling ahead without heed is real negativity. As you find issues, you can also look for solutions—a very positive experience.

Communicate the Plan

Once you have something solid, bring in your team and explain the intent. You've probably discussed the goal with your team before, but now communication is critical. Let them see all the requirements for what is still a preliminary plan. They're a part of it, so let them see what's in store and welcome any suggestions that might improve the plan. You're also likely to learn things that could affect your activities that you might not ever know any other way.

Creating Metrics

A plan is all well and good, but how do you know if you're following it? Easy! You use metrics. You must find ways to measure the progress of each and every part of your plan. In some cases the task is relatively simple, and you'll just want to know that the person responsible has accomplished it.

In other cases, though, metrics are more complex. You might be dealing with a long-term goal that seeks to change the way something occurs. For instance, a company might want to increase inquiries from prospects in a particular part of the country, or a nonprofit might be concerned with its fundraising for a specific project. In such cases, you will probably have targets that you're trying to reach by certain times.

Whether your plan is complex or simple, there is always a way of telling whether you are closer to a goal or farther away. If not, it's possible you haven't clearly enough defined it.

Set Things into Motion

Once the plan looks good, put it into play. Figure out how much you can comfortably load onto your team members and delegate, delegate, delegate. This will give them a feeling of ownership and increase the chances that your communal efforts will bear fruit.

Managing Goals

If you've analyzed your goals, diligently planned, and put things into action, you're well on your way to success. But there is still a road ahead. The most difficult aspect of goals is managing your progress while attempting to achieve them. For all that you've anticipated, you might still be surprised by problems, and then there is the daily slogging that happens for any long-term intent. As leader, you need to ensure that one foot continues to step in front of the other.

Monitoring Performance

You develop metrics so you can monitor performance. When there is a fairly objective measurement, you use the corresponding number to see how you're doing. When the interest is more subjective, such as group morale or the strength of a product brand, it may be difficult to find numeric measures (though you'd be surprised how often you actually can).

Sometimes you'll ask for reports from people. Other times you might be able to take the measurements yourself. The important thing is to get information so you can compare your performance with what you wanted to achieve in enough time that, should something go wrong, you can take corrective action.

Making Necessary Adjustments

Almost no progress happens in a straight line without deviation or delay. That is part of life. At times, progress on your goal will not meet your expectations. There are two actions you should take every time something like this happens.

First, examine your plan and how you are trying to reach the goal. It might be that what you thought would work won't, but with some modifications your plan can still put things right. Next, look again at the goal and ask yourself if it is realistic. Have you bitten off more than you can chew? If so, do you need to scale it back? Will it simply take more time?

Be flexible in your goal making and management. Adjusting a goal to something that is difficult but possible—like swimming the English Channel—is better than sticking to something amazing but impossible, like swimming the Arctic Ocean. Throughout the process, understand that change is part of life. Being the imperfect mortals we are, we should not hold our first intentions sacrosanct just because they were the first to come to mind.

Managing Conflicts

You can run into a conflict between goals or between the team's goals and the personal desires of the team members. These conflicts generally come down to a lack of ordering. When you treat all goals as equally important, you can't get any done; there is as strong a reason to do A as there is to do B, C, or D. The minute you pick a goal, you've started imposing order, but you need to keep the peace.

When you do have the occasional fender bender, take a step back. Which goal is more important or more pressing? Can you make progress on both through a little reordering of their parts? What is the nature of the conflict—scheduling, resources, or something more fundamental? Depending on the answers, getting everything back to normal could be easy, or it could drive you to distraction.

If the latter, you'll have to take a step back with your team, and perhaps with others in the organization, and decide on the appropriate priorities. It might be that one goal will have to give way, at least for a time, to another. Principles might have changed, and a goal might now be superfluous. Find a strategy that has the best fit with where the team should be and do as you must regarding the goal. Remember, it's ultimately the principles and mission of the team that are important. No goal is more important than those, so if you need to modify or even cut a goal, do it.

CHAPTER 7

Motivation

If leadership is the process of getting people to work together for common goals, then motivation is the art of getting the cooperation of the people you lead. This is one of the most popular topics in discussions of leadership and management techniques overall. In fact, motivation is the heart of leadership. It's also one of the most difficult things to do.

Matters of the Heart

One of the great leaders of the twentieth century was Dwight D. Eisenhower. Both as supreme commander of the Allied military forces during World War II and, later, president of the United States, he was a man who had to be a leader. Anything less would have meant an unpleasantly different world than the one we know. He defined motivation as "the art of getting people to do what you want them to do because they want to do it."

That is the essential problem any leader faces, no matter how grand or small the scale. You have to get people to willingly take on a job and to get it done.

Notice Eisenhower used the critical word "want" twice in his assessment. Motivation is not about proving to people that something is possible or arguing why a goal is worth your team's time. Like any type of selling, it is based on a completely emotional experience.

A Matter of Choice

Let's say it's a lazy weekend morning. You wake up and consider a chore that needs to be done, but then you roll over and consider the comfort of your bed. The idea of sleeping in and then treating yourself to a late brunch sounds much more appealing. What you might say under such circumstances is that you don't feel motivated. More correctly stated, you've considered your options and prefer what you would *like* to do over what you *ought* to do.

Humans consider themselves rational animals, but that's not the case. If you ask marketing professionals, emotion—rather than reason—is behind almost all of our choices. Until you can touch that emotional core in people, you won't be able to get them to do anything.

People always have this choice, and ultimately they will virtually always pick what they want. Sound surprising? Perhaps you are thinking of all the things you do that you don't want to do. For example, you might go to a job that you aren't crazy about, spend time on the weekend running errands and doing chores, and end up having dinner with some boring couple because your significant other is friends with one of them. All these are things that you don't want to do.

However, each of the distasteful actions is something you undertake to prevent something even more unpleasant. You work at the job because being out of work means being out of money, and finding a new job is not something you enjoy. You run errands and do chores because not having these things done makes you very unhappy, and it's worth the effort to have clean clothes and get new tires for the car. And dinner with the other couple? That's simple—it's easier to socialize with someone that you don't like than it is to face a fight with your significant other. In other words, in each of the above cases, you're doing something you don't like to avoid another something that you dislike even more. You're trying to find the most palatable solution.

Have It Your Way

One of the great secrets to marketing is the realization that people always do that which gives them what they want or think they want. Savvy marketing people will admit that you don't actually sell things to people. Instead, you find a way to let them buy what they want. The process is almost never rational. Even when you're in the market for something you might objectively need, like food, emotion controls the way in which you satisfy yourself.

Now put this into a context of activity. You'll see volunteers that put tremendous effort into a nonprofit organization because it gives them pleasure to do so. Contrarily, there are people who will join the same organization and do little, if anything, because what they really want is to perceive themselves as the types who do volunteer work. They don't really like doing the work, so they don't.

These decisions can be difficult to understand if you try to find clarity and logic. When you deal with what people want, you enter their emotional lives. Many attempts at motivation fall flat because they don't really deal with the emotions of others. Instead, they treat motivation as though it were a series of steps that could be checked off from a list. To really motivate, you have to grasp the appropriate emotional dynamics.

Motivational Sales Job

Motivation is a peculiar form of selling that is rarely recognized as such. When most people try to motivate others, they think their job is to pump people up to do a job better. That's an incomplete and even inaccurate view.

You are trying to get people excited about what they are doing—but that's just the surface. Look a bit deeper and what you're really doing is offering a transaction, something that is part and parcel of a sale. The customer (who in this case is a member of your team) is being asked to part with one thing to gain another. It's a quid pro quo, Latin for the phrase "this for that." Put differently, you're involved in a business transaction.

The Motivation Transaction

Let's begin to break down what really happens. When you try to motivate someone, you offer a product: a pleasurable emotional sense that team members feel when they actually want to act in support of something they believe in. This is heady stuff. A person has a chance to spend time, not at a grind, but at an activity imbued with full emotional investment as well as the distinct sense that he is doing what is right. What better way can you think of spending a day?

ALERT!

When you're involved in the emotions of people, you must tread carefully. If you enter into a transaction with the sense that you are looking to use other people—manipulate them—you will not motivate. Instead, you create a sense of distrust and perversely lower their motivation.

For this valuable product—does it sound like a sales pitch yet?—all you're asking in return is the commitment and effort to complete certain tasks that help advance the group's goal. To do that, team members must value the goal and understand the importance of their role in making it happen.

A Practical View

Don't worry if it sounds confusing at first. Consider your own experiences. When you feel motivated to take on a volunteer position, or you sign up for extra work at your place of business, or you do things around the house, you get a considerable emotional high from the activity. As you feel that pleasure, the effort you make feels light and you're glad to be doing it.

Contrarily, when you aren't feeling motivated, even something that is usually a pleasure can turn into a chore, whether it's cooking dinner, exercising, reading a novel, or finishing a report for your company. In that instance you're no longer connecting what you are doing to what is important to you, so you're acting out of obligation. No wonder it feels like a drag!

Making the Transaction Work

When you get a gut feel for the transactional process, you can begin to address how it works and what you need to do to make it work for your team. What you're really doing is becoming a salesperson in the highest sense of the term. If you do something that doesn't fit with the principles of these emotional transactions, you'll know that you're not really providing motivation.

Typically, you have a series of activities that can range from offering calculated compliments and hanging inspirational posters to some formal recognition of successful employees. But by taking a cookie-cutter approach and treating all people as interchangeable parts, you aren't taking into account each person's emotional needs. Instead, you've reduced the motivational activity to a string of physical actions.

FACT

The problem with motivational checklists is not that the activities are inherently incapable of motivating people. Sometimes they can be effective. But like any good carpenter knows, you can't use a pry bar for every problem. When you always reach for the same tools, you aren't trying to understand each situation on its own, and when you fail to do that, any motivation you manage to create is the result of pure dumb luck.

The effect is equivalent to speaking Romanian to someone who only understands Spanish. The two of you are talking different languages. Rather than offering a solution to a team member's emotional needs, you're looking for a physical solution to your own (specifically, getting something done to advance part of the goal).

Motivation and Meaning

It's fine to talk about satisfying someone's emotional needs, but it's important to look a bit more closely at what you're offering your team members. That means understanding exactly what motivation does for a person. When you know that, you will have a better sense of how to approach motivating someone.

That Connected Feeling

Think of a time when you've felt motivated. You've probably felt energy, a zest for what you were doing, and a sense of connection to the task. Paradoxically, when you feel like this, it doesn't matter what you're being paid for your efforts. The feeling is enough because, at that moment, your actions are aligned with what you find important. Your actions have significance.

For all practical purposes, that is the definition of *meaning*—the sense of connection between what you do and something higher. When you feel motivation, what actually happens is that, for that time, you're acting with meaning. There is a reason for what you do and for your choices. The invocation of meaning is what makes motivation so powerful.

Motivation and Vision

This may sound a little familiar. That's because motivation is strongly related to vision, which was discussed in Chapter 4. Remember that when people work with vision, they put what they do into a larger context of the team and organization. They can see the reason for their tasks and so are more likely to fulfill them.

When people are motivated, they also see what they do in a larger context, but in this case, the context is what has meaning for them personally.

Vision relates to the outside world of what could be. Motivation is about the *inside* world of what could be.

Why Motivation Often Fails

When you start realizing that motivating people means helping them act with meaning, it becomes clear why so many would-be leaders are terrible at it. They can't think about meaning because they're not interested in the people who are supposed to follow them. Instead, they operate as though they're dealing with so many interchangeable bodies that need to do work. To them, motivation is a series of tricks to get the bodies to do more.

Viewing your team as one group rather than as individual team members is one of the biggest mistakes you can make as a leader. When people get the sense that you are trying to manipulate them, you lose all credibility and goodwill. Even the perception of manipulation is enough to put your efforts into jeopardy.

It won't matter what these "leaders" do, nor does the amount of resources available to them make a difference. Some try to coerce people into doing as they want, which only helps ensure that those subjects of pressure will look to leave their teams as quickly as possible.

Others might try offering financial inducements to get team members to undertake a task, and that can work. In fact, there are special names for the financial inducement: *payoff* and *bribery* immediately come to mind. There's nothing inherently wrong with paying someone to get a job done. Chances are low that you'd show up to your job if no one paid you.

Have the Right Focus

However, neither coercion nor financial coaxing counts as leadership. Going back to Eisenhower's incisive definition, remember that the people on your team are not focusing on doing what you want because they want to please you. Instead, team members do things primarily for their own personal benefit.

The leader's relationship with the team is backward. To get people to focus on what you need, you have to focus on what they need, which is a connection to something greater. When you do focus on connecting them to something greater, they feel purpose and meaning, and nothing else is as compelling for most people.

Motivation is a type of sales: You are selling people into helping of their own accord. People sell best when they focus on what the customer wants and needs, not on their own goals and desires. Meeting quotas and goals comes as a byproduct from making the customer happy.

Focusing on the customer is one of the most difficult aspects of sales. A leader does need to be concerned with achieving the group goal, certainly. But to be successful in motivating someone, the leader must focus on how the goal can serve the emotional needs of the team member.

In other words, there is a time and place for everything. When you try to motivate people, you should spend your time doing just that. Success will turn into progress toward the goal because you'll have helped bring the person to the point of wanting to make the goal.

Using Motivation Correctly

With what you know about how motivation works, it's time to start considering its practical application. That happens more easily than you might think if you follow a few steps:

- Help make connections to goals.
- Focus on the big goal, not just the task.
- Find a balance of motivation tools.

When you put all these principles into play, you increase the chance that others will feel motivated and you'll improve your own leadership abilities.

Help Make Connections

People are motivated when they connect what they do to a sense of why they do it, at least one higher than needing to get a paycheck. The feeling of motivation isn't a passive sense of well-being or happiness. Rather, it's the byproduct of the active process of making those connections. A leader who motivates other members of the team helps them make those connections and complete their tasks with a sense of meaning.

Leader Misunderstandings

We've finally reached the heart of the motivation dilemma. The motivation process is not a series of empty practices or a check-list of must-do activities. For now, roll up the posters, postpone the group meetings, and don't sign those little certificates of appreciation. You need to forget knee-jerk reactions and habits.

To really motivate, you have to understand the different ways of making connections to meaning. You must know how that differs in group and one-on-one settings. Motivation is also a process that must always continue because, for most people, that's where the payoff for effort lives.

Team Member Misunderstandings

The same misconceptions are common to leaders and the members of their teams. Too often, people have had bad previous experiences being "motivated." They have misplaced expectations of what it means and what they can expect. Some people have also had the artificial high of getting pumped up, along with the crashing low that usually follows. This is particularly true of those who have spent time in sales organizations.

You will need to explain and demonstrate how your approach to motivation is different from what they've seen in the past. You aren't interested in a cheap thrill but rather in making the team experience meaningful. At first, many may think yours is yet another cornball exercise. Be patient and that skepticism will pass.

Expressions of Motivation

Remember that you're in the business of sales—trading real motivation for work done to get closer to a goal. However, it's tricky, because meaning is different for different people, and its manifestations will vary. Some people may have that cheerleader spirit while others might sit quietly and enjoy being creative in things they were already doing. For example, here are a few emotional responses that someone might have to true motivation:

- Joy
- Excitement
- Commitment
- Importance
- Hope

The individuals on your team have their own psychological predilections and belief systems. Reasons to take on a goal that resonate with one will leave another cold. Some might feel meaning in the challenge of trying to do something difficult, while others could feel more strongly about their obligations to others on the team or to some greater community. Meaning is an intensely personal experience, and there is no single way to motivate others.

Help Others Connect

Because meaning is such a personal expression, you will need as many ways to motivate as there are people in your group or organization. Motivating specific people is an emotional activity that you must tailor to them. To do that well, you need to pay attention to your team members, understand what makes them tick, and get a sense of what draws and what repels them.

Although you're interested in helping connect your team in an emotional way to your goals, start with the goals they have in their lives. Learn about their interests, which will give you an indication of what is important to them. The greater a sense you have of that, the more you can look for parallels between the team's goals and areas in the person's life that might provide a point of meaning.

For example, say that two people have been working on equivalent tasks that the group had to complete for a goal, but both are starting to flag. It can, and does, happen to all of us. How are you going to motivate them? That depends on the person. One might get enormous joy out of creatively solving problems; you could try helping that person reframe her task as a problem that needed a novel solution to get past the sticking point. That would call up the person's natural interests, reinstating her work on the project, which would then get done and thus bring the team member even more satisfaction.

What you are going to do is learn about the people on your team, but in a human way, not as a simple data collection exercise. To that end, you needn't pry. The best approach is to take a real interest. If you want to listen, people want to talk.

The other member might feel overwhelmed because other deadlines are making completing the task more difficult. Then, depending on the group's overall needs, you might help the person reassess what is happening as well as restructure the demands on the person to make life more bearable. You make the situation something that can be won, and the team member will reflect the goodwill that ending the unnecessary conflict has delivered.

Help Groups Connect

It's great to tailor your motivation for particular people, but that's not always going to be possible. There may be times when, acting as a leader, you deal with more people than you can practically get to know with any degree of closeness. At such times, you need a different motivational strategy.

Create the Atmosphere

The first step is to create an acceptance of the proper role of motivation. To that end, stop activities that ignore the emotional needs of others. Make everyone aware that mindless following of orders does no good. Insist on meeting the needs of the organization and people's legitimate self-interest at the same time.

Organizations that push their goals at the expense of their people are dysfunctional, and the problems generally systemic. Bad behavior is usually the result of official policies. Depending on the existing organizational or social culture, instilling an atmosphere conducive to motivation might require extensive negotiation with other leaders and re-examination of policies and procedures.

Structure Your Approaches

Different people will find different things meaningful, and you need a variety of ways to motivate them. Before you come up with the mechanisms, develop the approaches. Look at some of the different connections one might make with a given goal and see how to best express them. That way, you're not groping for a way to relate the goal to anyone in particular.

Good salespeople don't talk to prospects without preparation. They know ahead of time the types of objections they're likely to get, and they know what they'll say in those situations. That's the type of preparation you want here. When someone is not motivated, you need a range of possible tools and messages at hand so you can respond with something relevant. That way you're not flailing about, trying to find something to say.

You won't always have the appropriate answer. In that sense, a leader is very different from a salesperson, who is likely to lose touch with a prospect whose objections he is unable to counter. Your team members are still there. If one approach doesn't seem to work, go off and think more about how else you might help.

Plant Motivation Seeds

When you seed a lawn, you don't cover every single inch of ground where you want grass. You spread the seed around and water and fertilize it. The seeds start to grow and, as they do, they spread to fill in the blank spots. If you don't have the resources to motivate each and every person in the organization, try working with a select few to start. Positive attitudes are catching, so sprinkle your motivational work about and let it spread.

Work with Others

Don't assume that you have to do all the motivation, particularly if the group is large. Work with other leaders to create a motivation strategy. Are there approaches that might work in one group better than others? Could different groups with complementary strengths help motivate each other? Discuss motivational tools that all of you find useful so that each of you can learn and expand your leadership repertoire.

Interacting with Groups

You may have to address groups of people involved in the organization. Obviously, whether you're speaking or writing, you cannot literally relate on an individual level to everyone at the same time. But you can make sure that you touch on different motivational aspects that are common. You can keep particular individuals with different needs in mind as a way of focusing your communication and making it more grounded and practical in tone.

Focus on the Big Goal

When you first learned to ride a bicycle or drive a car, you might have noticed that it was difficult to keep a straight course. That's because new drivers tend to be tense and limit their focus, paying too much attention on the physical vehicle surrounding them. As you looked around, the rest of your body turned the same way, steering the bike or car off of its straight course. The more you looked, the more scattered your traveling became because you kept veering this way and that.

This is one of the big problems as you learn to lead—going astray, that is, and not wobbly peddling. In the riding and driving example, the answer would be to relax and keep your eyes on your goal. For leaders, you must focus on something other than just the immediate tasks. You have to remember the goal.

Put Goals Into Context

Goals can't be arbitrary. They have to relate to the principles that the group holds important. Indeed, if goals don't relate to principles, they are more or less arbitrary. When things are arbitrary, there's no meaning to them, and without the potential for meaning, there is no chance to motivate someone. People won't care about the goals because there is no particular reason to care.

Leaders must frame big goals in relationship to important principles. Also, goals don't float around as independent entities. Each goal rests on other smaller goals, and any goal may support higher goals. Therefore, each goal must be put into the overall context of the goals of the group.

Put Tasks into Context

When you are trying to accomplish something, it's altogether too easy to develop a myopic view of the world. You and your team have your heads down and are working hard to make progress. That's admirable, but it puts you back into the aforementioned driver's seat with a learner's permit.

A goal makes a poor reference point if you never refer to it, and by itself it is meaningless. To head somewhere and not get lost, you have to know where you are, find the right direction, and measure how far you've gone. Then you can double-check your destination, check your new location, correct any deviation, and again head that wagon train out.

All along the way, you need to keep oriented toward your destination and track your progress. To keep focused on your team's goal, you must take stock of where you are and check your progress. In other words, don't just look at the progress of all your smaller goals. Make sure you show the project's overall advancement.

Many organizations effectively use this approach on factory floors and other operational settings. They post company, department, and group goals in a prominent spot so employees have a tangible sense of how their efforts make a difference.

When you are trying to motivate your team, you must always keep in mind the bigger goals. Don't just talk about a task that needs doing. Mention how that task fits into the accomplishment of the goal. Relate everything, no matter how small, back to the larger picture of what the team is trying to accomplish.

Find a Balance of Tools

Now it's time to go beyond the basic principles and get a bit more practical. The result of the cookie-cutter approach is usually disaster because you're trying to adopt something intended for a different group of people with other needs and problems. As such, it is far from ideal. But there are techniques that can help.

Positive Versus Negative

A standard piece of advice that you may hear from motivation experts is that positive motivation is always the best choice and that negative motivation is bad. This is not entirely accurate.

First, negative motivation is an odd concept. You can't coerce or force someone's connection to meaning. Imagine trying to extort someone into being inspired. It wouldn't work. There isn't really such a thing as negative motivation. However, there are both positive and negative reinforcements. This is the punishment/reward model. You pair a pleasant reward for doing a task with a consequence for failing. That may work for trained animals, but it is belittling for people and unworthy of a leader.

There are leaders who use negative emotional associations to obtain their ends. Niccolo Machiavelli wrote in his treatise on power, *The Prince*, that it is difficult to be both loved and feared: "Men are less worried about harming somebody who makes himself loved than someone who makes himself feared, for love is held by a chain of obligation which, since men are bad, is broken at every opportunity for personal gain. Fear, on the other hand, is maintained by a dread of punishment which will never desert you."

Charming, eh? If people are so untrustworthy, they will continue to be so, even if you lead through fear. The world is full of stories of rats fleeing a sinking pirate ship. Not only are they still ready to desert you at the first opportunity for personal gain, but fear begets hate. Therefore, it's a safe bet that they will actively seek ways to make your life miserable. So much for the Prince's advantage.

FACT

In the early fifteenth century, Machiavelli was exiled from Florence—a sentence that was often considered equivalent to death. The year after being banished, he wrote *The Prince*. But there is debate over whether he was trying to charm the notorious Medici family or if he was satirizing something he loathed, the failed true republic the Medicis ruled.

Stick with positive motivation and leave the behavioral science for researchers and laboratories. If you're worried about the lack of consequences, don't be; they are always there. People can get fired or look foolish or be embarrassed. They already know this from a lifetime of reinforcement, so don't belabor the obvious.

Problem Solving and Barriers

You can't motivate people so dogged by practical concerns that they can't lift their heads up to see anything beyond their immediate problems. In such cases, you need to help your team move beyond these temporary barriers and find something more than bureaucracy. Concentrate on those problems and brainstorm to help people find ways around the blockades. When they see some actual progress, team members will be more receptive to motivation.

Motivation and Culture

Organizations and circumstances differ greatly. The cheerleading meetings of salespeople in a company might do little for a group of social activists in an inner city. But there's no way to be sure ahead of time what will and won't work for your situation. Try some intelligent experimentation.

Consider the demeanor, interests, and personality types of the people on your team. Then consider activities that would match and motivate them. Don't be too timid; if you are, you will never try anything that hasn't been done before, which means you'll keep doing the same things and expecting different results.

Do Your Part

If there is a single lesson to take from this chapter, it is this: Take on projects and tasks and get them done. Action is the surest form of language. Unless you have an unusually large share of charisma, giving rousing speeches and then retiring to your easy chair will get nothing done.

Years of exposure to political, business, and social figures who relaxed in constant comfort while others toiled has made most people mistrustful of authority figures. You can't change that.

What you can do is be sure to take on work yourself in ways that are visible to others on your team. Yes, leaders often do take on work that is invisible to everyone else. So? Many leaders make the same claim as a way of masking their considerable inactivity. If you want to motivate others, go the extra distance. Pick up a task that shows you don't think of yourself as ineligible for regular effort (and be sure never to complain about doing so).

Being fully engaged yourself sends a message to everyone else that there must be a good reason to achieve defined goals and that you don't ask anyone to do something you wouldn't do yourself. Combine that with finding ways to keep yourself motivated, and you send out the message that what your group does has real meaning—and that life doesn't get any better than this. Now that's powerful motivation.

CHAPTER 8

Coaching

Coaching is the process of bringing out the best in others. It's helping team members confront their own challenges and find their own solutions. Like motivation, coaching is a way to encourage and support others and help them achieve the best results possible. Based on an implicit trust and confidence in the abilities of others, coaching is the ability to foster growth and continued success in your team. If motivation is helping people find the why of what they do, coaching helps them find the how.

The Elements of Coaching

The Elements of Style by William Strunk and E. B. White starts with perfectly clear rules of grammar and usage, and then succinctly covers the elements of creating your own genuine writing style.

Coaching is one of those activities that lends itself to a similar approach: State the principles and let people apply them because there is no way you could anticipate all the variations that might arise.

ALERT!

Coaching is one area that receives more recognition in the breach than in the honoring. It's entirely too easy for someone to say, "I'm coaching now," and yet behave in an entirely autocratic and controlling manner—the antithesis of what it means to coach.

It's helpful to mention some principles of coaching before getting more into what it can do, what it shouldn't do, and how to offer it.

Someone Needs Help

Coaching isn't something you do to occupy your spare time or because you want to put on a show that others expect. Although there are general principles, coaching is always specific in nature. Someone on your team has a problem and needs help sorting it out. When you coach, it is for a particular reason. You're trying to help someone find a way to a defined result.

That means you can't just start coaching at any time. This is a tool meant as a response to a problematic situation or to a weakness of a certain team member. You must use it as such. Overuse will dilute its effectiveness and result in people thinking upon seeing you, "Oh, here we go again."

No One Has All the Answers

No matter how much we'd all like to think that we have all the answers, a little logic shows this to be impossible. All the answers means never making a mistake, being able to anticipate all oncoming problems, and generally being disgustingly perfect. That doesn't happen because it's not possible short of divine intervention.

Not being perfect, everyone has plenty of weaknesses. In the best of all possible worlds, people would learn to examine where they come short and work out ways to bridge the gaps as they see them. In coaching, you're helping someone else find new ways to bridge their own gaps—just remember that you have them as well.

Coaching is about helping your team members sharpen skills so they can cope with their tasks and goals. To that end, you can't be Answer Person, the super hero for the team. You don't have all the answers. Even if you have a lot of them, what good does it do to give people a shortcut? It might be efficient in the short term, but in the long run you build a culture of dependency. When everyone develops the habit of going to you for everything, you spend your time getting their jobs done and not your own. Besides, would you really look that good in a cape and Spandex?

An Exercise in Restraint

Coaching is an indirect and subtle activity. In a leader, much of it consists of listening, reflecting, and putting yourself into the shoes of the team member. Coaching is always individual—never a group activity—and its primary requirement is understanding the person you are coaching. Remember that all of us are imperfect mortals, and the coaching process has no room for a sense of superiority. You must always be truthful but kind as well.

Moving Beyond Comfort

When you are stopped by something within or outside yourself, you are not in your comfort zone. That is good. You don't grow when you are too secure in what you do. Coaching keeps team members outside the comfort zone so they have the psychological space to find new answers. So long as the risks are reasonable and the objectives within reach, people feel better about themselves and what they can accomplish.

Coaching Must Be Practical

Pointing out someone's flaws doesn't work. Honest and accurate critique is useless unless it's combined with functional suggestions on how the team member can get past an impasse. Otherwise, it's ineffectual, like telling a drowning man who never learned how to swim that he should do the Australian crawl to a life raft. Any advice must be adapted to the situation of the person (a dog paddle is a better first step toward staying afloat) and framed in a way that the person can actually accomplish. Refrain from judging people and focus instead on how to help someone change a given attitude, habit, or situation.

Power of Coaching

Coaching attains its objectives through influence and leadership. It builds better relationships among people, minimizes conflict, and reduces stress. It assumes that people are creative and that they have talent and something to offer. Instead of dismissing all that potential, coaching is a gentle process of releasing it and allowing it to be of use.

Coaching uses questions, active listening, and support to assist team members in developing fundamental self-assessment tools. If you do it right, coaching will result in increased productivity, skills levels, and satisfaction.

What the Coach Does

The coach helps team members solve problems on their own and encourages more creative thinking patterns. In this way, coaching becomes a communication tool that makes life easier for everyone involved. At its best, coaching can build stronger relationships between the leader and team members with a minimal amount of conflict.

By learning to accept that leaders don't always know best, you can use coaching to ensure a more respectful and participatory communication process where everyone wins. Coaching can build trust, boost morale, and help everyone grow and develop.

What the Process Does

Over time, coaching keeps everyone on the team involved. You and your team will catch mistakes or inefficient tactics earlier in the process. On completion of a project, you will have created an open environment in which the team can review what it did, fairly critique it, and learn lessons so that the next project will be even more successful.

Why Coaching Works

In short, good coaching is effective because the leader-coach treats the team member as a thinking, feeling human being worthy of respect. When you are fair and empathetic, understanding that no one—not even you—can move through the world without mistakes, you get an open discussion and encourage others to take initiative and accomplish things. It is a respectful, participatory, and mutual process of communication that honors different perspectives and everyone's valuable input.

Benefits of Coaching

Chances are that real coaching is going to be relatively new to you. Learning a new skill always takes effort, and coaching is significantly different from traditional concepts of management. Learning to do it can be a challenge. Developing new skills is easier when you know the benefits you'll see from them—it helps you keep your motivation boosted.

What Team Members Get

Which is better, having someone take you out for a fish dinner, or learning how to cook fish? Frankly, each has something to be said for it. Getting the fish dinner is convenient. You save money and the time and effort in preparing a meal, and chances are that the cook is experienced, which means that the food should be tasty. But then you go home without any idea of how to prepare fish on your own. Even if the restaurant experience is good, it is short lived.

But how often do people take you out? Dining in restaurants every night is expensive, and you never get the satisfaction of being able to prepare a dish on your own. When you do learn, though, you have a feeling of accomplishment, and you are no longer dependent. You also begin to develop the ability to deal with change. It doesn't matter if the restaurant is open at a particular hour, or if they've dropped your favorite trout preparation from the menu. You can make fish yourself when and where you want, substitute ingredients if necessary, and otherwise take control of what you need to do, no matter how circumstances change.

Team members who receive coaching to nurture their talents and improve their capabilities receive enormous satisfaction and confidence from the process. That also increases the meaning they find in what they do, which means higher motivation.

What the Leader Gets

If coaching offers satisfaction to the team member, it adds fulfillment to the experience of the leader. Helping people to become better than they were and to reach more of their potential is a wonderful experience. You have taken responsibility and left part of you with the people in question, literally making a mark on the world and leaving it a better place. There are few experiences in the world that leave you feeling more at peace with your actions.

From another practical view, coaching saves time in the long run. The less often someone asks you to solve a problem or make an adjustment, the more time you have to do what it is you should be doing. Additionally, solving a problem after the fact takes more time and other resources than anticipating the problem and making corrections before a situation gets out of hand. It's more efficient for the leader and is thus an excellent investment of time and effort.

What the Organization Gets

It is a natural assumption that when individuals and leaders benefit, so does the organization. By helping team members learn to perform better, no matter what the conditions, you also, logically, help the goals of your organization and group. Activities can only get better when all the people involved are smarter and more effective in their efforts. When people can solve problems themselves, they can head off disaster before it strikes.

In short, coaching helps team members improve what they do, helps make them independent, and brings forth sources of creativity and energy. That makes the entire organization smarter and more effective. It's a win-win-win situation.

What Coaching Isn't

It's always important to say what something is, but sometimes, because of many assumptions, you also need to say what it is not. Coaching is not standing behind someone and snarling, "Work faster, work faster!" Coaching isn't providing a detailed minute-by-minute breakdown of what your team members should be doing. It's not throwing your hands up in disgust and resignation when a person makes a mistake. Coaching is not a collection of dismissive, controlling, and worthless techniques that pass as managerial theory in too many companies and institutions.

The Managerial Flaw

Coaching and management are related in that both are tools intended to facilitate orderly and effective activity to achieve certain ends. Though they belong to the same family, there is a fundamental difference between the two. Coaching assumes that people have tremendous abilities while also recognizing that they often need help reaching their potential.

FACT

Think back a few years to corporate scandals and such names as Enron, WorldCom, Adelphia, and Tyco. Managers at those companies were sure they were smarter than everyone else. Unless you include destroying companies and winding up in jail as part of the definition of smart, it would be hard to agree.

Management too often makes the fatal assumption that a special set of people, called managers, are smarter, more knowledgeable, and generally better than others in an organization. Traditional management is a paternalistic approach to making things happen. As such, managers are supposed to direct and control others as the only way to get things done.

Under the management model, organizations generally accept that the manager possesses the necessary knowledge, information, and decision-making rights. Here, others in the organization—whether employees or volunteers—exist only to carry out the orders of management. These people are not expected to think, to find solutions, or to improve how the group tries to attain a goal. Instead, those who are managers are to do as they are told.

This has been the popular approach to organized activities for hundreds of years. In fact, until recently, it was largely the way companies, religious organizations, nonprofits, and other entities operated. In the last couple of decades, leaders and academics have experimented with other ways of doing things, but traditional management is still widely prevalent. Because it assumes that only a small group of people is capable of intelligent and creative action, this approach wastes most of the talent in any organized group.

Something Else Coaching Isn't

The term *coaching* can lead to some confusion because it's not quite the same as in sports. There a coach observes athletes, looks for problems, and tells them what they must do to correct any flaws that are hindering their performance.

In leadership, coaching is more closely related to a horse-drawn carriage, and helping someone get to a destination. Instead of pointing the problems and solutions out to a player, you help the person develop a sense of how to make such diagnostic efforts and then create corresponding strategies and plans. It's truly a case of helping people find a path to self-sufficiency.

Socratic Coaching

In the writings of Plato, Socrates talks with people, continually asking questions, probing assumptions, letting the flaws in an argument show themselves, and helping the other Athenian citizens find their own way to greater reasoning and truth. He was the epitome of a coach.

Plato's chronicles of the teachings of Socrates are continuingly instructive. Watch the give-and-take between Socrates and other individuals and see how he brings people to new understanding by gently turning them back on themselves. Start with some of the simpler dialogues, like Euthyphro, where only two characters are speaking.

As the coach you must be willing to give up some of the control you have had. Coaching is based on leading and influencing rather than directing. You achieve results through questions and discussion rather than directives, through listening and support rather than controlling. As with everything new, the process may feel strange at first, but in time you'll get the hang of it.

Asking Questions

Asking a good question is difficult. Too often, people close down a potential discussion by framing questions in such a way as to telegraph the answers they want or to limit how someone might respond. You might as well not even ask a question in that case because you already know the answers.

Since you don't know the answers, lean toward open-ended questions, where answers are not simple. A query seeking a yes or no response can stop conversation faster than walking out of the room. With open-ended answers, you can keep asking questions, and the conversation continues.

The person is also as important as the task and problem. If a goal can't include concern for the people involved, it isn't worth the time. Bring team members to the present by first asking their thoughts and feelings about the project or task under discussion. As you get answers, you will find other questions coming to mind. Ask them as well. Follow the trail where it goes so you can see what the landscape is really like.

Listen Attentively

Asking questions is one step; you have to hear the answers for them to make any difference. Actively listen throughout the coaching session. Clear your mind of everything else. As the team member makes a point, paraphrase what you hear in response to be sure that you actually understand it. Don't be afraid to ask for clarification.

ALERT!

Actively listening is an immensely difficult thing to do. You can't go through a list of steps and tell yourself that you've got it. To listen, you must stop the rush of all the concerns, petty and significant, that you face in your life. What your team members tell you must become the only item of importance.

Using this skill is the key to success in coaching. By really listening, you suspend the all-too-human tendency to immediately judge someone. While you actively listen, there is no room for that type of judgment because you are concentrated on what the other person is saying and feeling. Always acknowledge a response, even if it doesn't seem to directly address the issue at hand. When you dismiss someone's words, you dismiss the person as well.

Investigating Deeper

The difficult step is to use the question-and-answer process to move the discussion—and the team member—along the path to self-discovery. Yours is not the art of the district attorney's cross-examination. Instead, your aim is to build a bridge to a new place by taking answers and connecting them during the conversation.

Keep in mind what you need to accomplish in the end, and then look at how an answer relates to that. Then ask another question that starts from the answer and moves closer to the needed accomplishment—and toward the team member's understanding of what is necessary.

It's difficult to describe how to use questions as a staircase to step deeper into an issue until you reach its foundation. Perhaps more than anything else in this book, this process isn't a simple set of reproducible steps. It's recognizing connections and their importance and linking them to form a guide.

You also ask questions in a circular fashion. That is, you start addressing different aspects of the problem and potential solutions so that the team member thinks more holistically. For example, if you were asking an employee about a report, you might inquire into the following:

- Information sources
- Sets of assumptions one might make
- Topics to cover
- Proposed structure
- Resources needed
- Time frame to complete
- Relation to group or organizational goals

Through your questions, you help the team member build a well-rounded view of the issue. The more thorough the grasp, the more likely the person will identify problems and see potential solutions.

Encouraging Seeking

As with the work of the Socratic philosophers, questions should never be used to belittle someone or to feel their own superiority. In fact, when people said that Socrates was the wisest man in Athens, he replied that it was because he understood how little he knew.

How many of us could claim even a fraction of his wisdom? Socrates asked questions to help others—and himself—better understand life. It might make sense for us to do the same. That sets the tone of the questioning. You look for a real exploration and a path to get to the goal that differs from what you imagined it might be. Just as the team member learns from the process, so will you.

The Coaching Process

Discussing the philosophical basis, if you will, of using the Socratic method to ask questions in coaching is like studying aerodynamics and then assuming you could fly a plane. There are important procedures and you need to have a grasp of them before you walk into a coaching session. Otherwise you could crash just as you think you're taking your group to new heights.

Look for a Purpose

Coaching is a tool for helping team members learn to examine what they do, find weaknesses, and seek answers to problems. What it cannot be is a regular activity that happens on a predetermined schedule. Routine coaching is like going every week to see the doctor whether you need to or not. Eventually both you and the doctor stop listening to each other.

If you turn coaching into an activity that happens rain or shine, then you will kill off its effectiveness. Restrain the impulse and focus the technique where it can do the most good.

Clearly Express the Reason

Let's say you want to get from one place to another. You can't figure out what direction to move in unless you know where you want to go. As with a goal—because coaching is one tool to help people reach intermediate goals on their way to larger ones—you need a direction.

But setting out that destination clearly is even more important in the case of coaching. You have the presumption that a team member is heading the wrong way to some degree, and if you cannot set out in words where the person should be heading, things won't improve.

FACT

Thomas Jefferson wrote that the the goal of the Declaration of Independence was "to place before mankind the common sense of the subject, in terms so plain and firm as to command their assent, and to justify ourselves in the independent stand we are compelled to take." That is clarity of reason, and the degree of specificity you must strive to attain.

You don't have to provide the exact statement of the goal. To really own the improvement, the team member will have to provide that. But understanding the reason for the coaching helps the person frame what must change, and that is a vital part of setting an attainable goal—and eventually to make coaching on the subject unnecessary.

Be Prepared

Coaching is meant to be a nonthreatening approach to helping people discover for themselves what they need to do and how they need to change. Despite that, it is a formal activity. Do not approach it as something you can wing.

Start with preparing yourself. Write down the problem, the reason for coaching, and what your goals are for providing it. Then prepare what the team member will need: a summary of what the coaching is to achieve as well as the exact date, time, and location for it to commence.

Be practical in the preparations. Be sure that the team member is able to attend—a larger issue for volunteer organizations, where people are not under obligations to provide their time. Keep the first session between thirty and forty-five minutes. You don't want to overwhelm the person, but you want enough time for questions and discussion.

Sell the Process

The whole point of coaching is to involve people in the problem-recognition-and-resolution process so that they create their own solutions. You need their cooperation and support, and you want them to see how all this relates to the organization's goals and, importantly, to your team members' own sense of meaning. Even if people are paid employees, you'll still need their help—in fact, you need them to do quite a bit more.

ALERT!

As much as you need to listen attentively to the team member, you should keep an ear out to yourself. Be aware of your tone of voice, the words you choose, and your body language, and evaluate whether you are offering mixed messages—or even a unified unpleasant one. A little unconscious reaction can undo all the good you might otherwise achieve.

Approach the coaching process carefully. Be relaxed and cordial and try to alleviate any stress or anxiety team members may feel. Help them understand why they are taking part in the process. Let them know that they will largely be the ones driving change—that you are actually there for support and help.

Incorporate Follow-Up

Chances are that you'll need to have more than one coaching session. You want to see how team members make progress toward the goals they've set, which means finding ways of measuring advancement.

During one session, agree to the next step and set the groundwork for the next session. Be prepared to follow up on your mutual commitment to progress. If you've set measurable goals for a future date, plan to meet regularly to update the progress toward them. Remember that coaching is an ongoing commitment, and both you and the team member are responsible for maintaining momentum toward the results you seek. Be sure to recognize advancements and achievements—be human. Otherwise, you are treating the team member like an unthinking and unfeeling animal. In fact, even an animal would balk at such treatment.

Continue coaching sessions until the team member reaches the desired outcome. There will be times when the person just doesn't get it. When you find yourself at this point, don't get frustrated. State a more specific direction and move on from there. You're striving to lead the person to discovery, not to have someone jump through hoops and solve a puzzle.

Watching for the Dangers

Coaching is a powerful technique. As with most things of value, it isn't always easy. It will take more time and patience than just shouting out orders and giving directions.

If you find yourself feeling uncomfortable in the process, examine your emotional reaction. Coaching can appear threatening for leaders who are not secure in their self-image or skills and may be uncomfortable in letting go of control. You may even find yourself asking, "What are they going to need me for now?" The answer is simple: to help reach goals by helping others grow and develop.

Although it is difficult, it is an incredible feeling to help someone achieve something that she wouldn't have reached alone. If you find yourself struggling with the process, don't be afraid to get help from a superior, a peer, or an expert. After all, you don't lose the need for coaching just because you are a leader.

CHAPTER 9

Building a Team

Know what they call someone without a team? A lone visionary. Or a lone crusader. Or any of a number of other things, generally preceded by the word lone. What you won't hear the public call such an individual is a leader. A leader by definition needs someone to lead, and an effective leader must know how to build a team. What you need to do will depend completely on the people you work with and your specific circumstances. However, there are various principles and techniques that can be helpful.

9

Basic Requirements

An effective leader's basic function is to guide a functioning team. There is a problem in discussing teams: Too many of us have some experience and, therefore, preconceptions about teams and teamwork. If you were on the school football or chess team, have volunteered time to group efforts, or participated in some special project at work, you've had experience in working with others. The problem is that there is no way to be sure that your experience is actually a good example of teamwork.

If you're a parent, you've probably seen examples of this unfortunate kind of ersatz team. Youth groups in which coaches direct kids to risky or callous behavior or in which parents literally beat each other over the results of a game shows just how bad leadership models can be.

If you did see good examples of teams as you grew, you probably did absorb some good lessons. At the same time, you never applied a critical analysis to understand what made a good team work. As a leader, you want to know how to reproduce that spirit and its possibilities in any organization you lead. That means looking in some detail at what teams do and how they work.

Team Benefits

Teams offer a way of achieving results more efficiently than a loose collection of individuals would. Instead of rigidly fixing how individuals interact, teams allow their members to reconfigure and tailor what they do to best achieve their goals. Because people work together, they can learn from each other, broadening their experience. But the way teams work depends on how they are structured.

What Is a Team?

On the surface, the answer to this one seems easy. A team is a group of people who work together to accomplish something beyond their individual self-interests. However, they don't work in just any old way, so not all groups are teams. What distinguishes teams from other similar-sounding groups is that a team isn't a collection of people simply following orders. To function, a team needs the following:

- Purpose
- Commitment
- Rules of operation
- Interdependence

Only when a group meets the initial definition and then adds these factors does it have the chance to become a team. You might say that a team is a group that works together to accomplish something beyond the self-interest of the members.

Purpose

A functioning team must have a purpose, a reason for existence. This animating principle cannot be "because someone said we had to." Members of the team need the answer to the questions, "Why are we here? Why is it us? Why now?"

As a leader, you help add this element by working on vision and communicating your vision of the team, as well as helping team members develop a personal vision. When people understand what they are to do and how it fits into the bigger picture, they have purpose.

Commitment

As purpose is related to vision, commitment is related to motivation. Team members must commit to undertake their tasks and to see the purpose of the team through completion. That requires motivation so that when things get tough, they keep going. This is perhaps the most significant difference between teams and other groups. Instead of toiling in an atmosphere of fear and intimidation, team members willingly undertake what needs to be done in an atmosphere of motivation.

Rules of Operation

Every group has rules, whether formally documented or not. When a person runs one in an autocratic fashion, then the rules don't matter so much because the true rule is personal whim. For a team, this is unthinkable.

For a team to work, members don't have to like each other so much as offer respect and honor each other's efforts. So a team is like a society in microcosm. There needs to be predictability in how people interact. Teams have established methods of interacting, being productive, and resolving conflict.

Sports generally have complex sets of rules covering everything that might happen, so there is no question of how to handle a situation. But consider what happens when a fight breaks out in the middle of a game. Suddenly the rules go out the window and fists fly. Lose the rules, and you can expect chaos and injury.

To some degree, the rules may be simple. For example, the team could meet on a certain day and time each week, or there might be a standing rule about not dismissing ideas immediately. There is no standard manual for such rules, and some will evolve out of the team's own dynamics. However, that doesn't lessen their importance; you need a framework in which people can find synergy and not simply depend on orders from the top to keep them going.

Interdependence

In most groups, people look out for themselves and their own tasks. On a team, it's the entire team that succeeds or fails. There is no such thing as a team member winning on her own. As such, the way people pursue tasks is significantly different. They must look out not only for themselves but also for how they work with others and how fellow members are doing.

This is perhaps the most difficult aspect of a team to nurture and instill. In this country, society trumpets the rugged individualist. We fancy ourselves ready to take on the wilderness and wonder why others aren't so equipped, even though we may have profited mightily from family help, society's infrastructure, programs, and other such aids that we quickly assign to our own efforts. Yet we still admire those who support others. That's the part of human psychology you want to tap.

Team Types

Teams all come down to the effective interaction of people. Working with a team will depend in part on the sort of team it is. Your approach might also change depending on whether you're building the team from scratch, inheriting a group, or facing a mix of the two.

Inherited Versus Chosen

The most obvious consideration is whether the team already exists and you are coming in to lead. If the team is in place, then the first thing you'll need to do is begin to learn as much as you can about its strengths and weaknesses because you are the newcomer. Although you may be in charge, you are not yet part of the group.

Whatever you do, avoid quickly deciding on "obvious" changes that need to take place. Even if you are correct, you'll create the impression that you are overly hasty and closed to hearing what people say. Before you can get the team working at its best, you need the people to accept you.

QUESTION?

How can I recruit the right people to my team?
Involve others in your team. Pay attention to their impressions; if a new person doesn't mesh well, teamwork will be difficult. Look for others in the organization who will interact well or who have equivalent background and expertise to judge their knowledge and accomplishments. Finally, don't judge by appearance or "signs" of value. Try to understand how people are and not how they seem.

You might think that choosing your own team from scratch is the preferred way to go, but that's not necessarily true. Yes, there are advantages: no existing clashes of personalities, no people who clearly occupy positions they can't handle. At the same time, an existing team is like the devil you know. When you put together a team—particularly when bringing in a number of people at the same time—you can never be sure how they will work together.

Standing or Ad Hoc

We're taking the terminology here from organizational structures and the practicalities of running an organization, but the intent is the same. There are standing teams, which means the teams are always working toward goals that are usually ongoing. You have greater stability in standing teams, but keeping people motivated and connected to the tasks can be more difficult because of a fatigue factor. The team members are essentially eating the same meal day in and out, which can get boring.

The other type of team is ad hoc, which literally translates from Latin as "to that." This kind of team is assembled to achieve a particular goal and then disbanded. Often such a team comprises representatives from different parts of an organization. Having control over who is involved is at best indirect. On the other hand, ad hoc teams don't tend to fall prey to tedium, and if the group dynamics are less than favorable, you can simply think to yourself, "This, too, shall pass. Soon."

Departmental or Cross-Functional

A departmental team is one where all the members come out of the same general group. They may be from the same team or closely related teams, but all the people are likely to know one another. That can make for easier operation because you avoid the entire getting acquainted period. But it can limit the range of experience the team might have.

Cross-functional teams bring people from different parts of an organization to form a team. By selecting members broadly, you increase the amount of information about the organization that you concentrate. However, decision-making generally is more dispersed, as the people on the team all report to different parts of the organization. More diverse reporting means more people ultimately having a say in what happens.

Leader- Versus Self-Directed

A team run by a team leader runs very differently than a self-directed team. On a leader-directed team, the leader sets the agenda, runs all team meetings, and delegates tasks to other members of the team. Sometimes leaders actually pick team members from different departments based on expertise they think will be relevant to a particular problem or issue within the company.

Team Dynamics

No matter what special conditions apply to it, a team is a group of people. Teams are subject to psychological dynamics—the invisible forces that influence the members of a group and that come about whenever people spend time together. The more you know about a team's dynamics, the better chance you have of helping them work effectively toward team goals.

Personalities

Undoubtedly in your life you've found people who were simpatico, with whom you hit it off as though you had known each other for years. You've also had the opposite experience of a new acquaintance, one with whom you mixed about as well as oil and water. With the vast majority of people, you probably don't have a particularly strong positive or negative reaction.

Telling people to stop having a problem with each other will do little good because they will often start internally justifying their actions. Through coaching, you can set each one on course to find a way to live with the other. They don't have to be good friends; they just have find ways of working with and around each other.

These personal attractions and repulsions are as potent a force as the effect you get when you bring two magnets together. They will happen, to one degree or another, between every two members of your team.

Ironically, either attraction or repulsion can be a source of either positive or negative outcomes. Either extreme can shut out others on the team. Two people who are thick as thieves may not let others in, and a pair that is at each other's throats can create a poisonous atmosphere. Still, a mild attraction can facilitate cooperation and smooth operations among all members, and a mild repulsion could turn into a competitiveness that, if harnessed by the individuals, could spur each on to greater achievement.

You cannot eliminate these forces, but you can try to get them to work in your favor. Encourage efficient working of the team without polarizing members. If there are strong personality forces at work, assign them to different aspects of the team's goals. You can even separate them physically if necessary so proximity does not breed either greater antagonism or focus. In bad cases, you might find that you have to replace one or more team members to keep things on track.

Looking for Cliques

Cliques might seem like something you left behind in grade school. Oh, if only that were true. But social dynamics from childhood often resurface. What makes them different from personality conflicts is that they are more complex. Not only does personality take a hand, but so do class, economics, status, and perception, among other things.

When you have cliques that have formed within the team—and that can easily happen if you are joining an existing one—you can't swap people out. At that point, you're potentially dealing with too many team members. Focus on creating circumstances under which people are forced to work with a mix of other team members. You can't keep people from socializing outside of the team's activities, but you can ensure a more inclusive mix when it comes to pursuing team goals.

Operational Processes

Why bring up processes in a discussion about people? Force people into bad processes, and you generally create bad moods. Aggregate those sour dispositions, and pretty soon you've turned the atmosphere in the entire building.

ALERT!

Improving conditions to heighten a team's dynamics and, as a result, operations, is a grand idea. But there is a natural limit. You can't always make life pleasant for everyone. After all, a sewer worker must go into the muck, even if you perfume it.

Luckily, this is one of the most easily controlled factors affecting team dynamics. There are many times you can improve conditions. Talk to the team members about their greatest frustrations and have them rank the problems. Find some that are in the top three positions on most of the lists. Work on the ones you can, and see how the atmosphere changes for the better.

Organizational Culture

Every organization has its own culture—like a personality. This personality interacts with each team member's personality. It's as though you had an extra person always hanging around. As with any combination of personalities, sometimes the mix works, and other times it doesn't. When it doesn't—or when the culture has an adverse effect on how two different team members interact—the results can be disastrous.

Unfortunately, changing a culture is incredibly difficult at best and impossible at worst. If you aren't head of the organization, the chances of changing the culture are virtually nonexistent; it takes that sort of authority to even attempt to modify it. In other words, getting people and processes to change is the only way to make a difference. You can always alter processes. It is a shame, but often when there's a clash between a team member and culture, the only answer is to find a replacement.

Fitting People In

There's a general assumption that all people fit into a team. But people fit in when you design the team correctly and recruit the right people for the right reasons. After all, each person joining the team must find a place to fit in. That place may have particular requirements, like a children's shape-sorter—that old-fashioned toy with different-shaped holes and blocks shaped to match each one. The piece only fits if it's the proverbial round peg in the round hole. Similarly, you need to take into account what the team needs.

Team Positions

In addition to the interpersonal forces, there are roles on a team that exist and need filling. Only you can state the exact positions on your team. Chances are that they will break out, according to the type of work necessary. As an example, think of a nonprofit organization devoted to building outdoor play spaces for school-aged children in your state. You might have one set of people devoted to raising money, so you would need people who excelled at sales. Another could actually build the outdoor structures, and so you would need people who could handle themselves in large carpentry projects.

Notice, though, that you cannot assume that someone who would fit well on one task is necessarily a candidate for another. So there are two types of roles: the positions needed by the team, and the natural abilities and leanings of the team members. Be sure to take the measure of the team members and then find the assignments that most efficiently use them to support team goals.

Team Roles

Then there is a different view of teams: the types of personal qualities that team members might bring. These are different from personality itself and refer to how people actually relate to the team as a whole:

- **Cheerleader:** Always there to boost morale, the cheerleader's natural enthusiasm can help motivate the team. This person will always try to accentuate the positive and eliminate the negative. Although not necessarily a bad person to have around, there may be some personality clashes with other members of the group (particularly first thing on a Monday morning).
- **Devil's advocate:** This person can seem argumentative but really just wants to get to the heart of the problem and find the best solution.

The devil's advocate focuses on the root of a problem and seeks accountability in all situations.

- **Muse:** The muse brings creative spark to meetings and inspires others to think outside the box. This person will bring plenty of ideas to the table and will look to others to help decide how to go about implementing the new plan.
- **Counselor:** Wisdom comes from experience and this person comes with lots of it, using firsthand knowledge and observations to provide unique insight into solving problems. Everyone's ideas have value to the counselor, who wants to make sure everyone is part of developing the solution.
- **Facilitator:** This person knows how to get the job done. Organization and delegation are the strengths of the facilitator. Facilitators can also have a tendency to become overbearing and might try to take total control of the team.

Each of these roles can provide an important contribution to the group as a whole. Having a diverse set of personalities, as well as skills, will help you ensure whatever psychological boosts the group might need. Try to include at least one person who demonstrates the traits of a strong facilitator, as such a person is an extremely useful asset.

Analyzing the Team

It's not enough to know that a team has roles and needs; you must examine the team and see where it is strong and what parts are weak. You want to know not just whether team members fit in, but how they fit. What the team needs is a matter of balance—getting enough of the roles and positions filled so that it can operate in as harmonious and effective a method as possible.

Team Needs

You can't analyze the team until you examine what it needs. Those needs are grounded in the team's goals, which must relate to the organization's goals and principles. Ultimately, the team needs people who will carry out the goals. But for a moment, don't think of the individual members so much as the team as a whole. What are the goals? What actions do those goals require? What types of expertise and experience and resources does the team need to undertake the actions?

You cannot answer this question once and decide that the team is set for eternity. Its needs will constantly change with shifts in goals and organizational priorities, changes in team members, and other fluctuations that affect what the team is trying to do. Plan on this as part of your normal duties.

Team SWOT Analysis

Strength. Weakness. Opportunity. Threat. Analyzing these four pillars is a standard tool for strategic planning. In the case of a team, the leader—and even the entire team—looks at the group's strengths and weaknesses as well as what conditions and situations could help or hurt it.

The point is not to drown in detail but to look for significant issues that can have a major influence on what the team does and how it proceeds. You want to involve the entire team because this is an area where the activities of others may help them notice significant topics that you might not recognize.

Reconciling Your Knowledge

You're now ready to analyze what you've learned. Look at what the team must achieve, what it needs, and the considerations that might help or hinder it. When you have that, you can consider what the team should be and what it must do to get there.

In planning, you need to not only consider the team as a whole but to see how the members fit into it. Here is where you can consider the strengths and weaknesses of individuals and how they can best help the team goals. It is time to make some decisions, which means you should consider how your team approaches decision-making.

Decision Models

A team decision-making model is a clear case of absolutely no absolutes. Every team must make decisions, but the process shifts according to circumstances and group dynamics. As a leader, you have to be sensitive. Balance the needs of individual team members to feel respected and important against the need of the group to get things done. There are a few general categories of decision-making to consider.

Authoritarian

Pure authoritarian decision-making can have its place. For example, if there is an emergency, you don't want a consensus approach to keep running while the chance to take action has passed. But this approach should only be used in emergencies. If it's used too often, you lose the insight that others with different experiences and knowledge can provide. It can also make people distrust you and decide that if they are just to be following orders, there is no reason to do more than punch the clock. Good employees will eventually look elsewhere for employment, and volunteers are certain to have something better to do.

Consulting

In consulting, team members get to make suggestions, but they don't necessarily have a say in the decision. This can be useful when working with group members when you want to retain the ability to drive decisions.

Democratic

Coming from a democratic society, you might think this would be the natural answer to the question of how to make decisions, but it's not. Democracy gives everyone a say, and depending on how the vote comes out, one thing or another will get the nod. But democracy can divide your team into opposing camps that make working together difficult, if not impossible. Yet there are times, particularly in questions of how the team will best operate, that you want everyone's views expressed. If the issue isn't divisive and full support of the team isn't critical, then it can make things move along relatively quickly.

Consensus

Another possibility for those times when everyone has a significant stake in the outcome is to look at consensus decision-making. In this, everyone has to buy into a decision. It's a slow process, marked by the need to facilitate discussion to reach a common understanding and to get people to be willing to say what is really on their minds. When the decision is done, though, you have real buy-in from all parties because it's a decision they all had to agree with. Save this method for decisions that materially affect the team's direction and mission.

Choose the Right Model

So which model will you use? As in all realistic answers, it depends. In this case, the following questions are the ones to ask:

- Where is the team is in its development?
- What is the nature of the issue?
- How urgent is the situation?
- Is there a benefit to the team in greater participation?
- Will greater participation help or hinder the issue's resolution?
- Is there a weakness in your leadership style that a given choice can help you address?

Depending on the answers, you might find that the situation calls for one technique over another.

ESSENTIAL

Look back at the discussion about leader- versus self-directed teams. These two different types will lend themselves more naturally to different forms of decision-making. The former will lean toward authoritarian and consulting styles, while self-directed teams will likely favor democratic or consensus-based decisions.

If the differences are immaterial in this case, then we suggest always defaulting to the most inclusive and participatory technique that will work. The challenge in learning to become a leader is learning to work with others. Presumably, you already know how to get along with yourself and your own decisions. The more you can develop relationships with your team, where their views and experience matter (because they can bring the synergy you seek), the better a leader you can become.

Team Development Stages

If you want your team to work well—or even exist with any degree of success—you will have to contend with team development. Teams go through stages, and these stages put different demands on the members and on leaders. The more you know about how teams develop, the better you can navigate the various stages and keep progressing toward your goals.

In this case, we're using a popular framework first published in 1965 by Bruce Tuckman, a professor of psychology at The Ohio State University. He called these stages by neat, rhyming names: forming, storming, norming, and performing. Despite their rhythm, the terms aren't so transparent, so this book uses some others in conjunction.

Creation (Forming)

There's a big difference between a group in which everyone is new to each other and one in which the people have learned to work together, anticipate what the others will need, and act accordingly. That's the difference between having an assemblage and a team. Any time you start a new team or even see significant changes in an existing one, you face creating the team.

In the creation phase, the members have to come to know each other and each other's roles in the team. If they are new to the team, they must understand its purpose and goals. If they were previously on the team, then they need to consider how changes may affect pursuing those goals. All members, new or existing, must consider boundaries between themselves and others, making enough room for people to have control over their work without stepping on the toes of colleagues. But really knowing each other takes time because in this stage people are typically on their best behavior.

Emergence (Storming)

As the team emerges from its creation phase and starts to more seriously pursue its goals, people lose the veneer they don to impress others.

Now they start to be themselves, and you'll find some team members getting irritated with each other. Certain people will overstep the boundaries. Disagreements will flare up on almost every topic: why the group exists, what it should be doing, how it should be working. This period is one of necessary strife. Team members cannot walk on eggshells forever.

As things get a little ugly, don't hide from the arguments. This process is absolutely necessary if a team is eventually going to become stable and productive. You'll have to re-establish vision and meaning, work hard to listen, and adjust operations as necessary. You might even find that the way things started weren't correct and that this period is good for making necessary changes.

Establishment (Norming)

People have slugged it out—hopefully, only in a figurative sense. Now the team members should be comfortable with each other or at least resigned to everyone else's presence. Everyone has more or less agreed on what direction to take and on the fundamental issues facing the team. Now they are spending time making decisions and getting work done.

In other words, the basic group dynamics and processes are accepted and working. Now you need to focus more strongly on goals and tasks.

Performing (Self-Direction)

This is the highest development point for a team. In this state, it is effective in what it does. People on the team understand their positions and what collectively they are trying to achieve. As issues come up, team members see them—even anticipate them—and take corrective action. The team should start to act from principle and not just wait to be told what to do.

Recycle

Unfortunately, development is often not linear and never something you can take for granted. There are teams that won't progress past some stage. A disruption, such as replacing a team member or dealing with a change in organizational intent or strategy, can even take a well-established team and push it back into an earlier stage of development.

At some point, and possibly more often than once in your leadership experience, you'll have to face rebuilding and redeveloping the team that you already thought was set. All you can do is dust yourself off, determine where you are now, and then take appropriate actions. Don't take it too hard; it's not generally a sign of poor leadership (though it can be).

Disbanding (Adjourning)

In 1975, Tuckman added another stage to describe what happens when a team breaks up. This doesn't affect the group's goals because when this happens, the goals are hopefully completed. However, it is important for the team members and their futures. The bonds between people working intently on a single goal can become surprisingly strong.

Help people recollect what they achieved and how they worked together to meet goals. Let them all bring up lessons they learned. Treat disbanding as a form of grief, and give people a chance to get the emotions out of their systems.

CHAPTER 10

Conflict

Strife and disagreement are all around us. You could look at the news for a quick reminder: war, religious battle, economic conflict, even class struggle (for those who read too much Marx in their formative years). But you don't need a view that encompasses the whole world. Think about your personal life, with everything from spats to full-fledged feuds with friends, family members, and work colleagues. When people interact, conflict is inevitable. It may not happen today or tomorrow, but eventually team members will butt heads.

Bad Responses to Conflict

Given that conflict is such an inevitable part of life, the answer to its appearance would seem clear-cut: Handle the conflict the way you would in every other part of life. Trouble is, there are too many people who try to avoid discord.

Fear and Anger

There is no single reason why people dodge conflict. Some subconsciously remember experiences from their youth and shy away from negative situations. Others might find that they get angry and cannot deal rationally with circumstances, or that they are flustered and unsure of how to resolve a problem. Perhaps other people seem to be aggressive, more powerful, and intent on having their way. Specifics change, but there are always two underlying emotions when people face conflict, and each one gives rise to one common set of reactions. The first is fear that can grow to terror when unchecked. This emotion spurs lying, hiding from reality, and other avoidance mechanisms.

The other emotion is anger. That is natural, as the two have been tied together for as long as the human race has existed. The product could be such things as egoism, aggressive behavior, and inflexibility.

It is a mistake to think that people feel either fear or anger exclusively. Anyone emotionally reacting to conflict will experience both feelings. The proportions of each will vary, and an individual might lean toward one end of the spectrum or the other, but both will exist. That is why, for example, some people who seem outwardly passive have simply suppressed their anger and express it in backhanded ways—the condition that many call passive aggression.

People Remain Victims

The problem for most people is that they are trapped within this meeting of fear and anger. They react blindly—that is to say, they don't see what is happening in themselves and fail to understand how it affects their relationship to the world. In short, they are victims. Those who don't learn to rise above their reactions will find themselves victims of their own natures every time they encounter conflict.

Breaking Free

We know that conflict is a mainstay of existence and, therefore, it will be part of any team experience. Match that with the reluctant understanding that most of us are uncomfortable, at least part of the time, with any form of discord, and the prospects are bleak for the smooth and effective operation of your team.

Your only choice is to handle the inevitable conflict in a productive way and to help your team members do the same. The place to start is at the beginning of conflict. Understand the nature of the conflict and the benefit it can actually provide.

Nature of Conflict

An underlying reason for the problems we all have with conflict is a misunderstanding of what it is. The fear and anger come from assuming that conflict is a form of attack. Two forces meet, each trying its best to subdue the other. No wonder people don't like the concept—it seems to ask for you to stand still while someone tries to beat you senseless. However, while that is one form of conflict, it's a limited view.

Conflict and Doing

Although it is common to associate the word *conflict* with a collision on some field of honor, the word encompasses a much larger conceptual meaning. The world is based on opposites. For every black, there is white. You breath in and you breathe out. Having the opposite is necessary or we'd all quickly die.

FACT

What would happen if your car were equipped with only an accelerator pedal and no brakes? You wouldn't be able to stop, and the outcome would be disastrous. There is great danger from an uninhibited force. Conflict is a natural way for two opposing forces to keep each other in check.

Conflict is the manifestation of opposites in the world. That's why it is healthy. Only conflict gives us a chance to gain control over our own actions and actually accomplish anything. When you pursue a goal, it is opposites—or conflict—that will let you intentionally moderate your tactics to stay on course.

Conflict and Thinking

Conflict is not only a necessary part of physically getting things done. It is a basis of thought itself. Ancient Greek philosophers had terminology for it: thesis, antithesis, synthesis.

Thesis is the idea that one person offers. Antithesis is the counterargument provided by another, creating the conflict. That process of back and forth is called dialectic. One side or the other might win out. But sometimes that doesn't happen. Instead, the result is synthesis, or a combination of the two points that result in something new.

FACT

Dialectic has been a favorite tool of many philosophers, including Heraclitus of Ephesus, Socrates, Plato, and Hegel. Even economic and political philosophers Marx and Engels made heavy use of the technique.

Think back, and this will sound like the idea of synergy discussed in Chapter 4. By combining things, you get a result that is greater than all the single elements put together. Because you need the clash of ideas, it is a process that really must take place in a group.

My Way Is Best

When things begin to drift in the wrong direction, different people have varying ideas on how to set things aright. If they all have goodwill toward the project—and, presumably, members of a team will generally have positive feelings toward collective success—each team member will honestly want to help.

Remember that these people will have varying views of what is wrong or right and effective or useless. All will be sure that their perception is correct. That means they will be certain that their approach to fixing a problem is the one that will work, and that significantly different ideas, at least at first glance, will cause harm. If that isn't a recipe for essential conflict, what is?

Good Versus Bad Conflict

You know the theory behind conflict, but how can you use this to proactively confront conflict among your team members? First, you must realize that you can't look at all team conflict in the same way. Some is bad and some is good. The difference between the classifications is the effect they have on your team.

Impact of Conflict

Those who think that all conflict is bad react out of fear. People who relish conflict and even go out of their way for a fight—no matter what the context—act out of anger. Both approaches are wrong. Conflict is not, of itself, always helpful or hurtful. The only measure of the quality of conflict is whether you can use it to help your team achieve its goals. If you can resolve the conflict and create something that advances the goals, then the conflict is helpful. If the resolution of conflict hinders progress toward the goals, then it is hurtful. This concept is slippery. A given conflict might be helpful to one team because of the particular strengths, weaknesses, and challenges the members face, but it might negatively affect another team member.

Sometimes you will be able to direct your team in moments of conflict. At those times, you can use the emotional and intellectual results as fodder. The material becomes a type of fertilizer that lets you improve and grow the results of your effort. At other times, conflict will hurt what you are trying to do. It might set one team member against another or could cause your team's goals to conflict with other important goals in your organization.

What Distinguishes Conflict

What makes the difference between helpful types of conflict and hurtful types of conflict? The answer comes back to conflict as the interaction process of thesis, antithesis, and synthesis. What you seek is to keep pursuing your team's goals, which means not being stopped. If you are to proceed, you will run into roadblocks and conflict as surely as rain comes to Seattle. Those conflicts are unavoidable if you are going to achieve your goals. They are useful because solving them is a necessary step in making progress.

If you fail to pay attention, you will end up blocked—often in subtle ways that will cause your team to fail by going off course while assuming it is still on track. Be alert for these types of barriers so they don't slow you down unnecessarily.

Conflict becomes a real problem when it's a manifestation of ego on the part of team members. If you have two personalities that don't mix, you must solve the conflict to keep moving, and so the conflict is helpful. If some team members have weaknesses that act as barriers, overcoming that conflict keeps you on course to your goals.

The real test is the permanence of the source of conflict. When conflict is the product of ego, personal image, and ambition, addressing the issue doesn't get you past an inevitable barrier so much as it removes a shackle from your collective leg. To resolve the conflict, you spend energy that could otherwise go to solving a real obstruction. This is useless conflict because it is not going to disappear as you move past this point. Instead, you are only going to face it again.

Transforming Conflict

Now for the no-leader's land in the middle. What might be useful to one group can be useless to another. That probably seems odd. How could a conflict that doesn't disappear become useful if it's just a waste of energy?

You want to transform the conflict by changing its dynamics. The conflict remains useless when it is conflict—or, putting it another way, when the solution is temporary. Even if you have a clash of egos, you can make progress by dealing with conflict if you move toward eliminating that source of contention in the future. What you need to do is find a way to move team members toward a new type of behavior or create a process that reduces or eliminates the problem. That transforms the useless into the useful. For example, if two people are blaming each other for a problem, get beyond the specific circumstances. Have them, with help, spell out their roles and responsibilities, evaluate where the two mesh, and decide what process they will use to eliminate similar events in the future before they become problems.

Types of Conflict

Whether good or bad, conflict can be one of many types: for example, personal, work-related, bureaucratic, societal, economic. Here are the types of conflicts that are most relevant to the topic of leadership:

- Interpersonal
- Ideological
- Organizational
- Operational
- Relational

Each type is a bit different and requires its own type of handling. You need to be ready to deal with any of them if you want your group to be successful.

Interpersonal

Interpersonal conflict is often the single largest source of dispute. This is when people don't get along, and it is often a useless type of conflict. What makes it such a difficult type to manage is its focus on the personal. A team works when it elevates its objectives above individual concerns—when it doesn't let the personal get in the way of the team.

But interpersonal conflict is exactly that: when personal considerations, in the form of a clash between team members, take precedence. If you are around people having this type of conflict, you'll hear that personal aspect. Those involved will frame everything in terms of their own concerns, feelings, and reactions. People in the throes of an interpersonal conflict never say something like, "Oh, darn, I hate how this run-in distracts me and keeps me from pursuing our group goal." No, what you'll hear instead is, "That so-and-so! I'm tired of having to deal with him when he does that thing that bothers me!"

What you must do is turn attention back to the team goals while understanding that people have a right to their own feelings. Sometimes the feelings are justified. Sexual harassment isn't a trifle, for instance, and you can't tell a victim to just ignore it. But you also don't want to elevate every spat to a legally actionable issue.

ALERT!

When working with conflicts between team members, don't go for the easy solution. Try to get them to devise their own solution. The means by which team members resolve their conflict should have a broad enough structure that the people involved are able to continue to work successfully to make sure the problem doesn't recur.

When the conflict does not rise to that degree of seriousness, work with the team members. Although they may want to focus on proving their points, get them to look instead at what is happening to the team's goals. Ask them how to resolve any issues to enable the group's work to continue. The more you can get them to look at what the group needs, the less they focus on themselves, averting the head-on collision.

Ideological

You'd be surprised how often ideology in its many forms can appear. A business can insist on promoting a given political, economic, or philosophical view just as much as any advocacy organization. Groups can hold to particular ideas and so can individuals. Strong belief is a powerful force, a form of motivation and vision.

Belief can also be a limitation. When people insist that the world works in a given way, they sometimes refuse to acknowledge anything to the contrary. Cognitive scientists and linguists refer to the condition as a *framework*. We all have frameworks of culture and experience, but to solve problems, you must not let preconceived thoughts blind you to possible solutions.

ALERT!

By its nature, ideological conflict is difficult to overcome. People literally cannot see that they are stuck. The way to fight ideological conflicts is to start throwing away assumptions. You must insist on re-examining areas where things seem blocked. Investigate and use creativity techniques to break mental associations and find new ways to view situations.

The best way to avoid ideological conflicts is not to get into them in the first place. That means standing guard against the problem. Your principles and the need to support them can help you avoid ideological conflicts. Focus on them and toss other assumptions out the window.

Organizational

If you want to achieve a goal, you organize your efforts and structure your solution for success. Think about the word *organization,* which describes a selection of people gathered to achieve something. The way you structure the interaction of people, responsibilities, and hierarchy understandably corresponds with the way you get things done. However, you can do things well or badly.

Speak to experts, and you'll hear that the wrong organization is one of the biggest challenges a group can face. If it's possible to have the right people in certain positions, which is critical to building a good team, you can also have the wrong people. You could have the right people, but problems arise if you structure your organization so that communication doesn't happen easily or at the right time.

Your team may face problems with achieving its goals when there are no conflicts between people or obvious roadblocks. Consider whether your approach to organizing the team doesn't work well with what you are trying to achieve. See if members are getting the information they need on a timely basis directly from the people who have it. Ask if people with the right set of talents or experiences are working together.

Operational

Organization can provide conflict, and so can operational issues. The term *operations* describes how your team structures its work flow, the chain of events that drives what actually happens. Just as proper organization promotes communication, good operations enable action, and it's action you ultimately need if you're going to achieve anything.

Tasks that take too much time and effort to achieve are a sign of operational conflict. Your method of actually getting things done clashes with what you are trying to do. There may be too many steps or duplication or even some activities that send you in the wrong direction before doubling back.

Making a chart of what happens and how it occurs can do wonders. Such a flow chart forces the team to think through every step it takes. If you've never undertaken such an exercise, be ready for some surprises; chances are you have more conflict between your operations and your goals than you think.

Relational

There is an entire world out there, and your team and its goals don't exist in isolation. This is the biggest class of conflict, and it includes some of the most difficult things to change. Your team might find that aspects of the larger organization make it difficult to achieve anything. There might be societal pressures or environmental conditions working to your detriment.

Now you can see why this is the biggest—and toughest—class. When conflict is limited to the team, at least you have control. When it is outside, you only have partial control at best, and too many factors are independent of what you decide and which actions you take. Sometimes the best you can do is adapt to circumstances.

Managing Conflict

Although there is no one solution for all conflict, there are people who peddle such promises, and it is wise to walk away from them. But you can apply some principles to resolve conflict within your organization.

The Right Focus

It may sound odd, but you can't focus on the conflict. A clash is just a symptom. You can't directly address the conflict, and you don't want to. That was just the sign something was wrong. It is the actual problem your team faces that causes the conflict, and it is that problem you work to eliminate. Concentrate on what you are trying to achieve and how to get there.

Identify the Challenge

Keeping the right focus gives you the next step: recognize the problem. That might sound trivial, but it isn't. People constantly tilt at windmills, thinking that they are solving what bothers them when they're actually chasing phantoms. Misidentifying problems is much easier than you might think. Usually, mistakes are made because people are trying a solution that is suited for a completely different problem than the one that lies before them.

ALERT!

Misidentifying a problem is distressingly easy. Consider a mechanic. If the automobile is losing power, it could be the car's computer, a leaky gas line, a sign of an impending engine seizure, or any of a number of other things. The mechanic must get beyond the initial signs of conflict and see the details of the problem.

If you've picked the wrong challenge, you run the risk of wasting your time. Worse, there is a good chance that you can make a situation worse than it already is. Say you are faced with two people who aren't working together well. They may misunderstand each other, using similar terms in very different ways. If you think the problem is that they don't talk enough, you'll only increase the frustration by putting them together even more. Instead, you should be helping them understand where their communication is going wrong, or find someone who knows what each is saying and is able to translate.

What to Do?

When you see conflict and the underlying problem, many issues may come into play. But it can be refreshing to remember that you will only do one of three things:

1. You can abandon the team's goal, which may be sensible if that goal turns out to be poorly formed and capable of actually setting things back.
2. You can overcome the barrier and continue progress toward achieving your goal.
3. You can create a combination of your current approach to your goal (thesis) and the barricade (antithesis) to reach a new and more effective path to the goal (synthesis).

Your only imperative is to solve the problem and keep moving toward your goals. Use whatever approach lets you do this while maintaining your team principles and those of you and your team members. At times, one of these tactics will work, and in other conditions you might need another.

Resolving Principle

One of the basic concepts in this chapter is the thesis-antithesis-synthesis cycles. All three of the major categories above use a form of synthesis. That makes resolving conflict an art more than a science.

FACT

Many of us believe that only direct force clears the path for progress. Not so. In many endeavors, from art and architecture to engineering and science, brute force does not solve a problem. Solutions may come effortlessly. If you are working hard to find a solution, you may be on the wrong track.

The art comes in working with unpredictable conditions, goals, and people. The science is in the theory itself. Although the exact form of synthesis is not something you'll know in advance, you will need a resolving principle. You need the resolution of the conflict to move in a specific direction. You find which of the three general techniques gets you closest to your goal while not disrupting other goals of your team or organization. If more than one technique will do the job, then use the one that is easiest and least expensive in resources to implement.

Encouraging Others

Even if you could single-handedly resolve all conflicts for your team, what good would it do? Your team wouldn't know. In most cases, team members are the only ones able to see the conflicts and take appropriate action. If the conflicts are personal and you want a lasting solution, the involved members will have to take part.

As much as possible, using coaching and mentoring, you must help your team manage the conflict it sees. An implication is that a leader can never know about all conflict from direct perception. Many times the other members of the team will be the ones who see evidence—another reason why communication, particularly active listening, is so important.

Personal Conflicts

Conflicts between people are extremely common and can be debilitating for a team. Using the old eighty-twenty rule, you can bet that 80 percent of your conflict problems will come from a small portion of conflict types. As life goes, that nettlesome minority is usually all personal.

People Ignoring People

Useless conflict between people usually happens when one party feels a personal agenda ignored by the other. Some of the reasons it can come about include strong negative feelings, either from situations at work or home, or from unclear communication. But the real villain is often disagreements, because they tend to be the longest lasting. Disagreements may come about from differing perceptions or attitudes like prejudice, resistance to change, or a bias against change.

Get the Private Story

You have to start by understanding the reason for the personal conflict. You'll likely need to speak with the team members involved and listen to their versions of events. Often, the people may not be able to articulate what exactly is bothering them, or they might give one explanation when another is the true issue. You also might need to speak with other members of the team to get a clear view and one less tinted by the conflict.

ESSENTIAL

Before questioning someone before a jury, a good attorney performs extensive research. The lawyer wants to avoid asking a question without knowing the answer in advance. By having the likely information ahead of time, it's possible for the lawyer to plan on how to move through the testimony and emphasize certain points.

What you are doing is gathering material to further your own understanding, not to make a judgment or a decision. Talk to team members one on one or else there will be so much potential struggle that you might grasp with the issues.

Get the Public Story

Speaking with everyone involved all in the same room at the same time is also mandatory. You want them to get back to work with each other, not with you. Present the issue without emotion, blame, or judgment. Speak in the first person, such as, "I see that there is an issue with such-and-such," and not in the third person, because that helps keep you from making value judgments that will repel one or both sides. Clearly convey what you have learned without blaming any person or group. Make sure all parties express their points of view, and listen actively and without judgment. Then give your point of view clearly. Have the participants repeat it in their own words.

Ask for Help

In case it hasn't been clear, you need to involve the team members in the resolution. That should help increase cooperation and somewhat reduce anyone's feeling of being attacked. The more everyone helps to create a solution, the more each person has invested and the more likely he will be to actually make the agreed-upon changes.

Start by trying to build a common objective. People cannot agree to a solution if they don't agree on what they should be trying to do. Brainstorm to find possible solutions. Identify more than one way to end the conflict without actually evaluating each option. If you look at only one idea, someone will feel forced. On the other hand, if you have a number of ideas, people have some choice.

Next, select the solution that has the best chance of meeting everyone's needs. Evaluate the proposed solutions, keeping in mind that sometimes the best solution will be a combination of several suggestions.

Plan for Action

Develop a realistic plan of action and determine who will do what, when, where, and how. Using the chosen solution, plan what actions are necessary to ensure its success. Make a schedule and give a copy to everyone involved. Decide how each party will know if the solution is working and what criteria will tell you that the objective has been met.

Work the Plan

You implement the jointly developed plan and plan on following up to keep things on track. Evaluate the success based on the joint objective. Be sure to schedule time to meet so that the people involved can review progress and develop revisions or even alternative solutions if necessary.

Well Enough Alone

There is one option that hasn't been discussed: not doing anything. Not everything needs to be fixed. Many people who study forestry have become convinced that one of the big reasons we see so many large forest fires these days is because for years, people in charge of the vast land tracts tried to suppress every flame. As a result, the burning that happens as part of nature was never able to help clear underbrush and reduce the amount of fuel littering the forest floor. When a fire happens, it's as though someone has stockpiled cordwood for a New England winter. There's plenty of material for the fire to consume, and the blaze soon rages out of control. Sometimes the wisest course of action is to stay out of the way.

Pick Your Battles

There is a difference between true conflict that threatens progress and the everyday tensions that adults must learn to manage. Don't move in quickly at every sign of trouble. Often, you're only seeing one small facet of a more complex situation. Would you take a significant corrective action every time someone who works with you makes a mistake? More importantly, would you want someone to eliminate all mistakes from your life?

Absolutely not. In addition to being invasive, the atmosphere would be insulting, as though you were incapable of taking care of yourself. Furthermore, if you try to wipe out mistakes, you also remove the chance of learning.

Don't treat every hiccough as a call for the emergency response squad. Definitely take action when you are faced with real conflict that threatens to delay or derail your team's progress toward its goals. Yes, taking action earlier rather than later can mean the difference between a small fix and a big one, but make sure that conflict resolution is actually in order. If you try too soon, you tie up resources that might be more effective elsewhere and run the risk of being the boy who cried, "Conflict!" A wolf of a real problem will trip you up when people have grown tired of mobilizing for nothing.

Minimize, Not Remove

Don't assume that you must absolutely remove every conflict. No, you don't want them to come back, but some conflicts won't return. If what you see is timely in nature and not evergreen, then do enough work to get it out of the way, and then leave it behind you. There are times that the best way around an obstacle is literally to walk around it, not to yank it up and toss it to the side. If the blockade is a naturally occurring mountain, you won't move it anyway. Try for the wisdom to know when circumvention is the only tactic worth using.

Things Fall Apart

Notice that failing isn't an option. There's too much of that in the world already, and if it happens, you'll know soon enough. No individual or group smoothly reaches every goal, and at times you will be stopped dead in your tracks. Then you have to decide, honestly, how critical that agenda is to your overall progress and whether you really need it. If not, let it go and focus on important issues. If so, then dust yourself off and start over again.

CHAPTER 11

Empowerment and Delegation

Leaders and teams. The two concepts are indispensable. History has many examples of leaders who convinced their followers to participate in everything from strange rituals to wars to economic insanities. Leading teams means working with others—effectively and efficiently. Anything else would be a waste. This chapter deals with delegation and empowerment as ways of involving members of your team and reaping the benefits they can provide.

Leading Isn't DIY

U.S. culture has an odd view of responsibility and leadership. People often perceive leadership as being about the individual rather than the team. You hear about the quarterback who saved the game, but you don't hear about the rest of the team. Politics and public affairs become the story of a different type of sports: horse races where office holders win or lose. Business? It's all the CEO. Science? The result of brilliant people who are beyond the mental ken of ordinary men.

Singular Mythos

This may seem to be moving back into the touchy-feely realm, but sometimes there is more that is concrete in psychology than in mathematics. A mythos is the collected set of cultural beliefs one generation hands to the next. It comprises the complex and interrelating stories that help us hold a sense of who we are and what the world is.

FACT

Joseph Campbell was well known for his writing about mythology. His idea was that a common set of myths provided the foundation for most of our stories. We react most strongly to forms of entertainment that reinforce the myths. One of the strongest is the idea of the hero who faces dangers to achieve a quest.

The mythos embedded throughout American history—rugged individualists carving out fortune and a new life, leaving tyranny behind—forms the seat of how society teaches us to view leadership. To lead means to embody everything we see as the essence of individuality: to be the ultimate hero, powerful and alone.

Set the Record Straight

This is a false image. No one does anything alone. The greatest scientific discoveries were only made possible by those who had gone before. As Sir Isaac Newton said, "If I have seen further, it is by standing on the shoulders of giants." Only a fool of a military leader would walk alone onto a modern battlefield. Great business executives have help from hundreds, thousands, and sometimes tens of thousands of employees working hard to make everything happen. Great painters learn from copying the canvases of masters that have gone before.

Even for original genius, no one really stands completely apart from the efforts of anyone else in the world. Now remember Eisenhower's definition of leadership: the art of getting people to do what you want them to do because they want to do it. You can't be a leader if you aren't getting others to willingly do that which must be done.

Understanding Power

We think, deep down, that virtually everyone actually knows that it takes a team to accomplish great feats. Outside the odd megalomaniac, people have a sense that they can't do it all on their own. And yet if you look at any organization, from charities to for-profit companies, you'll find many people who insist on acting as though they can be it all. They can't, but as they try, they cause many problems. They believe in a myth of power because they act from the mythos of individual power.

Power Defined

Power. People use the word all the time but often with little thought about its nature. Stated most simply, power is the ability to do or act. Of course, there is power and then there is *power*. Technically, you can think because you have the power to do so. But in the context of teams, power is more expansive. It is the ability to not just do something yourself but to have someone else do something and to make decisions and take action in the name of the team or organization.

Many people mistakenly think that power is the ability to tell others what to do, but that is like saying that cooking is the process of slicing vegetables. Power over others in a given context might be part of power, but it is an empty explanation because on its own there is little to it. Power must always be about achieving something; otherwise, it is an empty exercise.

ALERT!

Some people horde power without consciously thinking about it. There are two giveaway signs: the desire to keep people from advancing to higher positions, and the need to stockpile information and keep it away from others. If you find yourself doing either of these, chances are that you worship at the altar of power.

Positions of Power

There are different sources of power. Some people have power because of natural gifts, like charisma. These are great to have, and they can make being an effective leader easier. Ironically, they do not aid in all aspects of leadership, like sharing power. Because they are personal characteristics, they don't lend themselves to being passed on.

From the view of sharing power, two sources are important. One is the power people get within an organization because of the positions they occupy. When people work within an organized group, they make implicit and explicit deals concerning what they will get for something in return. You might work in a large company and receive a salary and other forms of compensation. In exchange, you perform certain duties and also accept conditions about the group. One of the conditions is that when people occupy certain positions in the hierarchy, you agree to provide them with certain degrees of respect and obedience. If people make decisions within their granted authority, you abide by them.

What a leader must do to share power effectively is to create positions of authority for team members. These positions might be officially on an organization chart or more informal in nature. What is important is that you trust the team members to take on certain jobs and make the decisions necessary.

Knowledge Is Power

Equating knowledge with the ability to do things is an old and valid concept. Knowledge of hunting and agriculture, of weather, of building and weaving has kept people alive and dry and clothed for thousands of years. The more self-knowledge people have, the better their chances of leading the lives they want.

In an organization, people also have power based on knowledge. They might already possess this information or they might obtain it through the organization. Knowledge can be power if it lets you affect conditions or if people need it and you are a trusted source. Keeping hold of information is a subtle form of trying to keep control. To share power, a leader must share both the information that people need to accomplish something and the knowledge to understand how.

Power Trip

Mythic and historic aspects of culture have helped develop the image of the lone leader—an amusing conundrum, if you think about it. How can you lead if no one else is there? Yet many people have this view so deeply buried in their psyches that they can't easily get out from under it. Instead of leading, they look to directing, commanding, and micromanaging.

That is a major reason why some people within organizations seek power. They've been told all their lives that it's what they should do. But, at best, this is crude and ineffective. The people taking the orders are rarely committed to the goals of the organization and so are either giving allegiance out of force or from their own psychological quirks.

QUESTION?

Are all examples of following authority simply false power?
No. The military, for example, is full of people who follow strict orders because they strongly believe in the goals of the organization.

However, the upshot is that if you're exercising power over people who feel compelled or are twisted in their own way, you don't have any. One person cannot possibly make every decision in any concrete undertaking outside of trivial examples. We've all had experience in dealing with micromanagers. Things don't get done any better, and the process is exhausting. Real power for a leader comes from working with a team, from providing responsibility and authority to them, and from harnessing the results in a positive way to actually accomplish something.

Hoarding Power

If you've never done it before, giving up control can be scary. It leaves you feeling vulnerable. There is the chance that team members won't pull through, so things go poorly and you are left with egg on your face. Perhaps you're remembering a team situation in which things went badly, whether you were leading or not. Luckily, these feelings are actually phantoms.

You aren't any more—or any less—vulnerable than you would be without giving up control. If you have been working with others on a project or goal, you have already been dependent on them to do their parts. The biggest problem leaders generally have is actually refusing to give up power. Either they become micromanagers, or they give team members responsibility without the necessary corresponding authority. That's like putting people into a kitchen and asking them to prepare a meal, only not letting them use any of the pots and pans, knives, or ingredients. Why bother?

Sharing Power

Everything changes when you start sharing power. You clear the air and your head. You can't actually keep on top of everything and take care of every little detail yourself. By letting others take on areas of responsibility, you remove a lot of unnecessary pressure from yourself (because you don't have to be superhuman) and from them (because they are no longer handcuffed).

When others take on tasks and accountability, you divide the work of pursuing a goal. Progress can occur more quickly, and you increase the team's ability to cover all the details necessary to success.

Giving Up Control

To share power really means to give up control—or, to be more precise, to let go of an illusion of control. This is one of those paradoxical situations in which the only way to have something is to let it go. You just need to understand how to give up that control and when.

Setting the Conditions

It would be wrong to suggest that giving up control is like wiping your hands clean, walking off, and waiting until the real work is done. That would be like driving a car by turning away from the steering wheel—an experiment that would not be recommended. Nothing could be farther from the truth.

There is a difference between giving up some control and surrendering all of it. You must create the proper conditions in your team so that sharing power actually works. Giving up control is a measured, and measurable, activity. When you do it correctly, you make it possible to get more done while reducing the risk of people not doing their part.

Pillars of Power Sharing

Although sharing power with members of your team may be concerning and a bit difficult, it is possible. What you need to do is establish two aspects of power-sharing that allow you to do so safely and effectively. One is empowering employees to make decisions and delegating responsibility to them. If you don't give people the authority to do things, they won't be able to do them.

The other is delegation. You actually have to extend responsibility outward to team members so that you don't become the final bottleneck on everything the team tries to do. As team leader, you're still ultimately responsible. But you extend responsibility to others, deputizing them so they take over something on your behalf while still responsible to you.

Empowerment

The first aspect of sharing power is giving team members the ability to do things. That means a number of things, including providing the knowledge and resources they will need as well as creating the proper atmosphere. Your team members have to believe they can make decisions and that they have the backing to do so.

What It Is

Empowerment has become the organizational equivalent of a New Age term, bringing more sentiment than change. But it is the ideal word for what you need to do: give the basics of power to everyone in an organization who can use it. Concretely, empowerment is the process of giving people on your team the ability to make decisions and do things—in short, giving them power.

Convince the Team

But it's not enough to tell people they have power. That's the problem with the term *empowerment*: Its overuse has lead to a cheapening of the concept. When people hear that they are about to get the right to make substantive decisions, they often doubt it. Given the number of times they're promised something that never comes through, who can blame them? Not only must you propagate the idea that team members are valuable contributors to the success of an organization, you must convince them as well.

Empowerment can be more difficult to establish when the team already exists and the overall organization does not support the concept. Then you must find a way to enable a degree of power for team members and undo the psychological damage of established dysfunctional organizational behavior.

Empowerment can work for everyone on a team. However, if people are not used to the concept, you may need to bring them to the point where they will accept this new level of authority. You might find that people resist because they have either lost the belief in their ability to be effective or never developed it in the first place. In that case, you have a tough row to hoe.

Re-establishing Self-Confidence

When people lack the assurance to take on power, there is something wrong. Watch some children—even at play, they are daring and willing to create worlds and imagine themselves with tremendous abilities and futures. It is only as adults that many people find themselves limited, beaten down by life. These are people lacking self-confidence because circumstances have conditioned them to believe that nothing is possible.

If you have team members with this degree of reluctance, you will need to help them develop self-assurance, at least concerning what your team does. This will likely be a tedious process of giving them small amounts of responsibility, helping them through coaching and mentoring to succeed, and then expanding the scope of what you expect them to do. There is no quick way through this. At the same time, chances are that there is no quick way for your team to reach its goals, so you have no reason to rush.

Making Space for Others

Even if team members have self-assurance, you as a leader also need poise and confidence. It may not come naturally, and you'll need to create your own process to increase your acceptance of the strategy. You'll need to convince both yourself and others that you mean it when you use the word *empowerment*.

Persuading yourself is like persuading team members of their own worthiness. You hand off some power, see positive results, and then try more. When it comes to winning over others, you must show through daily action that you mean it when you talk about empowering people on the team.

Delegation

Giving people power means offering both the authority and the responsibility. The authority part is empowerment. Responsibility you provide through delegation. This is more difficult in many ways because it is in delegation that you actually release your grip on what needs to be done. With empowerment, you face the theory of change; delegation commits you.

Conditions for Delegation

Although both empowerment and delegation are fundamental to power-sharing, the two have an important difference. Empowerment, as an embodiment of authority, is more general in nature. When people are empowered, they are entrusted with the ability to do something. However, that isn't the same as having something to do.

That's where delegation comes in. When a leader delegates, the other team members shoulder part of the leader's responsibility as a way of helping achieve the team's goals. Because delegation is more specific, it requires a more specific set of steps:

- Matching the right people with the right tasks
- Creating oversight and metrics
- Marshalling adequate resources

By taking these steps for each team member, you set the foundation for sharing power in such a way that you more efficiently approach goals.

Match People and Tasks

This step relates to building a team. You need the right person for the right role. That said, right is a relative term. You might choose to have people do what they are already good at, or you could ask them to take on something new, broadening their experiences and developing the ability to have various team members cover the same responsibility. Consider what other responsibilities team members have before recruiting them for additional ones. Also, keep in mind how specific team members work together and who would come in contact with whom.

Create Oversight

If one of the factors driving people to hoard power is the concern that important things won't get done, oversight is the answer. You don't need to micromanage people. What you must do is set up a way of tracking what should happen and when it should happen. A master schedule is a must. There are only so many details the average human mind can juggle without help, and the total is generally in the single digits.

Don't plan out every small step of the way. Focus on milestones where you can actually see the results of progress. If you try for too much oversight, you'll end up with a distorted myopic view and make other team members feel as though they have neither authority nor responsibility.

The milestones should represent natural metrics that let you monitor progress. Again, don't get too fancy. Think of high-level indications of whether all is right with the world. For example, if you're fundraising, then you might watch the number of contacts the team makes with potential donors.

Come up with a formal way of tracking all the moving parts of whatever your team is trying to achieve. Paper is an underrated method, though there are developed systems that can save time. Project management software is another choice and has some significant advantages, including graphic displays of complicated interrelationships of tasks.

You may be tempted to focus exclusively on the end results your team wants, but that would be a mistake. With fundraising, it's important to know where your team stands in terms of the money it wants to raise. You don't control the generosity of the donors or even whether they are in to take a call. Where you do have control is in the number and quality of your collective efforts to find donors.

Marshall Resources

When you do everything for yourself, you can pull in the resources under your control as you need them. But when you delegate, everything you'd normally have on tap must be shared with your team members. As carefully as you monitor progress on the various delegated tasks, you must be even more diligent in ensuring all team members have what they need to accomplish their tasks.

Taking Stock

Many companies are fond of discussing giving power and authority to employees, usually as part of some bland and indecipherable mission statement. The only problem is that often the loftier the talk, the less power sharing actually happens. Yet the people in charge at these places will generally swear up one side of the street and down the other that they really are interested in sharing power. Unfortunately, what people think they do often conflicts with what they actually do. Before you make enlightened plans, it's best to look at your own actions.

Team Structure

Because an organization is as much about structure as the particular set of people in it, look at how your team is organized. First study the overall hierarchy. Do you have an abundance of people reporting directly to you? If so, you're effectively trying to keep too much under your direct control. Some management studies suggest that a workable number in many organizations is between three and eight.

Ask yourself some questions. How often do you include other team members when trying to develop solutions to problems? Do people have a significant say in how they perform their duties? The less say they have, the less empowerment and delegation you have in your team. A giveaway is if you find yourself constantly thinking, "I should have done this myself."

Team Member Clues

Just as the organization itself can provide clues to how the team operates, so does the behavior of the team members. Do they behave as though they were responsible for the success of the organization and their duties? Are they trying to be helpful to others on the team?

Examine your results for patterns. If people are willingly involved and energetic, and if they get to use their creativity and talents to solve problems for the team, then you're passing power along. On the other hand, if you don't empower team members and delegate to them, the patterns will be different.

The only way you can be successful as a leader is to engage the potential of everyone on your team. You must be ready, willing, and able to recognize the value that each employee brings to the table. Everyone will have different strengths and weaknesses, but each can play a crucial role.

CHAPTER 12

Retention and Recognition

Perhaps you have pulled together a team whose efficiency and effectiveness should become the stuff of graduate school case studies. Congratulations! Now you must keep your team happy and functioning or you risk failure. There is a difference between team members strolling out the door with regrets and fondness and team members sprinting out the second an opening appears. The latter case means significant loss to the team and organization. A leader needs to understand how to retain team members and to recognize their contributions and accomplishments.

Impact of Loss

If you've ever been on a team—whether it was a group in the military, a sports team, a theater group, or a dedicated volunteer group at a church or temple—you know that there is a cohesiveness inherent in teamwork. There is also a sense of loss when someone leaves. The loss breaks an emotional bond, but beyond that you must consider the significant impact the departure has on your team.

What Leaves the Team

If you think of a team as something organic that works to achieve goals, then every loss of a person means a loss of a part that knew something and did something. When people leave a team, they take with them part of the team's ability to do. It is possible to eventually overcome the loss, but it takes time. People aren't objects that are swapped in and out like mechanical parts. When you change one person, you potentially alter the dynamics for the whole team. That can affect everything that every team member is doing.

ALERT!

Even if you found the perfect replacement for someone, it takes time for new team members to become effective in new surroundings. It can take anywhere from a good six months to a year or even longer for someone to become fully acclimated and functioning, according to management experts.

In addition to the human aspect, it takes time, energy, and—in most cases—money to replace people. Because the newcomers don't get up to speed for a significant period of time, that means lost efficiency and knowledge that can set you back on your pursuit of goals. Think about what the cost would be to train someone from the outside to know how to work with the team.

Secret Loss

It's not easy to calculate how the loss of a team member will affect your team, and many times the real expenses might be invisible. When someone from your team goes, you may not even be able to identify what goes with the person. It is a bitterly funny paradox of organizations that even when you think you know what individuals do, you often never get past the surface.

To know every detail of what someone does, you essentially have to micromanage the person, which is enough to drive team members away. Frequently it is the undefined contribution that makes team members so valuable. In effect, it is this long list of contributions to the organization—undefined, unknown, and probably unknowable—that makes retention so important.

Turnover

The rate at which people leave an organization and must be replaced is known as turnover. That amount can get surprisingly high. For example, there are companies with turnover rates that run 20 to 30 percent and higher. On the high end, that means every year, you're replacing close to a full third of the people in the organization. If you've ever had to recruit people, you know that's a painful prospect.

People Have Choices

There's a saying in smart business: No one owes you an order. It's true, and the concept is actually broader. No one owes any organization loyalty, hard work, or constancy. To expect that people must remain loyal to their employer is as outdated as the concept that a company will take care of the fiscal needs of its employees for life.

For corporations, when the economy is booming, it becomes increasingly difficult to retain people, who always assume that there is something bigger and better waiting for them elsewhere. The tough thing for the corporation is that this is almost always true when the industry is doing well.

When the economy isn't doing so well, companies can't afford the inefficiencies that get masked in better times. Knowledge and experience going out the door can cripple an enterprise. And the problems aren't limited to the for-profit world. When all is right with the economic world, people have lots of options for their spare time. Crank back household income, and you might find volunteers thinking more carefully about how they handle their time.

FACT

Not long ago, companies thought outsourcing was the solution to all their problems. Moving work overseas would drop costs and reduce the need to deal with their own employees. But now those outsourcers are actually outsourcing their work—back to the United States. Dealing with employees didn't go away—it just got more difficult.

Turnover Happens

No matter what, you will always experience turnover, and often it's good. You want people to learn and then to move on to greater opportunities and responsibilities. Such growth is actually the sign of a healthy organization. Sometimes team members want more growth and responsibility than you can offer. That is healthy turnover.

However, it is unhealthy when an organization effectively pushes people out. It's a pity, but this is by far the more common type of turnover. Sometimes the *effectively* turns into *actually,* as organizations fire employees and kick volunteers off committees. In either case, when recruiting replacements seems to become a full-time activity, then you can be sure your organization is driving people out unnecessarily. To reduce the costs of losing people, you must begin to think more strategically.

Unhealthy Loss

There is something inherently wrong about an organization repelling the very people who can help it. But in an objective assessment, we live in what is often a peculiar world. There is no other way to describe entire industries that consider a 15 percent annual turnover rate to be normal. It's not necessary; it is possible to get quality people to stay for extensive periods of time. But before we look at what it takes to keep people, we have to look at what drives them away:

- Poor communication
- Unclear policies
- Compensation problems

- Low team-member involvement
- Low satisfaction

When you know what goes wrong, then you can get an idea of what you need to do to improve it. If you don't take that step of understanding the problem, you make the same mistake as many other organizations: feel-good programs that offer no substantive help.

Poor Communication

People get frustrated when they don't know what is happening or when they can't find out what they are expected to do. It doesn't matter how well you try to use vision and motivation; if you don't communicate, it does nothing.

In the most exciting activities, there are stretches of tedium; think of the old saying that war is long stretches of boredom interrupted by brief periods of terror. You cannot make any position constantly exciting. However, you can help team members connect what they do with the team's goals and their own senses of meaning.

You also aren't the only potential broken communication link. Often people have no concept of the organization's vision or direction because no one bothers to tell them. Communication can break down anywhere in a hierarchy, and, unfortunately, you will bear the responsibility of making it work.

Unclear Policies

This is even worse than poor communication. It means that there is no clear understanding of where the organization or team should be going. At its worst, there will be contradictory policies or procedures, so that no matter where you look, things will be muddled. Such confusion comes from a lack of invested thought and planning. It's understandable why people wouldn't want to take part in something ill conceived. Chaos will only make their efforts painful, ineffective, and frustrating.

Compensation and Respect

Although not directly an issue for volunteers, compensation is a difficult area for companies. There is the obvious issue of paying two people with the same job responsibilities two different salaries. Should the lesser-paid one find out, at best you'll have some explaining to do regarding preferential treatment.

You simply cannot win arguments about compensation if the employee correctly views true performance peers as getting more. Don't bother saying anything about others asking for more, as the employee in question will rightly think you were trying to take advantage of a less aggressive nature.

However, just as likely is the chance that the employee will start looking for another position and leave as quickly as is convenient. The issue isn't just raw dollars but the perception that the organization doesn't value people evenly. That immediately brings preferential treatment to mind, and people, finding themselves on the wrong end of the preference, are unlikely to stay. Even if they do, you've shattered an important link of trust, and it's unlikely that you will reforge it. The employees will consider it demeaning to have to ask for more money, and they will view the organization as indifferent to their real value.

Compensation is just one form of respect the organization can provide, and that means even nonprofits and volunteer groups can have analogous problems. Volunteer groups have been torn apart when the leadership developed a systemic dismissive attitude toward members. People who volunteer time—and even donate money—don't want to be treated as minions. If you do so, they will leave.

Low Team Member Involvement

Tying in to the need for respect is team member involvement. People feel respected within a group when leaders ask their opinions and involve them in the decision-making process. When people feel left out of the process, they also feel neglected. You don't get involved in an organization to punch a clock. You want what you do to be interesting and challenging, and you want to be able to use your talents and intelligence. All the high-sounding mottos on all the motivational posters in the world won't disguise how the organization actually operates. Action is the truest and most persuasive form of language.

Low Satisfaction

People want to be respected, certainly, but they also want more: They want satisfaction in what they do. Few people want to think that what they do doesn't matter to anyone and doesn't contribute to anything. Satisfaction is a need; people want to feel useful, motivated, and even inspired. Smart manufacturers have learned this, taking what might have been mind-numbing factory work and giving employees enough authority and responsibility to help make a difference.

Looking for Trouble

You now have some sense of the problems that can increase turnover and hurt the organization, which puts you in an interesting situation. A classic problem in trying to solve a dilemma is to confuse symptom with cause. Often, people work to eliminate the symptom and forget that there is something instigating the trouble. Right now you're in exactly the opposite situation. You have some idea of the causes but haven't been looking at the symptoms. Now it's time to change that.

Using Diagnostics

No matter what type of situation you are trying to appraise—whether medical, electrical, or mechanical—you take the same basic approach. Proper diagnostics requires an understanding of what can go wrong and a keen eye for the signs of a problem. You work through the signs to trace back to the causes. Keep in mind that there may be more than one cause and more than one symptom, so when you find one problem don't assume there are no others.

You also need metrics: numbers you can use to measure how well a certain activity is going. For each diagnostic concern, you should find something that gives you a quantifiable grasp of how your team is doing. If you can't measure something, then you are left with hunches, suppositions, and guesswork. That is fine if you guess right, but most people tend not to.

You don't need to entirely ignore your hunches, though. You must measure what is happening to get a realistic sense of changing conditions. But don't take things to such an extreme that you miss another early warning sign. Often, your subconscious will piece together observations you don't even realize you're making and reach an important conclusion.

Planning Ahead

Diagnostics can be used two ways. You can start them when things obviously aren't working right, but then you're trailing the problem and the impact it has. The other choice is to work actively and monitor for troubles before they surface. Staying vigilant may seem like more work up front, and it is—a bit. But the cost in time, money, and aggravation compared with trying to clean up a mess after it has spilled everywhere is like taking your car to have the oil changed versus dealing with a seized engine.

Common Problem Indicators

The following is not an encyclopedic list of danger signs, but it should give you some idea of where to look:

- Sudden problems with "customers"
- Recruitment or training costs
- Low productivity or morale
- Sudden elevations in accident or illness rates
- Unexpectedly increasing expenses

Notice that in each case there is a specific result that would suggest a problem in team member attitude. Take all the definitions loosely. For example, customers could be people who buy products or services, other parts of the organization that depend on what your team does, or people from outside your organization who interact with your group. Recruitment or training costs could be all so-called soft costs, like team member time spent on getting new people up and running.

Any one of these can be the result of some systemic problem, such as a product with a design flaw, inadequate safety training or gear, or a flu epidemic. Nevertheless, each is also closely tied to team member attitudes. They can show displeasure as expressed through such things as doing little, doing tasks badly, or leaving. And if they aren't the result of existing negative attitudes, you can bet that they will quickly breed some. The bigger the difficulties you have in these areas, the bigger a warning you have that something is not right with your team members.

Understanding Dissatisfaction

If you do see signs of employee dissatisfaction, you need to better understand the problem to know how best to take action. There are several ways to do this. One is to study your team members' behavior. It might be that the actions they take will indicate something about the problems. For example, you might ask yourself some of the following questions:

- Are people highly motivated?
- Are team members eager to attack a new problem?
- Do people help each other solve problems, even if they are not directly involved?
- Do people feel comfortable asking questions?
- Are people willing to take chances and possibly make mistakes?

Such questions help you understand the impact of the organization's environment. It is this environment that has the greatest impact on retention.

Another approach is to ask the team members directly. It may take time to get them to open up and admit what they're thinking and feeling, but it can be the most effective way to learn. Finally, if people leave, try an exit interview. This can be a useful way of pinpointing possible problems.

Structuring Retention

Keeping people associated with your organization is never an accident unless you are the sole large employer in an isolated geographic territory. Barring the only-game-in-town syndrome, if you are successful at keeping people, you are doing something right. By the same token, if you want to improve retention, there are measures you can take to do so.

Satisfaction, Not Happiness

When you ask many people what they want from life, they answer happiness—but that's fuzzy bunk. No one can be happy all the time, and happiness is not some vague but pleasant cloud. When you are happy, it tends to be for a reason. Perhaps you recently achieved a goal or overcame a personal barrier. It could be that you're approaching the world with a positive attitude or you see—at least for a moment—that things can be better than you often perceive them to be. People say they want happiness the way businesses say they want profits, and yet both are results, not causes. To increase retention, you need to find out what causes happiness in your team members and then work toward making them happy.

ALERT!

A person's entire life—the happiness/unhappiness balance—will not be made by what happens in an organization. Sure, if you're miserable at work, that can color a lot. But if the rest of your life is unhappy, having a rousing good time in the office won't improve things.

It's important to go back to the basics of feeling motivated and connected with what you are doing. Hopefully you've had that feeling in your life. If so, you know that the result isn't traipsing about in delirium. Instead, there is a satisfaction in what you are doing because you are doing it in a way that is connected to what you find important. That's what your team members want, and that's what any program designed for retention needs to deliver.

Stupid Retention

Some organizations come up with some interesting ideas for how to improve retention:

- Recipe exchange
- Weekly positive outlook activities
- Come-in-costume days
- Giving employees toys when things are tense
- Organization sports leagues

These programs bear some resemblance to the stupid pet tricks that you might see on late-night television. Some organizations treat a collection of activities as the program itself, like a series of palliatives that people in charge smugly implement as a way of keeping team members complacent. However, such a laundry list won't really work because people simply aren't that dumb. The most common reaction is to mock the effort.

A good type of activity is a celebration, where team members come together in a formal acknowledgement of what they actually accomplish. That could be project milestones, an innovation, a great new idea—anything that's related to the goals and principles of the organization. Whether you do this with a pizza party at lunch, a dinner out, or just a brief gathering and chance to feel good about success depends on your organization's culture and how substantial the achievement was. This is a source of some of the best fun you can have because it's a result of something real happening and not an artificial happy dance.

Smart Retention

On the other hand, some activities generate a sense of fun and bring people together. What makes the difference is atmosphere and intent. When things are generally working well in your team, even if they have been a bit off base, an activity that reminds team members of working together, of creativity, and of playfulness in the service of a goal can be powerful. People don't generally mock the proceedings because they have a positive attitude toward the organization, or at least the group.

A retention program cannot be separate from the operation of your team and organization. If that happens, you are undertaking it in a cynical manner, and it will be obvious to everyone. At the same time, if you focus on creating a meaningful work environment, where you and other leaders share power and everyone has responsibility, then special activities and programs serve to reinforce what you already do.

Be Something

One of the best retention policies is to be expansive. People aren't going to feel enormously attached to someone else's self-interest. But that is what too many organizations actually represent, because people in charge—those who should be leaders—aren't interested in anything greater than what they personally want, whether it's career, money, or power.

Motorcycle maker Harley-Davidson defines its business culture with five values: tell the truth, be fair, keep your promises, respect the individual, and encourage intellectual curiosity. The company works to embody the values, and it is known to have a loyal work force.

If you get the sense that your organization is at all like this, do something different: Operate from the values your organization espouses. For example, ask team members what they would like to do. If you are going to share power, try this basic exercise. Too often, would-be leaders assume they know what's best for people on their team. What a numbingly arrogant attitude! No wonder people so often up and leave; they get tired of being insulted.

A Good Environment

Make sure everyone on the team receives equitable treatment. People generally don't mind limitations and demands if they fall on all equally. You start down the path to trouble when some individuals suspect there is bias toward others.

You know it is illegal to discriminate against classes of people, but beware of the small issues that might make someone feel discriminated against. For example, if you are in a company and let one employee leave early without any challenge, but you then ask a second person a series of questions before granting the same permission, you've created an appearance of discrimination. Say you are in a volunteer group with a friend, and you give that person details of what is going on that you don't share with others on the team. You've just demonstrated that there is an in-crowd.

Be direct and honest with people on the team. If there is a problem, say so, and get their help to resolve it. If someone is doing particularly well, don't be shy in telling the person. Also, keep your word. Don't change the ground rules on people, whether in terms of responsibilities, pay, or opportunities. If you don't know what to expect, particularly when there is no good reason for the suspense, then you're in a stressful situation.

Fostering Recognition

Retention is an enormous problem for most organizations—and recognition is an important aspect of retention. Study upon management study has shown that people have many needs and expectations in organizational settings. They provide something to the group and need something in return. Ah, but the question is, "What do they need?"

Team Member Needs

Money is rarely the sole—or even the most important—consideration for most people. Yes, there seem to be natural-born mercenaries in the world, but they are relatively few and far between. Studies have generally shown that the three biggest concerns for most of us, in order, are these:

1. Being recognized for the work we do
2. Being part of the organization's larger picture
3. Getting help with personal problems

In other words, people have pride and want to be valued, respected, and recognized for what they contribute to an organization, not treated as replaceable cogs. At first glance, this seems easy enough to accomplish. But it's not, and the strategy you use to create recognition is crucial.

Crazy Making

A lack of recognition is not just a situation of being snubbed. In organizations, it actually creates a form of temporary insanity. There is a concept in psychology called *cognitive dissonance,* defined as a clash between what a person knows or perceives and new information that contradicts it.

Think about it, and you might recognize the essential struggle between thesis and antithesis first mentioned in Chapter 10. In resolving conflict, the healthy approach is to work for a synthesis. Too often, however, leaders of an organization effectively ask people to act as though their perceptions of reality didn't exist. There are situations when a supervisor takes credit for the work of a direct report, who was then expected to act as though that were the case. Or leaders hold people responsible for their mistakes, yet act as though they weren't also responsible for their successes.

FACT

Scott Adams catches the essence of the insanity of corporate organizational behavior in his comic, *Dilbert*. Adams has directly acknowledged the role that cognitive dissonance plays in the strip, saying the humor is in the absurd conflicts that arise when a company essentially requires people to ignore reality.

In healthy versions of perceptual conflict, a person comes to a more sophisticated and mature grasp of the world. In unhealthy episodes, those caught in the Kafkaesque conditions literally get a little crazy. They become, in varying degrees, distraught, anxious, and even obsessed. There is nothing inherently wrong with these people. Poor leadership causes the problem when those in charge insist team members resolve what cannot be resolved and pretend that reality is something other than they perceive.

Private Versus Public

What can really push the insanity is when there is an additional dichotomy in how the organization deals with recognition. Some groups make a big fuss at certain times with a public show of acknowledgement, yet they don't extend that attitude to regular actions. In that sense, private recognition is far more important than public because it creates the touchstone moments that give people a sense of how leadership thinks and what the group's standards actually are.

The issues most important to employees are the items easiest for a company to provide. But they must be supplied in a sincere, consistent fashion. You cannot make employee recognition a program that happens at a certain time each year with bells and whistles and fancy awards. The creation of a positive employee-recognition strategy demands an ongoing commitment to employees as people and as partners in the company. It must be real, and it must be part of the day-to-day culture of the organization. The annual awards ceremony will be meaningful and have impact only if it is the highlight of an organization that demonstrates recognition and respect for all employees all the time.

If recognition, and the respect it conveys, happens almost as a begrudged requirement, then it will be seen for what it is—a cheap attempt at emotional bribery. If it is part of a company's essential makeup, it will be something that people value.

Types of Recognition

Like formal retention activities, a recognition program can be a useful addition to a culture that regularly acknowledges the contributions of team members. Any such program can be whatever you want and should reflect your personal style and that of the organization. First decide on what you want to recognize. Suggestions include the following:

- Individual achievement in a team member's role
- Individual achievement in the organization but outside someone's role
- Individual achievement outside the organization
- Team achievement inside the organization
- Team achievement outside the organization

With such a mix, you encourage people to do well in what they are supposed to do, in thinking in larger terms, in excelling throughout their lives, and in working with others. You might use a public announcement, a plaque, even a signed thank you note. The particular mechanism isn't important as long as you are consistent. The more you can do this in every-day and simple ways, the more easily you can apply it as warranted.

You should also make it possible for team members to suggest others for recognition. If your organization is like most, there are unsung heroes who go out of their way to help others, both in the group's activities and in their own lives. The higher you are in the organization, the less likely it is that you hear any of these stories.

Benefit of Recognition

Not only do team members get an emotional lift from recognition, the organization benefits in a number of ways as well. It helps increase retention—that, after all, is the point of this chapter. But there are additional benefits. You encourage similar behavior on the part of everyone else, and you create an atmosphere that attracts whatever types of customers your group serves. Your organization becomes the kind of place where everyone wants to be.

CHAPTER 13

Handling Change

For years we've appreciated the saying, "Change happens." What makes it appealing is not whimsy but its universal applicability. In the real world, a better authority is Ecclesiastes, from the Old Testament: All is vanity because everything comes to an end. You can nod in theory, but for a leader, this concept has significance. No matter how you organize a team, no matter what processes are in place, no matter how many problems you solve, all of it will end. It's a reality we all face, and leaders must know how to work through change if they want to succeed.

Nature of Change

Why me? You've wondered it, and so has everyone else. As the saying goes, the only thing that is constant is change. No matter what you do, it is there, waiting. The first step in dealing with it is to get a better grasp of the concept.

No Straight Lines

There is no such thing as a straight line. To ensure steady movement—physically, psychologically, or organizationally—you'd need to have a constant force that could always point accurately in the right direction with no sort of obstruction or resistance to change your path in even the smallest way.

That, of course, never happens. When a pilot flies a jet from Los Angeles to Chicago, there are hours of slight changes involved. Try to make yourself think of the word *elephant* for an hour; you will have forgotten it long before you reach the end of this chapter. Some will say, "But I achieve what I set out to do all the time." Nonsense. If you are honest and compare the results with your intent, either you'll find differences from your specific initial plan, or you'll find that you started with a general picture that left plenty of room for the compromises in execution called experience.

Change Follows You

Change isn't something that happens here and there. No matter where you go, there it is—and no wonder. Life is a complex interaction of millions of factors, all connected to each other. If any one thing changes, so do all the interactions, sometimes in imperceptible ways.

FACT

According to some scientists, the beat of a butterfly's wings can cause significant changes in weather. The wings connect with air that strikes other objects that create eddies that eventually compound and cause a storm.

You live in a world where everything is changing. It's not that change stalks you. Instead, since change is everywhere, it is already where you are heading.

Change Isn't Cataclysmic

Just as things seem to be going well, something happens to overturn the cart. That view isn't realistic. Usually people are so tied up with their concerns and interests that they don't notice change as it happens. The concept that things stay in place is an illusion. You're either moving forward or falling behind every minute, and so is everything else. Eventually positions shift so much that you become aware of them.

Change Is Quick

At one time, change was slow. Movements like industrialization took decades to really take hold, and societies were relatively static. It could take centuries for the basis of an economy or political system to shift. Think of the time it took to move out of feudalism and into a broader concept of private property. Even as recently as the early twentieth century, significant social change still took years, even decades, to occur and people had some time to adjust.

FACT

Talk to experts and they'll tell you that back in the sixteenth century, it took a good fifty to seventy-five years for a change in fashion to move from political capitals down through a chain of connections and into a country's backwaters.

The Internet turned media upside down in less than fifteen years. Change literally bombards us in fashion, in the economy, through the media, even in climate. We no longer have time to adjust to change.

Change in an Organization

To recap, change will happen, and at a dizzying rate. But what does that have to do with being a leader? There are millions of influences on organizations—global economies, human ingenuity, tastes of the public, fickle attention of the media, cultural trends, natural disasters, fads, competition, employees or volunteers, management structure, and regulation, just to name a few. Every factor breaks out into another rainbow of shifting elements, and as they move, so does the nature of your organization and what it tries to accomplish. If you are going to lead, you must grasp the nature of change in your team and organization and how to handle it.

Source of Change

First examine what exactly is changing. There might be a shift in team members, modifications of someone's responsibilities, a different location, an alteration in the nature of the organization's goals, a difference in a market, or a shift in the description of your customers.

Change can be either accidental or intentional. Other people in the organization may make decisions that force change throughout, including within your team. Such changes can be even more disruptive than anything from the outside.

There are times that the metrics you've set in place will indicate that change is in the air. Sometimes you learn of it through team members who are closer to the fluctuations than you are. Someone who constantly interacts with customers, vendors, or business partners is more likely to see the early warning signs of change than are you. Then there will be occasions that a source of change is so obvious that it's impossible to miss, like a company you are working for being acquired by another.

Good Change, Bad Change

Change isn't necessarily good or bad; it just is. We impose value judgments on change after the fact, and such judgments are relative. If a change opens possibilities and gives new ways of approaching goals, then that change is good—for the person who sees the opportunities. If change prevents someone's efforts to pursue goals, then it will seem bad. In fact, one person can see a change as positive, while a neighbor swears that it's the scourge of the earth.

Does this sound familiar? It's very similar to the topic of conflict discussed in Chapter 10. The desirability of the change all depends on where you are and what you are trying to do. Before considering how to deal with change, you must identify how it is going to affect your team and the organization. It may be that the change will open possibilities and allow new levels of efficiency. Or—and we might as well be frank about this—it could be that some genius at the top of the organization has decreed an "improvement" that is supposed to catapult the organization to new heights but in reality is more likely to drive people to find the nearest metaphorical cliff and jump.

Change Process

Since change always happens, there will be many times as a leader that you'll have to address the issue. It's best to do so in as systematic a way as possible although the particulars will always be different. Here are the basic four steps:

1. Become aware of change.
2. Plan a response.
3. Implement a response.
4. Examine the results and adjust.

Be warned that while change is almost always challenging, getting an organization to adapt as necessary is one of the most difficult tasks. In fact, major management consultancies will devote extensive study, time, and billing to what they call change management.

FACT

Change management is a large part of consultancy practice because change is so pervasive. Any time you want to improve an organization, you must alter the way it works. That means you have to institute change and find a way to keep things functioning during the process.

The process of change is not difficult to understand intellectually. Much of change, however, occurs in the realm of emotion. Most people hate change—but we'll get to that shortly.

Become Aware

You can't solve a problem if you don't know it's there, and you can't take advantage of an opportunity when you sleep through it. The first step in handling change is being aware of it. Sometimes that is easy because circumstances thrust it into your face. Other times it takes work to recognize something is afoot.

Rude Awakening

The worst way to learn about change is at the last moment. Unfortunately, that is often how people come across change. Sometimes there is no other choice. The forces that create change present themselves suddenly, and you have to deal with them.

All too often, the need to adjust to circumstances with little notice is a product of our reaction to the idea of change. We tell ourselves that things actually do go in a straight line; otherwise, we're left with the scary realization that life is more uncertain than we'd care to think.

So we bury out heads and insist that everything is supposed to progress smoothly. Often, part of that insistence is the attempt to believe that change really isn't happening. We basically convince ourselves that the signs of change aren't there, and so we don't take action early.

Reading Data

If you have built a series of metrics and created some kind of monitoring process for your team, you will be a step better off. What you do is first create a baseline set of numbers that indicate "normal" activity. This isn't a measure of optimum conditions so much as usual ones. You might even take readings for a month, or even a quarter, and average the results to get a more representative set of numbers. When you calculate the average, also track how far the numbers vary, low to high.

Now you have data for typical conditions you might expect—both the average values (the mean) as well as how far they can shift away from those values (the range). On an ongoing basis, you can watch for trends, possibly using a moving average. When you see an overall shift in a number, you know that there is a change happening.

FACT

A moving average is an average over some period of time—maybe a week, a month, or a quarter—using a longer period of time for more volatile data. On any day, you take the average going back the given period of time. It helps you spot longer-term trends without being distracted by the momentary ups and downs.

Be aware that watching internal data has limitations. One is that it only tells you something is happening but doesn't give the reason—the what, not the why. You still must determine the underlying reason for the trend if you want to understand the actual change happening and formulate a plan to adapt to it. Another limitation is that data won't let you catch everything—only what you can directly measure. For example, if you're in charge of a customer service group, overall customer satisfaction numbers can't warn you that one of your best team members has decided to leave.

Third, what you learn is no better than the data you collect. You have to choose metrics that are actually meaningful, a more difficult prospect than you might think. Many people become drunk on data, collecting massive amounts that do nothing but drown them in detail. The trick is to choose only what gives a telling indication of a fundamental influence on your group. Finally, although data can help indicate trends, it often is next to useless in catching sudden unpredictable changes.

It is often smart to look for external data that might help pinpoint changes you should address. If you were involved in a community outreach program, you'd want to know if a shift in demographics meant your team would need some fluency in a particular language to be effective. As with internal data, take in only what is telling, and realize that you may need that data less frequently. In the outreach example, you'd only check a population breakout at most once a year. It takes time for neighborhoods to change and, just as importantly, more frequently updated information would be unlikely to exist. Many sources of external data may be refreshed only every few years.

Reading Signs

In organizations, the harbingers of change are often nothing measurable. They may be modifications in operations or spending patterns indicating that someone is emphasizing one aspect of the organization at the expense of another. A new directive might itself be a reaction to some form of change, requiring adaptation by your team.

FACT

Various occupations use these sorts of skills. You might turn to them for training or support. They would include business analysts, competitive intelligence specialists, equity and financial analysts, forensic accountants, and strategic planners. Classes or books on these subjects cover different aspects of reading an organization.

Although this topic alone could be the subject of a book—and getting a grounding in it will help you learn to read your own organization—the basics are largely common sense. You are looking for signs that suggest the real interests of the group and the people running it. If there is a change in spending, consider what different factors might trigger it. A reorganization will offer clues in terms of the hierarchy, who is now on top, and what particular skills or orientation they bring to their positions. A new strategy can be an acknowledgment of different stakeholders, emerging competition, or the failure of past approaches.

Reading People

Perhaps the best source of information is other people in the organization. As people's thinking and feelings change, so do perceptible indicators, such as attitudes, emotional signs, body language, and behavior. Sudden frostiness or warmth, inclusion in or exclusion from meetings, distraction, and unexplained closed-door activity are all clues.

As you would with data, take a benchmark of how people usually act. When you see changes, you can expect that something is causing them. The difficult part here is understanding the source. Someone might be having problems at home or working a large project that is consuming a lot of attention—or there may be change afoot.

Often people will not admit to changes, but you should still ask what is going on. There are few things as toxic as an atmosphere in which you perceive that secrets are being kept and you are not allowed to ask about them. When that happens, you operate completely based on fear. You're now in a psychological condition in which you cannot really lead because you're too busy running away from something. So turn around and deal with the conflicts around you. At worst, you'll find that things are as bleak as you fear, and then you can make plans and take action. At best, you may discover an innocent explanation and find you've been turning yourself inside out for no good reason.

Simply approach people who might know what is going on and ask their opinion and advice. People on the line, so to speak, often have a more accurate sense of reality because circumstances force them to face it. There is no insulation between them and the outside world; they are the insulation. By the time changes show up in metrics, they may have been happening for a while. The time lag can be enough for a change to achieve momentum. Think of this process as part of empowerment and delegation.

See the Need

You can see change coming from various directions, but that isn't enough. Not all change is imposed, and there are times you'll see the need for a change. The same indicators that let you understand what is different might also give you insight into something that needs to be different. Generally things grow or decline, and if you find that conditions seem stagnant, they probably suggest that your team is in a rut.

Plan

Noticing change (or noticing the need for change) is the first step in managing it. To make the plan work, you will need to involve your team and get the members to buy into what will happen.

Compare Change to Goals

The way change affects your group depends on how the team operates and the goals it works toward. As you plan how you will manage a change, you must first determine what impact, if any, that change will have on your team. Identify exactly what aspects you need to address and adjust. You may need to do nothing or you may need to overhaul many aspects of the team. The main point is not to react but to understand and take appropriate action.

Get Buy-In

The single biggest mistake is to pretend to team members that change doesn't exist. To do so is patently insulting, treating your team members as though they were children and you were the parent. You also lose the opportunity to get their help. Remember that these are the same people who often have a better practical sense of what is going on than you do. Ignore what they can teach and you might find yourself setting down a path that, for various reasons, cannot possibly lead you anywhere positive.

Not being honest with your team members creates an uncomfortable atmosphere that is not conducive to effective activity. Your team members are the very people who can scuttle any plan you conceive. It becomes like trying to coax a group of people to follow you when they've sat down on the pavement and locked arms in protect.

Change management experts strongly recommend getting buy-in from the people that the change will affect. Many organizations make the mistake of treating that as part of the implementation of change. By then the resistance is generally in place. Instead, bring team members into the planning process as early as possible.

People tend to give more enthusiastic support to ideas and changes that they helped to engineer. They are more understanding of change and aren't as resentful or obstructive as when they feel that someone is forcing change on them.

Review the Plan

Before you put a plan into place, wait some time and have a review. This is why it is so important for leaders to establish a trusting and open environment in which people can ask questions and get straight answers. People scrutinize change and often expose incomplete thinking, poor judgment, or the need to review other options before moving ahead. Better to find problems with your "baby" than learn in retrospect that it included ill-conceived initiatives. By reviewing the plan with all your team members, you also continue giving them a sense of ownership of the change.

Implement

You've got a plan in place, which is good, but it's hardly enough. It's time to make your plan work, and you'll need help. Ironically, the same word that describes the shift of things around you is the one that describes the process of dealing with it: change. As upsetting as changing conditions can be to people, so can the change you must put into place to accommodate them.

Meeting Resistance

The basic problem you face in implementing the plan is that no one likes change. It's a quirk of being human, this need to have things remain as they are. If people were as adaptable as they'd like to be, then quitting smoking, losing weight, starting a new career, and otherwise doing new things wouldn't be the major challenges they are. Yes, we know there are factors that make each of these difficult, but no factor is as large as the human unwillingness to change, when people think they can get away without it.

Facing Resistance

You have to assume there will be resistance. If you aren't prepared for opposition when it comes, success will be difficult—if not impossible. Don't rely on memos. Have direct meetings. The air of uncertainty and suspicion that would come about from hiding change—really the result of being unprepared to meet it—can still occur when change is no longer a theory but an incontrovertible fact.

ALERT!

Fear will be evident in your team members. But don't forget that you will have your own bouts of fear and doubt. Don't deny the feelings. Unwatched, they will undermine your goals. Accept them and focus on the necessary steps in the plan.

When change occurs, people often erect all kinds of barriers, often without realizing that they are doing so. They will ride emotional waves—some positive, some negative. Your plan for change may include some unpleasant actions. People will push back, not out of antagonism but out of fear and unhappiness. Don't react. Just keep moving forward, and give people the room for the emotional adjustments they will need to make.

Addressing Team Members

Hopefully, you've involved the team members in the change-planning process, but sometimes you won't be able to do that as well as you'd like.

Appropriate actions might require painful actions, including laying people off. You may not be able to legally provide information in advance. Then again, even those involved in the planning may find that discussing change is easier and more pleasant than actually undertaking it.

Your strategy for working with team members and getting buy-in doesn't stop after planning or the beginning of implementation. As you (hopefully) asked for help with planning, continue to seek it. Provide team members with as much information as possible during the process. Be open, honest, and upfront as early as you can when you recognize the need for change.

Follow-Up

Once your team is through the implementation process, there is still work to do. Things don't suddenly end. For success, follow-through is everything, like swinging a golf club or baseball bat. And there are a number of things you must continue to do to ensure that the changes take and thrive.

Keep Goals on Track

During periods of significant change, people can become so engrossed with the details that they forget the bigger picture. As a leader, you need to keep your team's overall goals in mind. If not for that, then the entire change process would be meaningless. The changes must become part of the processes and structures that support the organization's principles.

Continue Buy-In

Even if you have worked to get team members involved as part of the solution through planning and implementation, you need to do it again. Old habits die hard, and even after you think things are changed permanently, they can move back to where they were. Procedures mean nothing if people don't use them.

You must work with your team members to continue their understanding and acceptance of the necessary changes. This isn't something you need to do forever, but it can take a long time. Don't shortcut the process.

When leaders fail to continue working on buy-in, people quickly go back to their old habits and ways of working, undermining all the previous efforts.

Consider Training

A major problem with change is that you can't count on anything to remain the same. Activities and procedures that once supported the team's goals may no longer work correctly, and everyone on the team will need to get used to working differently.

Consider whether you need to institute a training program for everyone to reinforce new ways of operating. Although it can be costly, it is far cheaper than offering inadequate training and seeing all that hard work at change going right down the tubes.

Take Stock

Once things have settled down, you'll have a chance to take stock of what has happened. Do so. The entire reason for heading down this road was to adapt your team to external or internal changes so it could pursue its goals more efficiently. Watch metrics, talk to team members, and get a sense of how well the team is performing. If you find that performance is off, don't be so wedded to your existing plan that you value it over what the team is supposed to be doing. If things are going off track, reinitiate the change evaluation process. Better to spend time making adjustments than to end up doing worse than you did before.

CHAPTER 14

Using Meetings

Making jokes about meetings is like decrying traffic jams: Who could disagree? Everyone has spent too many hours in meetings for no perceptibly useful reason. But to write off meetings as nothing but collective time wasted would be unfair. There are times when you need meetings of various sorts. When conducted properly, they are an important part of a communication strategy and an effective way to work with team members.

Meeting Madness

Meetings have become a way of life. There are staff meetings at work, PTA meetings, meetings for social organizations, and even family meetings. Think of the word meeting and you have a sense of what is supposed to happen: a gathering of people who want to exchange ideas and knowledge. There are some good reasons to have meetings, and there are even more bad reasons to avoid them. As a leader, you must separate the two and support the useful type while trying to eliminate the unhelpful type.

Why We Meet

Humans are social creatures, spending considerable time, money, and expense to spend time with others for no discernable practical reason. Oh, we all have rationales for congregation, whether the setting is a service at a church or temple, having drinks with friends, scouting a potential someone for a personal relationship, or sharing an interest in amateur theatre, sailing, books, or antique cars.

ALERT!

We often organize much of our lives to enable more meetings. There are special interest groups, associations, impromptu gatherings, parties, and many other occasions and excuses for gathering with people. Try to see your own inclination to attend and even arrange all manners of meetings.

However, there is generally little action in meetings. Although there may be some effective decision-making when a meeting has direction and effective structure, most of our meetings are really for emotional needs. It's okay to spend a period with friends, show off, and share some good fortune and fellowship—so long as you remember that's what you're doing.

Meetings Go Awry

Unfortunately, meetings have become one of the biggest wastes of time in our lives because we default to using them whether we need to or not.

How many meetings have you attended where people could have more easily addressed issues through a short note or memo? However, we have eons of social history and inclination that gives us a drive to be around each other. Compounding that are some enabling inclinations in modern organizations:

- Meetings satisfy a need people have to visibly justify what they do for their pay.
- When people decide in consort, they are safe from individual responsibility and blame.
- Activity is often so scattered that multiple people from around the organization must agree to a course of action.
- Meetings have become a modern jousting field for power and control.
- People have developed a habit of having meetings.

Between our natural inclination and these organizational factors, we tend to believe that any answer starts in an official meeting. Sometimes a meeting is a good venue to accomplish something, but often it isn't.

Meeting Pitfalls

Admittedly, not all meetings are bad. But many are, and generally there's a small set of reasons that makes them bad. People let meetings get away from them and take on their own lives with remarkable consistency. If you are going to use meetings effectively—and, as a leader, there will be times you must—then you have to be sensitive to the potential danger areas.

Too Many Meetings

People love to get together and even subconsciously will create reasons for doing so. Add those organizational incentives and habits, and you have people meeting all the time, whether they need to or not. Unless a meeting is the most efficient way to achieve what you need to do, your team is wasting time and energy. A further problem is that you unnecessarily annoy people, making them less receptive to making the meeting work and to further meetings in the future.

Too Little Preparation

How often have you walked into a meeting only to get a packet of information that you were expected to speed read and instantly understand? It's annoying and useless; people can't possibly comment intelligently or make smart decisions under such circumstances. Things get even less useful when you consider how few meetings have clear agendas or objectives, how poorly most are run, and how seldom people keep adequate notes. When people drone on and drift from one irrelevant topic to the next, they put everyone else to sleep.

Too Little Follow-Up

If the previous steps have left any trace of usefulness, here's how people manage to drain it out: letting things drop after the meeting. They don't follow up with any summary of the meeting. They don't have anyone follow up on assigned action items, and, whatever they do, they don't look back and evaluate on how the meeting might have gone better. These are all classic mistakes leaders make; the meeting itself won't accomplish anything.

Making Meetings Good

Unfortunately, these poor practices are more the rule than the exception. Because bad examples are rampant, many people who volunteer in organizations and work in even the largest corporations assume that such meetings are the way to take care of business. They aren't, and you certainly don't need to have meetings simply for the sake of having them. If you want meetings to work, you need to focus on getting the elements right before, during, and after.

Proper Preparation

The way to run a good meeting is for you to start long before it does. There are two aspects of preparation. One is to lay out, as clearly as possible, what you need to cover and what you want to achieve. That way you can keep things on target during the meeting because you'll know where you need to go. The other part is giving people everything they will reasonably need to prepare in advance.

Meet from Need, Not Habit

Don't have meetings because you're "supposed to." Like any other form of communication, a meeting should take place because it's necessary to pursue common goals. If you do not need to have a meeting, or if the meeting will not achieve something more easily and efficiently than another activity, simply don't have it.

FACT

Meetings are not always the best choice for a group. For example, if the intent is to get a status update from everyone, let each person write a brief memo and circulate it to everyone else. Then you can have a meeting on those items that people feel they need to discuss.

That bit of advice is pretty standard if you read anything about how to manage a meeting. However, like so many things, it's easier said than done. You're battling your own inclination to have meetings, and it may take some time to nudge yourself out of the almost physical urge for a get-together. Don't be afraid to try some innovation, like using high-tech methods to replace sitting in a room with others.

However, be aware that you're not the only one who may think in terms of meetings. Everyone else on your team thinks meetings are good to some degree, to say nothing of an organization that sees meetings as proof of productivity and any outside individuals and entities that may deal with your team. In the beginning, be judicious and cut as many meetings as possible. Be realistic and know you can need a meeting for many reasons, including, at times, having one because someone else insists. Just control it to the degree you can, and work to lower the number over time.

Meeting Intent

If you've ever walked into a meeting uncertain about what was going on, you understand why you must thoroughly address the question of intent and what you hope to accomplish. Announcing a meeting, even with a quick mention of the subject, is not enough. You must address the following:

- Who is calling the meeting
- Who is attending the meeting
- The subject of the meeting
- Meeting location, time, and duration
- Meeting objectives

Individuals need different types and amounts of information to prepare themselves for a public interaction. Even if some of this seems irrelevant to you, it's better to distribute it and not need it than to withhold it and leave some of the participants uncomfortable or even hostile. Some of the items—particularly the subject of the meeting and its objectives—will be vital to everyone. It's best to send this out first to be sure that you can set up the meeting in the first place. Once you know that you can, it's time to proceed to the additional information you need to send.

Provide an Agenda

Distribute a detailed agenda to the participants in advance. You should send it long enough ahead of time that people can raise questions and suggest agenda items before you enter the meeting room. This will let you incorporate the concerns of others in a coherent way while giving them a way of responding to and, yes, buying in to the entire process. But don't think of an agenda as a simple list of points. It's a road map you design to start at one point and end at a different point, accomplishing your objectives along the way. The agenda helps attendees better know how to prepare. Just as importantly, it forces you to more thoroughly consider what you want to do in the meeting. Use it as an exercise to understand how the meeting—and its objectives—relate to the team's goals.

Get the Backup Out

There are two reasons to distribute materials at a meeting. Someone could be presenting some sensitive information that you want to keep under control, or you could want to use the emotional wave of surprise in a group setting. If the information is relatively simple, then, by all means, have a blast at your event.

However, you might also want people to digest complex data, consider an in-depth study, or otherwise use their brains and talents to do something useful. In that case, the only sane thing to do is to send out reports, charts, and packets of material ahead of time. A meeting is a constrained and artificial environment. If you wait to hand out your materials at the beginning of the meeting itself, there is no conceivable way people can actually pay attention to them, as well as to everything that happens in the meeting, and appreciate the work that went into them. Plus, by setting up a difficult situation, you make people resentful, which means you can likely kiss goodbye the chance that they will do anything after the meeting.

FACT

A new trend in meetings of corporate boards of directors is to provide more extensive advance preparation than for regular meetings. Experts suggest that the board's chair send out full packets of all information to be reviewed far enough in advance that directors have time to review and understand it.

The solution is simple. Before the meeting, arrange to circulate all the necessary materials and data so everyone has time to review them. You want productive time in the meeting, not a show of people reading. Just as an agenda gives you a chance to think through what you want to achieve and how you want to achieve it, the backup documents serve the same purpose. If the agenda provides the road map, the documents describe the terrain and what you need to do to succeed.

You can also increase buy-in and participation by having other people attending the meeting prepare necessary items. Often the material must come from them anyway because they are responsible for the appropriate areas. So let them be completely and visibly involved.

Smart Execution

You've prepared for the meeting, and now it's time to make that preparation useful. Watch out for common problems: letting the discussion get off track, letting the meeting run too long, and not getting participation you need.

Have the Right Roles

Inviting the people who need to be at a meeting isn't enough. You need the right roles. If you remember some of the team roles mentioned in Chapter 9, you'll have a sense for who you need here. Someone has to lead the meeting. You might think that should be you, as the team leader, but not so fast! Someone else might know more about the topic or actually be in charge of the aspect of team activity. In that case, take a back seat and let someone else take the position. The person might need some help in learning how to run a meeting, but you can always provide some coaching, and this is a great way to empower and delegate.

You'll want a facilitator to make sure everyone adheres to whatever rules you establish for the meeting (for example, no interrupting another person). People in this role can also suggest tools, like brainstorming techniques, that might help achieve specific ends. The documenter is responsible for taking notes for later distribution, and the timekeeper keeps an eye on the clock for everyone.

Stay on Time

You cannot afford to have meetings that start raggedly and end unpredictably. A meeting should have a hard end time. If you legitimately need to go past that point, then you can call a follow-up meeting or try to address as much as possible through the normal working process. What you want to do is keep everyone as on point as possible. You might need to limit aspects of discussion so that no one person takes more than, say, ten minutes on a given topic.

Stay on Track

Keeping people focused is difficult but essential to successfully running a meeting. The biggest meeting problem is aimlessness. To cure that, inject a dose of direction. The agenda will help, but only if you stick to it. Staying focused has an additional edge because it helps you stay within the time constraints.

There may be times when off-track issues are important. Make sure you note them down and follow up later, whether directly with people, through a meeting, or whatever avenue that makes the most sense.

Encourage Participation

A group gets together in a meeting to speak and listen. If you don't need the active discussion of others, then you are probably better off sending a memo or e-mail. You may find, though, that even if you need the participation of others, they may stay quiet.

You can directly engage them.

Try delegating some of the meeting responsibilities. Let each person take charge of something. That could be collecting data, making arrangements, or even running a part of the meeting. By letting other people take ownership of part of the meeting, you increase team members' stake and interest in what happens.

Create an atmosphere of openness. Demand a respectful attitude from yourself, and others will take note. Try occasional brainstorming sessions in which everyone offers as many ideas as possible without anyone criticizing or analyzing them. If some people seem painfully shy, you might ask them questions to draw them out. Request the opinions of those with expertise on specific topics. Make it a meeting, not a glorified lecture. At the end of any one discussion, when the meeting itself is about to conclude, leave some time to ask if anyone has any questions, concerns, or observations. Seldom will people bring something up, but for the few times they do, you'll be glad that you made this a regular feature.

Time Out

Pacing is important in meetings. You can put people to sleep or leave them scratching their heads, trying to grasp the details of what happened. It's fine to make the time restrictions you've set for the meeting, but don't do that at the expense of comprehension. Also, don't keep a meeting running longer than it needs to. If you've gone through the agenda, don't add things on. Everyone has things they need to be doing, and if you show that you respect their time, they're more likely to be cooperative in the future.

There are also times that meetings go long. Very long. There are even all-day meetings that you might legitimately need. Don't expect people to sit hour after hour. Plan frequent breaks.

ALERT!

According to ergonomic and health experts, prolonged sitting can cause pain and physical damage. Take five minutes out from every hour so people can move around as well as head to the bathroom or grab a cup of coffee.

Take Note

Go to a meeting and you'll see a collection of people sitting around with pads of paper, occasionally scrawling something down. They are all making a show of doing something, but they aren't, really. Now you've got a situation in which the participants, who may need to take specific actions as a result of the meeting, may or may not take adequate heed. This is why you have the documenter—someone whose responsibility it is to record everything of importance and to make the notes available after the meeting.

The documenter should work with a copy of the agenda at hand, so notes can refer to sections of the meeting. For a particularly complex encounter, you might consider having two documenters, each one independently taking notes. At the end of the meeting, you'll have two sets of notes that you can compare for a better chance of actually capturing all the pertinent information.

There are two schools of thought with documenters. One is that it should be a person involved with the subject. Another is that you should use a third party who is uninvolved with the proceedings, allowing those who are involved to participate. The former makes the most sense. If someone isn't involved with a project or event, it will be difficult for the person to take coherent notes or even to grasp what is happening. There are too many people who managed to successfully walk and chew gum at the same time—or participate in a discussion and take their own notes—to say it is impossible.

Types of Meetings

After a while, all meetings may seem alike, but that isn't really the case. There are distinctly different types, and each can have its own requirements.

Idea Generation

You're not looking to make decisions here. What you want is the opposite—to suspend decisions and simply generate ideas. You might use brainstorming, concept mapping, or other techniques, which emphasizes the role of a facilitator. After generating ideas, you might find you'll need an additional meeting to sort through the material and decide on which ones merit implementation. An idea generation meeting will have significant need for follow-up.

Work Meeting

If you're sitting down to actually perform specific work, the approach is different from open discussion and debate of issues. Agenda and focus will be particularly important, because there are things that must come out of the meeting. Slack off and you could find the meeting dragging on and on because you may not be able to adjourn until everything is done.

Review

In a review meeting, a group goes over some previously completed work. You absolutely need to get material to people in advance for this type

THE EVERYTHING LEADERSHIP BOOK

of meeting because it will otherwise be next to useless and highly inefficient. Participation is critical because, presumably, the people who did the original work need feedback before they can proceed to the next step.

ALERT!

Before scheduling a review meeting, see if you can replace it by circulating a document by e-mail. Using electronic review and comment features, you can gather comments and make them stand out distinctly, so that it's easy to identify any one person's remarks.

Status

A status meeting is generally one of the most abused forms. Always consider whether you can replace a status meeting with a memo or group of memos or reports. This is one of the best candidates for meeting by insistence—a meeting that doesn't occur unless one of the participants has a specific need to meet in person with the others.

Project and Kick-Off

A project meeting is one designed for the people working on a specific project or task. It generally involves some aspects of status, review, and work. Typically the attendee list is critical, and often you cannot hold the meeting unless everyone will be able to attend. Although often treated as a cheerleading session, a kick-off meeting is the initial meeting on a project. It lets the group members discuss each of their roles and responsibilities to help ensure a smooth working relationship in the future.

Regular or Standing

After the status meeting, this is the most over-used meeting type. Anyone who has sat through regular staff meetings might wonder what most of them were supposed to achieve. Most regular meetings feature selected participants taking turns reciting information they have on paper in front of them.

After the Meeting

Most of the work has already been done by the time the meeting is over. But there are some crucial things left to do that can reinforce what you achieved or quickly help undo it.

Distribute the Notes

You had at least one person taking detailed notes of the meeting and recording action items. But the notes do no good if they sit on a computer and nothing happens with them. You need to distribute them—within twenty-four hours, if possible. The more time that passes between the meeting and distribution of notes, the less relevant they will seem. If you had more than one person taking notes, make sure they have a chance to compare them and create a document with all the points each of them noted. Also consider creating a separate sheet of action items, so every attendee can, at a glance, see what they are supposed to do and by when.

Follow-Up

For people to ignore what they agreed to do in a meeting is to retroactively waste the time of everyone who attended. Nevertheless, even if you include a list of action items, the meeting leader might well check on progress. Otherwise, you have a list of commitments with no one looking to see if they were actually done, which, again, retroactively scuttles part or all of the meeting. The meeting leader might also consider creating a follow-up document—a spreadsheet or other schedule of what was promised, what happened, and what is still outstanding, attaching the names of the innocent and guilty alike.

Get Feedback

If you want to learn to produce better meetings, you need to hear how they went. Actively go to the participants of a meeting and get their impressions. What worked? What didn't? Talk out the issues with the people so they don't fear that you might perceive their critiques as attacks. The more you can learn, the more you can improve future meetings.

Using Technology

For those who want to expand the boundaries of meetings, technology offers new tools. From virtual meetings to sophisticated ways of reviewing information, technology can help you make some meetings unnecessary and allow more effective information sharing and presentation.

Review Documents

You have a number of ways to let people review information. Using the review functions of word processors, presentation programs, and spreadsheets will let you collect thoughts from a variety of people and, by distributing the document with all the comments, let everyone see each other's impressions. You could also use a format like Adobe Acrobat: create a document and then generate a PDF file and allow others to make comments.

Collaborate

Computer technology allows group members to exchange work, opinions, and even hold discussions without having to be in the same place at the same time. Collaboration software, Web sites, intranets, newsgroups, e-mail, and instant messaging software give your team wide options for keeping in touch. The real power is that all the communication happens asynchronously, with all parties connecting when they can, seeing what people have already posted, responding to them as they wish, and having access to common documents.

Remote Meeting

Audio teleconferencing, video teleconferencing, and Web-hosted meetings have become a boon to many organizations, improving communication across the board. When you have people in remote locations, this can keep them from wasting time in transit. Even though these technologies can't do everything that a face-to-face meeting can, they can let you reduce even further the amount of physical meetings you will need.

Technology can be a boon, but it can also be tricky as you look to more sophisticated uses. Particularly in remote meeting technology, you'll need to work with people who understand information technology systems and who can ensure that all the participants have the capability to participate.

CHAPTER 15

Leading from Within

Leading from within doesn't mean tapping your inner leader (though that isn't a bad idea). Most people have been conditioned over the years to associate being a leader with being in charge. If you wait for official anointment, you might not only get long in the tooth, but you might let one opportunity after another pass. You could squander chances to further develop your leadership skills and make a difference in how effective your organization could be. Instead, learn how to act as a leader, no matter where you are in a group.

The New Leadership

Not long ago, leadership was synonymous with having a position and title. Anyone with the proper spot on the org chart or political hierarchy was assumed to be a leader. It was an understandable assumption if you look at the political and social organizational history. Those responsible for the welfare of the many were authority figures of various forms. At different times they may have been royalty, land owners, captains of industry, or elected officials, but the public assumed that because of their station in life these people knew what they were doing. Sometimes, especially in the case of royalty, people believed their leaders were placed in their stations by a deity. It's tough to argue the illegitimacy of divine purpose.

In many cases, the people in charge actually were good at leading others. Even then, there was no guarantee that they exercised their power and knowledge to good ends. For every golden age, there have been religious persecutions, wars for territory, and literal enslavement. And in probably far more cases, those with the right position knew nothing of leadership. As a result, much of the activity that was called leadership was simply the bellowing of orders.

Leadership Changes

The view of leadership began to change in the 1950s and 1960s. For the first time, people stopped thinking of leadership as some quasi-metaphysical trait and began to study it as methodically and scientifically as they could. No longer was leadership the act of ordering people to do what you wanted them to do.

FACT

The new view of leadership was in major part the product of social change. Significant failings in political, educational, and social leaders, insisting on an unbending approach to changing time, created an opening for a new approach. People began to consider that a different approach might be more effective.

As people began to realize that leadership was a skill, they started to rightly connect the concept with knowledge, not privilege. Today, leaders are less often defined as "the boss" and more commonly defined as people who point others in the right direction. You no longer have to be a CEO, the executive director of a charity, or a manager to be a leader.

Path to Leadership

To be a leader, you actually don't need any conveyed authority at all. No matter what position you hold in an organization, no matter where you went to school, and regardless of whom you know, you have ways to lead. Being a leader has everything to do with accepting the role of leadership and what you do in the role once you take it on.

Accepting a role doesn't mean signing a union card or getting the name plate for your desk. To take on a leader's mantle means to act in the way a leader would. Whether you are in a position of authority or not, you can take on the persona, the responsibilities, and the outlook of a leader.

The New Leader

The first thing to learn about leading from within an organization is that you aren't trying to usurp someone else's authority or carve out some "position" for yourself. You want to act in a way that supports the organization. As a leader, you aren't just going through the day doing what you have to. You're going out of your way to do what you can.

Sense of Duty

Duty seems old-fashioned these days. You hear few people talk about it, but it is vital to leadership from within. Duty is a concept that says people have an obligation to behave in particular ways and undertake tasks because of an allegiance to something greater. One might feel a duty to family or friends, to an entity, or to an idea. The exact nature of an obligation isn't as important in this case as the necessity of fulfilling it.

The idea of duty is thousands of years old. You can see it in the aristocratic notion of noblesse oblige, extensive formal religious obligations, and even in the remnants of holiday traditions like wassailing. There were entire structures of interrelated duties people owed each other and institutions.

You can't lead from inside an organization if all that motivates you is your own self-interest. You can't dismiss self-interest, but, really, there are better and more efficient ways of serving it. And you can't lead inside an organization if you feel no bond to it and its mission. If you do have the connection, then you are acting from duty, which is something you can practice in many ways under different circumstances.

It's necessary to remember why you do something if you are actually to accomplish it. You can easily lose your way, winding up doing something completely different that doesn't really achieve what you wanted in the first place. Act from duty, though, and you keep the fundamental principle before you.

Be Committed

Acting from duty also isn't enough without commitment. It is one of the most common human traits to begin something and then, for whatever reason, to give up—usually while telling yourself that it's either not your fault or fooling yourself into thinking you accomplished what you wanted to. Listen to others and to yourself and hear the excuses. Don't beat yourself (or others) over this because it is part of human nature. To lead, however, you need to get beyond the willingness to give up. You must insist on doing what you have said you will do. Duty may support the end, but commitment is about the means and the process—the journey. You can't lead if you don't want to go where you must or if you aren't willing to keep putting one foot in front of the other. This is why duty and commitment are crucial.

Don't Wait for Others

People often abdicate their own responsibility and look to those in power instead. They assume the person in charge will take care of all the problems. But a funny thing happens. When you wait for the powers that be to ride in like the cavalry, they never show up. Ironically, that's largely because those authorities can't make things better. At best, they can rally others and help channel their help into useful action.

As you can see, the powers that be are actually highly dependent on all the other people in the organization. You wait for them, but in reality, they wait for you. It's a circle that can keep you chasing your own tail for years. The only way out is to become a leader by doing. When you stop waiting for others, they may find that you're the one they've been waiting for, giving you more freedom than you might think.

Must Do

It seems clear that if you're going to become a leader from within an organization, you need to take action. It's not enough to want to take action. You have to know that you need to take action.

ALERT!

It is amazing to find the number of organizations that fall into a rut or worse. Some see the problems and some don't, but when things don't change, it's because no one is convinced that it is necessary to take action.

People don't act without reason. What compels them may be selfish or selfless. They may work from intellectual curiosity or emotional fervor. Their motives might be well thought out or they might come on utter impulse. The one constant is that there is something they want. If they wanted nothing from the situation, they would do nothing.

You need a must, an imperative that comes from your belief in the goals or principles or even possibilities of the organization. It's good if you have personal reasons as well, but only if they augment the desire to help the group in its endeavors. If you act solely from your own desires, then you won't be leading. You'll be running a con job to get what you want—and people will know it.

When you act from something higher, however, you offer inspiration and vision because you are connecting action with principle, and that is motivation. You're offering an opportunity to experience something that is rare in the world. That's a big reason why people respond. They want a taste of that in their lives.

Taking Responsibility

Accomplishing anything requires the combination of responsibility and authority. Unfortunately, when you're trying to lead from inside an organization, you don't technically have either. What you need to do is learn how to achieve something as a leader. This means finding a way to create influence and bring others in the organization in concert with what you're trying to achieve—a complex solution.

Initiative Becomes Influence

You can gain influence by being willing to work. That can mean taking on jobs that no one else wants to handle. It also means working beyond the description of your position, helping others when and where you can, pushing projects though to completion, and even taking some risks.

FACT

When growing a crystal, you start with a small piece of well-formed structure, called a seed crystal, in a liquid saturated in the material you want to crystallize. The seed crystal acts like a model, providing the foundation for a larger structure that sets the pattern of growth. You want your initiative to become a seed crystal.

What you are doing is creating an atmosphere conducive to gaining the cooperation of others. Willingness is an attractive characteristic in the broadest sense. It gets people to act in compatible ways. Your active support of the team and its goals calls forth similar action in others. In that way, they willingly put themselves at the service of what you are trying to do because in that way, they are connected to meaning.

Active Advocacy

When you work to help achieve principles and goals that are larger than yourself, you're acting as an advocate for them. You can become the living embodiment as you try to bring them into existence. But you cannot do that unthinkingly. If you are going to be an advocate, you must be an educated one. Learn about the organization—its structure, hierarchy, and culture. Extend that knowledge outward to other areas that might apply to what you're doing.

Take Advantage of Organizational Values

Many organizations come up with grand-sounding sets of principles and intents. Sadly, this is often nothing more than talk. But it doesn't have to be that way. Specifically, you can take personal responsibility for implementing the values and putting them into practice. That helps the organization find its way. You help it start to actualize its aspirations—what it says it wants to be. When you connect action with highest principles, you create meaning, and that brings motivation into play.

In virtually every organization, people are dying—on the inside, at least—for something that has meaning. When you take a stand for something meaningful, you spark the hope and imagination of everyone else. When that happens, you'll find massive amounts of goodwill and help.

There is another practical advantage to embodying organizational values. It gets very tough for people at the top of the organization to push out those who are everything the group claims to be. You insulate yourself to a surprising degree from managerial reaction because people in power can't really take an obvious stand against what they said they stand for.

Becoming a Guardian

Being a leader isn't about getting a list of things done or even involving people in the team. You need to really care about what happens with the team and its members, the organization, and the goal. Another old-fashioned word that helps frame the idea is guardian. A leader, particularly within the organization, has to watch over everything and have a properly caring attitude.

Guarding the Goals

Paying attention to the group's goals and principles should be old hat at this point. But being a guardian of the goals is a touch more expansive. You no longer look only to achieve them. As a guardian, you keep a watchful eye over the goals. They become something you want to promote and even protect, which in itself orders what you do in the organization. When in doubt, you, as a leader, are there to make sure that the group moves forward toward the goals.

Guarding Others

As a leader within the organization, you know that it takes a team to achieve the goals, which is why you also have to be a guardian of your other team members. The welfare of the organization and its goals depends on the welfare of these people. Helping others to work for a goal involving principle helps them connect to what is important to them. You help them find satisfaction and remember that doing work for an organization is more than punching a time clock.

In guarding others, you want to be sure never to tell people how you view yourself. It would seem unspeakably arrogant on your part, which would reduce your effectiveness. As important, you don't want to mention this objective because of the danger that it will become part of an expression of ego and not of leadership.

There are times that guarding others means acting as the de facto group spokesperson. Listen to all that each person in the group has to offer: complaints, suggestions, and new ideas. Then you can communicate those ideas—diplomatically, respectfully, and without pretending that the ideas are all yours—to the people who institute change. You deepen your relationship with the other people on the team and come to be seen by authorities as the voice of the group.

Guarding Management

You'd think that people in the actual positions of power in the organization could take care of themselves. That is generally correct. But they have their own responsibilities that play into overall success. To be a guardian of the people at the top is to watch over their time, to be sure that the team takes care of virtually everything it can so as not to pass any problems upwards. You can also work to bring the organization's core principles into existence through action. By doing so, you help those in authority to see their vision come into being. That creates meaning for them and acts as a reminder that the underlying principles are important, even in the face of mounting bureaucracy.

Building Coalitions

Leaders are those who lead, which does imply working with others. When you're on the inside and not at the top, you can just start doing what is necessary. But that is insufficient at times. You may see something that needs to be done but that is beyond your authority. Help is especially important in such a case, and you may need to build a constituency to help you succeed.

Find Your Colleagues

People use the term *friend* too easily. The modern notion of relationships has become too simplistic, with people defining each other either as strangers, friends, or enemies. Colleague is an old-fashioned relationship whose time has come again. Less than a good friend, more than a stranger, and different from an acquaintance, a colleague is someone with whom you share an interest-based relationship. You and your colleague strive in the same arena and want to see it advance. When you pursue a goal, you want to consider finding colleagues who can help you. They bring new viewpoints, additional knowledge, and extra resources.

Find Supporters

In addition to colleagues, supporters will be helpful. These are others in the organization who may not have your drive but who view your desire and goals with sympathy and who are willing to help.

Work Across the Organization

To find colleagues and supporters, you must think more broadly than your organizational backyard. The most appropriate candidates may be people on your own team, in other parts of the organization, or even outside it. A suitable person isn't necessarily someone in a given position; it's someone in a suitable place who shares the passion to get something done and who is willing to work with others to achieve success. Such people may well be leaders themselves. By standing someplace other than where you do, their relationship to the goal is, of necessity, different. Another part of the organization suggests the availability of different knowledge and ability resources.

Networking

Networking is making useful contacts. The process is successful when you learn more about the organization and others know that you want to be involved. Essentially, networking puts you in the loop.

Establish who the key players are. Who can help you get ahead? Who has the information or knowledge that is of the most value to you in reaching your goals? Understand that the key to effective networking is to make it a give-and-take relationship. You should always start out by giving far more than you take. Of course, it will work only if you have knowledge, expertise, ability, or authority in an area where someone else is lacking.

Once you have developed the giving part of the relationship, then you can begin to get something in return. There is nothing backhanded about networking. It is an essential part of developing relationships in organizations.

Use Persuasion

You don't win others to your cause by complaining, begging, threatening, or demanding. Only persuasion can call them to help. Don't confuse being persuasive with flattering or a false bonhomie. Pleasantness and warmth do play roles, just not singular ones. In being persuasive, you combine elements of logic and emotional appeal.

FACT

Samuel Adams is known as one of the drivers of American independence. He became interested in the idea long before most others, but he knew that most wouldn't support what he wanted early on. He had to spend many years persuading those around him to eventually get the support he sought.

You're trying to show that what you want to accomplish fits in with the person's desire to support the organization and with the person's own goals. At the point that they think and feel that helping you does something they wanted to do anyway, you'll get their support. However, this can and will take time. Start building constituencies long before you need them.

Build Momentum

As much as we talk about building coalitions, not everyone will be open to working with you. Sometimes the most reluctant people are those in authority. That presents a sticky problem. The very people in charge may, for personal reasons, not want the organization to move forward, at least not when the efforts aren't directed by them. These people might even actively oppose what you are trying to do.

There are at least two ways of handling such an impasse. Pardon the emerging Machiavellian streak, but one is to manipulate the authority figures to either think that the efforts were theirs or to set things in motion and effectively give them credit early on, so that it becomes difficult from them to try and sink the activity. This is a dangerous game to play, and it involves behavior sneakier than many people may be comfortable with. You have to put so much effort into the intrigue that you can start losing sight of what it is you wanted to do. Such machinations can also backfire.

In the corporate world there is a concept known as a skunk works. This is an activity that is started out of view of anyone in power and often without official sanction. The group uses corporate resources to develop something that works outside normal channels and then presents its results upon success.

Instead, it is preferable to build organizational momentum. It's similar in some ways to manipulating the authority figures, except it is more indirect. You don't try to trick the people in question. Instead, you create a grassroots movement and start achieving results. You work around the uncooperative authority figure and, when you've had some success, announce what people in the organization have been able to accomplish. Make sure the results go not just to the supervisor but by official or even back-channel routes to the people above. There's still a chance that someone will squash the initiative, but it's more likely that those higher up in the organization will be delighted with the winning effort, which makes opposition virtually impossible.

Don't Lead Everything

We're all heirs of the concept that leadership means authority and direction. As such, we all are subject to certain weaknesses, like being the big cheese. Save those slices of Swiss for a sandwich. You want to be a real leader, which means helping the drive for the organization's principles and goals. You don't have to run everything to make that possible.

Choose Your Battlegrounds

When you are thoroughly in the middle of the organization, you don't have the power to force broad change, so don't every try. Look at what you want to do and see if it smacks of taking over the organization. You're highly unlikely to be successful, and you'll end up wasting energy in the process.

Instead, you want to consider where you could best influence the organization and other people. That means starting where you are, not where you might like to be. Step up in a project or function that needs help. Concentrate on the operations of the part of the organization in which you find yourself. If you focus and attain some success, you'll find that over time you can lead on a broader basis.

Not a Battle

You can run into trouble by becoming antagonistic. You don't want to do that because then you're involved in a power struggle, not in leading to get something done. Find a way to include others without trying to force them to take part. Leading is getting someone to follow the same course, not to drag them kicking and screaming. If you find things getting tense, review the conflict resolution techniques discussed in Chapter 10.

Office Politics

Be aware of the politics within your organization by paying attention to what goes on around you. Keep your eyes and ears open. You will be amazed at what other people know, even when they are in positions that you might normally associate with "scut work."

Know who works with others and whom to avoid at all cost. Know who does what and the best way to approach each person. Above all, remember that the ultimate goal is to gain respect from others, not make them resent you. Look for information, but don't descend into using people.

Recognize Others

A leader is someone who gets others to help achieve a goal. Nowhere in that definition is there a statement that a leader cannot work with other leaders, even on the same goal. In fact, all great undertakings—the Civil Rights movement, World War II, the drive to cure polio—involve multiple leaders. You can't be everywhere and do everything, so don't try to.

As you work to lead, you'll find that others in the organization will take up the call and start pushing to achieve and to uphold the highest principles of the organization. Welcome the company. Ultimately, you'll find that you need those companions to achieve your vision.

CHAPTER 16

Recovering from Mistakes

We all make mistakes—one right after the other. Whether you are already acting as a leader or want to in the future, you're going to make enough of a variety of mistakes to fill a small retail store. There will be minor ones and major ones and mess-ups that are so bad they will deserve their own name. And you'll need to deal with them.

Mistakes Will Happen

To err is inevitable. Although in theory it might be possible to achieve a goal without a single thing going wrong, you'd be more likely to win the lottery. You're going to make mistakes and so will every single one of your team members.

You Want Mistakes

This seems insane on the surface. Why would you want your team to make mistakes? Because it needs to—at least part of the time. Of course you don't want rampant ineptitude; you'd spend as much time correcting mistakes as you would doing anything else. Think about what usually minimizes mistakes: practice. As you do something repeatedly, you get better at it.

At first impression, that might seem like the best route for your team. All you have to do is get them to work on the same thing repeatedly, and eventually the task will go more smoothly. There's only one problem: Your team is trying to achieve multiple goals, not the same goal over and over again. You may have continuing tasks that can benefit from practice. However, if the team remains in the same place, not going anywhere, then you aren't a leader so much as a caretaker.

Mistakes are the axel of choice and opportunity. Progress depends on movement, and you can only move if you are free to pick the wrong direction or action. Otherwise you'd be in a rigged game, where there was only one way to make things work, and you'd virtually never make a wrong decision. You can't always know what is right, but usually a mistake becomes obvious. Mistakes are the ultimate teacher. Given a set of circumstances or a type of task, they help you discern the proper direction by underscoring all the wrong ones. You want to embrace the mistakes that help the team progress while holding their number to a minimum.

Your Mistakes

You will make your share of mistakes. Learn to accept this and don't allow it to paralyze you. You should not ignore mistakes or assume that they cause no problems. However, the worst course you can take is to become so afraid that you avoid decisions as a way to avoid error. Inaction can be far more detrimental than making wrong decisions. Leaders must take calculated chances and learn from their mistakes. Moving past these issues allows you to lead in a meaningful and productive way.

FACT

Even experts can make mistakes in their areas of knowledge. Daniel Boone was a pioneer and an American folk hero, famous for his wilderness skills. In answering a question about his navigational infallibility, he reportedly answered, "I have never been lost, but I will admit to being confused for several weeks."

Accomplishment always requires a degree of risk, which is not inherently bad. Every day you take risks, even if you don't realize it. There is a chance of being injured in doing many everyday things, from driving a car to using a paring knife, that you think you've mastered. By the time we become adults, most of us learn to handle some degree of risk management. Look both ways before crossing a street. Grab a pot holder before lifting up a hot pan. Wear a seat belt. You use your experience and knowledge to apply sound judgment based on what you learned from your mistakes in the past. As a leader, you do the same thing for the team: Stay informed and use common sense. Make sure you and the others on your team have all the information you need to make smart decisions.

Team Member Mistakes

It can get frustrating to deal with other people's mistakes, but you must get used to it. If you can make mistakes, why expect the other people on the team to be perfect? You'll only get frustrated and things will never work any better. Mistakes will happen on the team, and you need to learn to deal with them.

Don't try to reduce error by creating an atmosphere of fear. Many who have gone through the management ranks lean on this behavior, as wasteful and counter-productive as it is. How do people react when they are scared? They indulge in that ancient heritage, the fight or flight response. Either they become belligerent and defensive, denying the mistake and even continuing on the same path, or they run away and hide, ignoring the problem and your demand to fix it.

When fear is the motivator, the result is a positive feedback loop, which, ironically, is anything but positive. In positive feedback, a system reinforces what is happening, like turning a car wheel in the same direction that the front is moving during a skid. The result is that things spin out of control.

The team member errs, the leader becomes angry, the team member compounds the error to avoid facing it, the leader gets more angry, and so the cycle goes around and around—a complete waste of time. Keep the atmosphere, and either the leader discharges the team member or the latter, having had enough of the nonsense, leaves. When someone new comes in and inevitably makes mistakes, the cycle begins anew.

ALERT!

As the team size increases, so does the chance for mistakes. If you had five people, each with a 75 percent chance of doing his or her part correctly, the chance of everything going right is about 23.7 percent. Increase the number of team members to ten, and the chance of perfection drops to only about 5.6 percent. Something will go wrong.

Whenever possible, keeping people in place after they make mistakes is the economical action. You save money, efficiency, time, and goodwill among team members. There are some areas in which mistakes are intolerable—generally in the realm of law and ethics. However, if people haven't absconded with the funds, caused death, wreaked havoc, or otherwise decimated the reputation of the organization, keep them on. Why would you want to remove someone who has just learned a lesson that would cost you as much to repeat for the next candidate?

However, you do want to minimize the number of mistakes necessary to learning. Start people on smaller projects that have a greater chance of success. As they gain experience, you can increase the complexity of responsibility and the difficulty of the assignment. Throughout it all, make sure team members learn how to handle mistakes and learn from them.

Making New Mistakes

We've said that mistakes are part of life, learning, and progress. They are, but not always. When you make the same mistakes a second, third, and fourth time, you're wasting time. But many people do just that, and more often than you'd think in an organizational or business setting.

Insane Activity

There's an old saying that insanity is doing the same thing twice and expecting a different result. Such is the reality of too many organizations. Even when a course of action seems fruitless, management, faced with challenges, will try to do more of the same.

ALERT!

Often a kiss of death in organizations is the phrase "We don't do things that way," and all its variations. It is a sign that the people in charge are actually terrified of any change and will work to keep things as they've always been.

When you think of this in relative peace and quiet, it does seem mad. For example, when a company is not making enough money, it might set higher quotas on salespeople, assuming that revenue is some mystical issue of will power. The big three American automobile manufacturers are classic examples. For years, leadership saw that people weren't buying their cars and reacted with discounts and interest-free loans. They focused on price rather than improving the quality and design of the products themselves.

The practice isn't constrained to things an organization has done itself. It extends to ideas and procedures that become established in an industry, study, or area of endeavor. You can do the same old thing without having been the one to do it the first time.

Reason for Repetition

Back to Chrysler, Ford, and GM for a moment. During the long periods of declining sales, managers could have asked themselves what Toyota and other companies were doing to capture the interest—and dollars—of the public. But to invite the question was to consider acting differently than before. Yes, we're back to that biggest of bugaboos: change. Life doesn't proceed in a direct way, and we humans don't like that.

ALERT!

What bigger change can you face than dealing with a mistake? Suddenly, what you have been doing falls apart and all your good intentions fail. Reality suggests some major change, but the human animal doesn't like that alternative—in change lies the recognition of mortality and our own fallibility.

Another reason we continue with the same practices, particularly when others do them as well, is because all those examples can't be wrong. Could so many people really be ignorant and not know that they were wrong? Oh, yes, indeed. At one time, many people assumed that the world was flat.

Rationale for Repetition

We don't like change, and so when we make mistakes, we all too often return to our first plan of attack. Only that's not what we tell ourselves. Instead, we rationalize our behavior. You might tell yourself that the problem was not what you did but the way you did it—which, to be fair, is sometimes true. You might tell yourself that many others do the same thing. This chosen course of action must work or all those others wouldn't do it. Maybe the rationalization is that others in the organization wouldn't accept something different. That, too, is sometimes true.

But this is all rationalization. You must remember that there is nothing wrong with mistakes—yours or anyone else's—so long as they are honest in nature and you learn from the experience.

Anticipating Problems

You can correct a mistake after the fact, but, oh, what a wearying chore that is. The easiest way to deal with mistakes is not to make them. You certainly are going to make your share, but you should also avoid more than your share. Some presence of mind and preparation can go a long way to reducing time, money, and energy

Do Some Research

One way to avoid a mistake before it happens is to work with information and not out of ignorance. If your team is going to undertake a task, the members should be doing basic research. How have people successfully solved the problem or similar problems in the past? In what ways does what you are trying to achieve differ from what others have done? What are the requirements of the customers (again remembering to use the term broadly)? Do you know the organization's expectations? Are there reference books or experts that you can draw upon for insight? The research process is really one of directed questioning. Assume that you don't know the answers ahead of time and find out what others with experience think.

Avoid Rationalization

Learning alone won't keep you from all errors, and some of the dandiest you can commit involve the misapplication of what you've learned. One of the biggest is rationalization. Often, particularly in a corporate setting, people for some reason decide on what they want to do and then look for justification. The reason to do research is to increase understanding, not create something to blame.

The surest sign you're going down a blind alley and into a brick wall is if you start looking for statistics as proof of a position without spending the time to understand what the numbers actually mean—which is often different from how someone presents them.

There is a variation on this, in which people effectively create rationalizations though blind assumptions. Instead of having someone tell them to concoct an excuse for a decision, they operate under beliefs without testing their validity. That is an extreme form of rationalization: the assumption of infallibility. That's a grand way to make horrendous mistakes.

Remember Your Experiences

You've made mistakes before, so use your experience. Look forward to similar situations to avoid future problems. The result is like a form of time travel. Your imagination builds a picture of what could happen, based on your experience. Knowing what can land you in that situation lets you make plans to avoid it. In a fanciful sense, you see the future and come back to tell yourself how not to wind up there.

A simple example is locking yourself out of your car with the key in the ignition. You could do this time and time again, but why should you? Knowing that you have the propensity for forgetful behavior, you might choose a number of actions that would keep you from the same situation. You might train yourself to only lock the door from the outside with the key, rather than locking the door before you close it. Another solution would be to keep a spare key hidden in a magnetic container under the car or slipped into your wallet. Alternately, you could get a car with a combination lock or a car that recognizes when you've left the key inside and won't lock until you retrieve it.

Seeing Mistakes

Stopping mistakes before they happen is the best solution, but often that isn't possible. You must learn to meet mistakes head-on and deal with them. By recognizing and handling them analytically, you can minimize the damage and maximize the learning.

Mistake Methodology

Mistakes may be an inevitable part of life, but there is no reason to shrug your shoulders and accept the aftermath. You must learn to be prepared to avoid mistakes as often as you can, and, when you can't, accept and learn from them.

FACT

Kimon Nicolaides was a brilliant twentieth century artist and teacher who wrote the book *The Natural Way to Draw*, described by one source as the best-written how-to on any subject. Nicolaides wrote, "The sooner you make your first 5,000 mistakes, the sooner you will be able to correct them."

However, nothing says that you have to be inefficient in dealing with mistakes. You can take a methodical approach to see what went wrong, fix things, and avoid similar problems in the future:

- Identify the problem
- Analyze the mistake
- Develop and implement a correction
- Develop an alternative approach

You will learn to find out what went wrong, fix the problem as best you can, determine how you could have avoided the situation, and learn how to recognize it in advance next time. The first step? Know what happened.

Identify the Problem

The first step in dealing with a problem is knowing that it exists. Although you might think this is simple, it's not. To know something is wrong, you have to be able to see it, and there are factors that can keep you from doing so.

The problem facing you may be subtle and you might not grasp its ramifications. Someone on the team who made a mistake might be hiding it out of fear or embarrassment. Effects of the problem could be removed in time from the cause, like the error in an auto assembly line that doesn't become obvious until months later, when someone buys the car and puts it to use. People responsible for noticing a problem may have fallen asleep at the switch, or you and others could be so invested in success that none of you pulls back enough to accurately judge the effects of your actions. Your team must proceed to achieve its goals with enthusiasm and a certain degree of watchfulness. Keep an eye on the metrics you create for signs that something is off course.

One of the most important skills a doctor can develop is good diagnostic ability. So many disorders have similar symptoms that determining what ails a person can be difficult. The physician must learn the subtle differences that indicate a patient has one illness and not another.

Analyze the Mistake

Knowing that you or someone on the team made a mistake is one thing; understanding how it happened is another. You are sorting through the difference between what happened and how it happened. The former is recognizing the problem, not its cause. A problem might have multiple causes. You'd want to know whether a factory product broke because of the user's treatment of the equipment, a design flaw, the factory worker's improper technique, or a substandard part.

In your efforts as a leader, a problem could be as obvious as a physical aberration. However, chances are that you are looking at an activity, not an entity, that went awry. The cause might be systemic—the result of a procedure or flow of communication that is unsound. But you're dealing with the work of people, and there's as good a possibility that the source is psychological in nature. Think of how many people you know who couldn't see their own weaknesses—or, perhaps, you've found yourself in that situation, causing a problem because you forgot about some quirk in your character that trips you up.

According to experts in statistical quality control, most problems are systemic in nature: Someone made a mistake in the design of a policy or procedure. As a leader, that generally means that any problem is the fault of the organization, and a solution will take the cooperation of the entire team.

At times, you will have to deal with human weakness. To uncover this type of problem, you must be ruthless and unflinching while remaining kind. Because we're such complex creatures, you can't assume that Rudy or Phyllis could never do something like what you see. It may be highly unlikely, but don't write off the possibility. Kindness lets you search for the source of the mistake without scaring everyone so much that they go into hiding.

Fixing After the Mistake

You know what went wrong, how it happened, and why. That forms the foundation for taking action. There are two parts to taking care of the mistake: cleaning up the aftermath and finding a way, if possible, to keep it from happening again.

Corrective Strategy

You're facing a situation in which something went wrong. The team needs to find a way to correct the results. Start by isolating the problem's impact from the problem itself so you can treat the result as an entity in its own right. Find a way to control and heal the symptoms. You might find that there is little or nothing you can do. For example, there might now be a delay in reaching an objective with no way to speed the process to meet an original deadline. Customers might cancel orders because they aren't willing to wait longer. But it's imperative that you do what you can to deal with the issue.

A corrective strategy will have a few parts:

1. Identify what or whom your team has affected.
2. Acknowledge the problem to the injured parties.
3. Get those parties to help formulate a working remedy.
4. Implement the remedy.

Leaders and organizations most often go wrong in the second and third steps. They pretend that nothing out of the ordinary happened, either to save face or out of real concern about potential legal liability. They compound the problem by deciding on a remedy without checking to ensure it will actually help the affected people or groups. In fact, if you're so out of touch with your customers that this could easily happen—and it is far easier than you might think—you've got a good lead on one source of the problem.

Alternate Approach

Corrective strategy is a way to take care of the immediate damage, but you don't want the problem to happen again. That's why you need an alternative approach for the future. You won't change what just happened, but with some hard work and good luck, you might be able to develop a permanent solution so that the problem cannot recur.

In short, it's time to return to the drawing board. If the mistake was one of those rare occurrences that was nothing but the single error of an individual, there is little you can do. It's far more likely, however, that the mistake was the result of a systemic miscalculation. Somewhere, someone made a wrong choice in setting up a process, a strategy for achieving a goal, or some other long-lasting undertaking.

What you do is start from the beginning. Treat the process or strategy as something new, using all your research and adding everything you've learned from dealing with the mistake. Given that you were able to create the previous version, you should be able to build a new one and design protection into it. The reason you act as though you're completely starting over is to avoid the temptation of a bandage solution, where you do something to patch up the issue. If you look over the whole process, you might find that the fix must extend to other parts. Ignore that, and chances are you'll make things more complicated and error-prone than they need to be.

Correction in Process

Next to stopping a problem before it happens, this is the best way to deal with a mistake. You have to catch the mistake early enough so that results aren't set in stone. Then you apply the same analytic deconstruction and rebuilding that you would use for fixing a mistake after the fact.

Complications set in when you remember that you're trying to affect a work in progress. Proceed with caution, and avoid radical corrections. You don't want to push something to the point of introducing new errors while you're trying to fix the original one.

Common Mistakes

The errors your team makes will be specific to its structure and goals. However, there are some mistakes that everyone makes.

Not Asking for Help

No one has super powers—and that includes leaders. You have skills, but the essence of teamwork says that you can't get everything done yourself. Take advantage of the resources available to you. Empower team members and delegate. In addition, when you are beyond what you know how to do, find people who can provide the necessary information or expertise to let you succeed.

Inflexibility

It is important to deal with change. One aspect is being flexible about the way in which your team achieves its goals. Organizations may change budgets or shift deadlines. Environmental factors can suddenly make a strategy unworkable. Shift with conditions as necessary; the more you try to stay with what no longer works, the bigger a mistake you will create.

Forgetting Your Origins

When leadership involves an official position of authority, there is the risk of thinking that you're better than the other people you're dealing with. That is foolish. At many smart companies, the top salespeople make more money than the CEOs because they are the ones who help bring in all the revenue. People in power aren't necessarily more important than those who aren't. Be thankful for what team members do and their willingness to help. Don't talk down to them, and don't think that they are there to simply follow orders. They are there for the same reason you should be: to help the organization achieve its goals.

CHAPTER 17

Leading As a Volunteer

You can be a leader anywhere. When you do so in a volunteer-based group, you face a number of special considerations and opportunities. You can get a lot out of such an experience, so long as you're prepared to deal with the idiosyncrasies. Some will make your leadership experience more difficult, and some will make it easier. Here are some highlights of what you need to know.

Why Volunteer?

You, as well as other volunteers, have your own reasons for offering your time to a group. You could believe in what the organization is trying to do. There could be a personal payoff. Or you could have a long affiliation with the group and offer help out of affection and sentiment. You need to understand why others volunteer and why you do, as well.

Belief in Mission

This is the most important reason to volunteer. Without it, any other reason will eventually give out, and the person will be a volunteer in name only. There are so many volunteer groups, each with its own priorities and view of doing good, that you can find one that fits your own tastes and personality. But with this emphasis, you have to make the group's focus your own. When doing volunteer work, the most important thing is to advance its interests.

Group Identification

Some people are interested in the cause, but even more volunteers identify with the organization itself. Some people have been associated with a given organization for a long time. A few will jump in headlong from day one. Such people have a long-term dedication, but it may be to the trappings of the entity and to specific other volunteers. They may be highly supportive and willing, but in times of great change, their attachment may become strained.

ALERT!

This can be the least useful reason for your own affiliation if you're interested in being a leader. Being too glued to the organization can make it difficult to distinguish between its goals and the interest in maintaining the group for its own sake.

Personal Benefits

Almost all people work as volunteers in part at least for their own reasons. They might be interested in virtually anything, ranging from the feeling of contributing to a cause, to having an interest in meeting a potential romantic partner. Depending on their reason and the balance with concern for the organization's goals, the person may be an effective team member or might offer little more than the presence of a warm body.

Working as a volunteer to expand your leadership experience or to gain other benefits, like professional networking, is a fine motivation, but it cannot be the primary one. If it is, then you're not working to serve the organization's goals but trying to make them serve yours. That is the complete inverse of real leadership. However, you can be smart about volunteering and let your own interests serve those of the organization. Take your growing experience and put it into the service of the team's goals. Also remember that your initial motivations for joining may not be the same ones that keep you in the organization.

Types of Organizations

There are all types of organizations, and the type will affect how a particular group approaches its goals and how you can exercise your skills and learn more about leading.

Ad Hoc or Standing

Latin for "to that," the ad hoc group is one that exists only so long as it works on a specific task. There is an intended finite lifespan. The positive aspect is that with such a focused existence, you should have an easier time concentrating on the team's goals. However, there will be less infrastructure and organization to lend a hand in accomplishing things. The majority of ad hoc groups seem focused on politics and social change. Depending on your interests and leanings, you might find that standing organizations and their goals are a better match.

Because of the ephemeral nature, any hierarchy is likely to be at least somewhat disorganized and malleable. Under the circumstances, the best approach to leading is probably using the techniques of leading from within. Another consequence is that your leadership opportunities will likely be short-lived, and there won't be an ongoing entity that could easily provide a reference.

A standing organization is one that has continued existence. Some of the strengths are actually the inverse of the ad hoc group. By being around over time, they have the opportunity to develop more robust structures to support their goals and provide help to you and the team you have or build. There is a hierarchy, and so you might have opportunities for positions that might add to authority and ease some of the issues of dealing with volunteers.

FACT

Sometimes an ad hoc group will turn into a standing organization if it achieves its initial aim. The classic example is the March of Dimes, originally organized to raise money for polio research. It found itself out of a job with the advent of the Salk vaccine, so management reinvented it to address the problem of birth defects.

Professional Versus Volunteer

Many nonprofits have professional staff and volunteers. The paid workers are necessary to maintain continuity and to provide the amount of time that would be impractical for virtually any volunteer. People can donate time while still working for a living. However, the paid staff will generally have control over the organization, either explicitly or as a result of handling the daily operations. You might find a ceiling past which you cannot move.

An all-volunteer group suggests that there are more opportunities for leadership at the highest part of the organization. But donated time means that things might not move as smoothly as with the presence of a paid staff. The organization depends on people arranging their schedules and finding openings to keep things on track. If you're trying to learn to lead, removing one potential area of uncertainty could make the process easier.

Nature of Volunteers

Working with volunteers means understanding their nature. If you don't grasp that, if you act as though such an organization is the same as a for-profit company, then your tenure as an effective leader is going to be short. This is because, in the team relationship, the members have the upper hand. If you don't grasp the dynamics and act accordingly, you'll be leading a group of one.

They Have Their Reasons

As mentioned earlier, all volunteers have a set of reasons they donate their time to organizations. There is a mix of altruistic, selfish, and even slightly neurotic impulses that can come into play. Whatever the set, however, if you are going to be a leader, what you do must cohabit with the interests of each member. If people don't find a way to satisfy at least the bulk of the reasons they have for volunteering, they will drift off and you'll be without anyone to lead.

ALERT!

If you are trying to lead a group to accomplishment in a volunteer organization, a big mistake is to push people too hard. They are looking to be part of something, not take orders and feel like they often do at work.

Demand Respect

One quality that people who work for corporations share is that they often find themselves pushed about. Corporate management is often locked into the command and control model—directing every aspect of what employees do. The employees are often stuck because they need to make a living and don't necessarily have other immediate options. Even if they decide to walk away from a company, the change takes time; this is true except under the most extreme circumstances, in which they decide that a continued association is intolerable. If people only continue to work under oppressive conditions because of economic necessity, what happens if the practical need evaporates?

Have Options

Volunteers always have a world of options; they don't have to spend time helping an organization. There are other groups, other causes, and completely different ways of spending time. You can't compel a volunteer, except for those performing court-ordered community service. At any time the volunteer can stand up and announce, "I'm outta here!" If you're going to keep volunteers and get them to willingly do what you need, you'll have to put reasons, respect, and options together and coax them.

ALERT!

An organization is actually in competition with other activities, demands, and opportunities in the lives of the volunteers. If you are a leader in a volunteer organization, you must hold your volunteers' attention and make them feel their contribution to the organization is more valuable than their other opportunities.

When it comes to volunteers, a leader should expect to use many of the same tools, only a bit differently than usually. Vision and motivation are important, but you have to place even greater emphasis on how they connect to the person. An employee is stuck doing something and so is willing to make the effort to gain a more fulfilling and pleasing environment. However, volunteers aren't stuck, and they don't have the same degree of incentive to make the connections themselves. Mentoring is important, not only to help volunteers perform better but to establish a direct connection with them and aid in making them part of the organization's fabric.

Working with Volunteers

It's important to know something about the nature of volunteers and the organizations with which they work. You need to adapt your way of leading so that it works effectively in this type of setting. At the heart of being a leader in a volunteer organization is learning to work well with the volunteers.

Volunteer Grapevine

Volunteers talk constantly, and they compare notes, aggravations, and lists of real and imagined grievances. Because they don't have the restraints of employees, the talk can turn into action and even, in extreme cases, mass disaffection. Paid or not, volunteers may still possess information and skills that are critical for the organization.

FACT

Market research has shown that, in business at least, customers will, on the average, tell four to six friends, family, and associates about positive experiences. For negative experiences, however, that number jumps to the nine-to-thirteen range. Bad feelings and ill will spread like wildfire.

In a volunteer organization, team members often have leverage in their relationship with leaders. At the same time, you can't be a pandering pushover. Seeking cooperation and using indirect methods in dealing with people will be a necessity.

Limiting Expectations

If you've been developing your leadership skills in a corporate setting, you must learn to moderate your expectations. Even when using the tools of a leader, you can still order people who work for you to do things. When necessary, you can single-handedly set a strategic direction or make an adjustment for some change.

That doesn't work in a volunteer organization. People might want to help you achieve goals, but it's likely a second priority. Even with the complete buy-in you need, you'll have to moderate your expectations. You can still achieve what you need; it just takes additional planning and volunteers.

Staff-Volunteer Bridge

In nonprofit organizations, you might have to work with volunteers and paid staff to achieve a goal. Both have different sets of motivations and conditions. Staff members are there to advance the organization, but they also have the regular duties of employees. Volunteers don't have the impetus of a paycheck, and yet they have more flexibility because they lack the strict organizational demands on their time.

In such an organization, you'll have to harness both types of help and get them to be productive together. Volunteers need to understand why staff may not be at their beck and call, while the employees have to know that the unpaid contributors are vital to the group's efforts.

Levels of Leadership

As in a corporation, you can be at different levels in the organization and lead in varying ways. You must find the type that allows you to be useful while exercising your leadership skills.

Activity Volunteer

You might be a regular volunteer, in which case the best outlet is to focus on projects the organization needs done. This is the perfect opportunity to sharpen your skills or gain new ones. The easiest way is to seek out and take on ownership of tasks that need to be accomplished. Sometimes this is relatively thankless work that no one else wants to do, and that is fine. Fundamental to leadership is being willing to do what must be done. When you take on such work, you actually create authority—ethical, moral, spiritual, or psychological—within the group. Your willingness to roll up your sleeves engenders respect and makes people more willing to take you seriously. Demonstrate skill and effectiveness, and other volunteers become open to taking your guidance.

In your interest to expand your leadership abilities, don't forget to enjoy the act of volunteering itself. If you don't believe in the organization's aims, you won't be effective, and you'll miss part of the joy in leadership: doing something you think is worth your time.

As you develop this baseline authority of effort, you can then take on projects that will involve more people. Work on your skills of listening, motivation, and empowerment, as you're in a forgiving environment. After all, no one is paying you, either.

Position of Responsibility

After some period of time, you might find an opportunity to become part of the volunteer "management" of the group, but you should stay away from such a position for at least six months to a year. You will need to understand the people and organization so you can try leading with some success from an official position. Take that time and gain the knowledge.

FACT

If you do take a controlling position in a volunteer organization, it can charge your learning about leadership faster than most other experiences you could have. Almost no commercial experience will put you into positions of authority and responsibility as quickly.

When you do take on such a role, remember that you're still a volunteer among others, and you will still need the help and goodwill of the team members. Because of the dynamics in a volunteer organization, this is almost a perfect atmosphere to learn what it really means to be a leader. Few will vest any sense of awe or fear in who you are, so you will find yourself having to coax and convince people to do what you need. This is a great foundation for future leadership roles.

Officers and Board Positions

Being asked to serve on a board can be flattering, and it can be an incredible opportunity to learn more about leadership. However, sitting on a board is a huge responsibility, far beyond what most volunteers realize or expect. Be sure you understand what you are agreeing to do and think carefully before accepting.

What Boards Are

A board can be many things, depending on the organization. One thing that always holds true is that a board is a form of oversight. The organization may have officers that have specific tasks, and it may even have paid staff. The board is there to ensure that the group stays true to its mission and that it operates in a way consistent with its own principles and any applicable laws.

Expectations

An organization expects volunteers to help. When you are on a board or acting as an officer, the expectations may change radically. Someone may have to represent the organization to the press, to work on promoting the group, and, often most important, to raise money. Look at large cultural institutions and you'll see that the board members are often well-placed to find donors and help establish important relationships with businesses, government, and other organizations.

QUESTION?

Will I be expected to donate my own money?
Board members of volunteer organizations generally do donate money to the organization. But the group will mainly expect you to use social and business connections to introduce the organization to influential people who could become significant donors.

Organizations need such help, and there is nothing wrong with asking board members to provide it. However, you need to understand exactly what you are getting yourself into. Talk to current and, if possible, prior members of the board. Be certain you understand all the requirements, whether formally stated or implicitly understood.

Remaining Open

There are many examples of organizations in which the board or officers come from the ranks of volunteers, and then become distant. It's all too easy to acquire an elitist attitude. This manifests itself in a variety of ways. Among these are the mistakes of assuming that only the board might have a sense of what the organization needs, assuming that you're too busy to do the "grunt work" provided by other members, and mainly associating only with other members of the board.

This is a good way to unlearn any positive lesson of leadership and to embody a set of habits that will make you incapable of leading anyone. If you do find yourself in an official position, know that it means time in addition to ordinary volunteering, and not a substitution for it. Be sure you continue working with others on the everyday tasks that need doing to keep from thinking that you're too important to do so.

Understanding the Organization

There is one level of understanding an organization that a volunteer needs and another level that an officer might require. But a board member had best become immersed in the organization. That will include reading the bylaws and becoming familiar with how the group is supposed to work. To allow the group to step outside of the bylaws is to invite tossing them out the window; if you don't need to pay attention to the rules for one issue, why should you for another?

Bylaws may seem a form of petty officiousness, but they are actually like the rules of a card game. If you change the rules, the game no longer exists. Although it may seem like needless bureaucracy, you must become a defender of the bylaws as they exist at any given time to make sure that the organization has proper continuance.

Legal Responsibilities

As a board member, depending on the form of organization and the geographic area in which it exists, you may have specific responsibilities under the law. That might include fiscal responsibility, duties to ensure that certain types of meetings take place, or obligations to produce certain public records of activities. The board might have to engage legal and accounting professionals to certify the group's proper operations, and it might have responsibility for hiring and firing paid staff.

Leadership Considerations

To successfully lead volunteers takes a twist on what might work in a corporation. You have to be sensitive to people's needs and adjust your leadership activities accordingly to satisfy those needs.

Importance of Recognition

Anyone performing volunteer work does so at least in part for personal reasons. Even if they don't admit it to themselves—even if they protest the attention—most people want at least some degree of recognition. Give them what they are looking for. It's an expression of proper respect and manners. Ensure that recognition and feedback happen on a regular and consistent basis. If you don't, volunteers will perceive that you are favoring one group over another.

Don't Take Dedication for Granted

Be genuinely thankful for all the time that people are willing to donate to help you achieve something and at the same time to provide you with an opportunity to expand your leadership capabilities. You don't necessarily need to make a show of gratitude. The internal recognition will guide the external expression and will help you learn the important lesson that team members are every bit as important, and often even more so, as leaders.

Selling People into Helping

Persuasion is everything when it comes to working with volunteers. Without being heavy-handed, you must constantly sell them into continuing their work and increasing their commitment. Often this takes just a bit of creativity. You could simply ask someone to sell raffle tickets at an event, which isn't terribly inspiring. Instead, explain why the raffle is important and how it is vital to the success of the event as a whole. Help volunteers see the context of what they do; in this way, they will understand why their time and effort are valuable contributions.

Firing Volunteers

If you've ever spent time doing volunteer work, chances are that you've run into unpleasant and negative people. We all have our off days, and an occasional bit of ill humor is something to overlook. But some people are so divisive and petulant that they repel other volunteers and thereby oppose the organization's goals. Sometimes you can help correct a problem, but other times you may have to ask someone to leave.

Reasons for Negativity

You might wonder why people who seem so unhappy in doing volunteer work would put their time into it. They might actually believe in the espoused cause and simply be blind to the results of their behavior. Unfortunately, there are also people who are genuinely negative. They might enjoy the opportunity to feel put upon, see volunteering as a way to undertake a personal interest in an overly aggressive way, or could even be predatory and see the group as easy pickings.

Handling Negative Behavior

You must handle the two types of people differently. In either case, you want to defer to paid staff or to those in official positions in the organization if possible, as they will have the responsibility for any fallout. If you must be the one to take action, first consider if the behavior is an honest lack of understanding. Then you must work, in as nonconfrontational a way as possible, to help the person see his or her effect. This is where coaching comes into play, as it would in any leadership position. It will take a bit more finesse because, unlike holding a position in a corporation, you cannot simply tell volunteers that they must cooperate with the process. Be sensitive because this is a harder conversation for the recipient than the deliverer. Work to get buy-in from the person all through the process.

When People Must Leave

Should the person display behavior that is extremely disruptive or even illegal or if there have been previous conversations about changing behavior, then the only choice for the good of the organization might be for the person to go. The organization should have a process for this, and you must follow it down to the last letter. There will likely be several warnings, all documented.

At the end, you personally might have to fire the volunteer. You must rid yourself of anger and never fire someone with even a hint of vengeance. The meeting must happen in a private setting, preferably with a third person of the same gender as the volunteer. Know that the reaction is likely to be unpleasant. State the reasons, and give the person a copy of the meeting's purpose in writing. Don't make personal comments, and get any organization property, including keys and identification. Above all, remain calm. If the volunteer has friends in the organization, go to them immediately afterward to say that the person is no longer volunteering, although without providing any personal details. Do not agree to provide a letter of recommendation to the person.

CHAPTER 18

Leading at Work

This book has been generally upbeat, but this is the one chapter in which the sledding gets tough. The problem is that leadership is difficult enough to do in the best of circumstances, but it's perhaps the most difficult to exhibit it in the workplace. That's ironic because companies are usually in desperate need of strong leadership. You can be one of the people to provide it by remembering how to navigate your way through corporate life.

Management Conundrum

Corporations are often terrible places to exercise leadership because they too often place an emphasis on management. That might seem reasonable on the surface. How can you have a company without management directing the operations? You generally can't, but the question becomes what form of management is in effect.

Control Versus Guidance

Businesses face their greatest management challenge when the people in charge think they must take control. Sometimes it may be true that someone has to make a decision from among a number of possibilities. Unfortunately, when managers focus too long on the moment of that final decision, they may lose sight of the prior deliberation and discussion process.

Management-speak has a term that applies: command and control. When an organization uses such a structure, it relies on highly centralized authority that only allows operations and initiatives to happen by order from above.

Organizational Interest Versus Self-Interest

Another major factor is the interest that directs the actions of managers. Everyone has reasons for doing what they do. You've heard of doing the right thing for the wrong reason and the other way around. Sometimes the intent doesn't change the outcome of what you do.

As some of the great corporate governance disasters of the early twenty-first century suggest, people at the top are sometimes more interested in their own bank accounts and futures than those of the companies that employ them.

But intent can make all the difference in the world because it drives individual choice. Different interests may occasionally spawn decisions that seem identical on the surface—though not when it comes to the role the decision has in a larger context. More often the choices go in diverging directions.

You'll get one type of result when people keep the interests of the organization front and center. Emphasizing self-interest, on the whole, produces self-interested employees. When people approach management with themselves in mind, they will, on the average, make choices that reduce the participation necessary for leadership.

Silo Setbacks

A third problem for organizations is a subtler remnant of business history. For many decades, management structured corporations into separate pieces. Whether formed by business function (called silos) or independent business units, these different divisions or sections each had their own budget and strategic aims—all well and good, except that eventually it was realized that the goals could conflict.

What should be important in a corporation is the company's overall health and success. Breaking the organization down into pieces, each with its own measures of success, can wreak havoc with the success of the whole business. The manager of each division has incentives to meet the goals for that group, but they may conflict with the goals of another division.

FACT

Suboptimization is the term experts use when a company optimizes for the performance of every part separately, but that process doesn't take into account whether that actually results in better operations for the business as a whole. Instead of working together to achieve a necessary balance, divisions try to do the best that they can.

You could imagine an automobile company in which the design engineers looked at each system as completely separate from the others. The people creating the body might use an abundance of heavy steel for safety without considering that the extra weight might be more than the engine could power.

Having departments focus on their own needs is similar to letting people make decisions based on their personal needs. The motive may be slightly different, but the impact is about the same—individual need versus the needs of the organization.

Working with Company Goals

If you're in a company with forward-thinking management, it already works on principles that will work with your interest in leadership. But no company behaves consistently in this manner. Even the best of corporations have pockets that resist the practices conducive to practicing leadership. Some will seem hostile to the practice. No matter where your employer comes down in the scale, there will be times that you'll need to lead effectively in spite of contrary conditions. A major tool at your disposal is a publicly stated company goal.

Existence of Goals

All managements make grand pronouncements on a regular basis. It's sometimes window dressing, but it can be a sincere interest in the stated principle. Generally it's some mixture of the two. They may be expressed only to employees or to the world at large.

Motivation doesn't really matter in this case because the company says it throws its weight behind these statements. The concept of using such corporate goals is simple. The more closely you adhere to the publicly stated aims of the corporation, and the more you can demonstrate that your goals would advance them, the more difficult it is for someone to publicly or privately criticize you or your intent. How can you take someone to task for trying to achieve the stated company mission?

Using corporate goals in this way might seem manipulative—and it can be—but it's ultimately good for the company and the other people working there. Using principles as a rallying cry puts them front and center. Supporting them only advances the organization outside of people's incompatible personal goals. Every time you help advance the highest corporate aspirations, you help improve the atmosphere, making leadership easier to undertake.

Identifying Goals

The first step is to research stated company goals and principles and make a laundry list. You might find them in a number of sources, including the following:

- Corporate mission statements
- Annual reports
- Company newsletters
- Press releases
- Financial reports
- Top management quotes in news stories
- Company histories
- Biographies of managers

The same goes for departmental and group goals. Hold to them—and show how your goals will support them—and you make it difficult for people to oppose you, even if they would rather spend their time focusing on their own interests.

Goals and Positioning

As much as possible, you make your goal and the company's goal the same. This is an example of what in marketing or public relations would be called positioning.

FACT

In politics, positioning has become an art. Pay attention to the names that congressional representatives attach to bills and laws. There are many examples of a title being the polar opposite of what the sponsors actually want legislation to achieve.

Ironically, people can use such techniques to try and advance aims that they actually intend to benefit their own careers. The difference is that you must keep honor in mind. A sure sign that people are playing a positioning game is if, when they are successful in getting authority to do what they wanted but the result is failure, they then try to blame someone or something else. Don't go this route. Play above board, and if things don't work as you planned, avoid pointing the finger at everyone else. You'll be uncomfortable at times, but team members will respect you more, and others in the company won't feel as though you'll try to saddle them with unwarranted responsibility if they help you and you fail.

Toward Greater Leadership

A company has many parts, and each has its own interests. Each part requires attention. Dysfunctional businesses are pulled in multiple directions by all the people who are trying to build their empires. To lead, you will need to learn to navigate these different interests and bring them together when possible.

Study Corporate Dynamics

The more you understand how the company works, where the parts tie together and how they interact, the better you can marshal the forces necessary to accomplish something. So be a corporate geek. Read organizational charts, dissect the company newsletter and press releases, look through financials and annual reports—in short, consider looking at all the sources to identify corporate goals. Most companies are like jigsaw puzzles, and few people take the time to put the pieces together. When you do, you'll have a better idea of what parts of the company you'd need to involve to get something done.

Develop Relationships

No one likes to be chatted up simply for a favor, and it's an unsatisfactory way to do business. You don't know how the other person works and communicates, which makes smooth cooperation difficult. Develop relationships with key people in other parts of the company in advance. Offer help to them in your area, and ask them to help you better understand what they do. People love to talk about their own occupations, and you gain valuable information in knowing how the company fits together, not in theory but in practice. Then, if the time comes when you need help from a given department for a team goal, you have someone who can help or at least point you in the right direction.

Find the Data

If few people put together the jigsaw that is a corporate entity, only a tiny fraction do the same for data in the company. People tend to assume that whatever they need is available. It probably is—if you know whom to ask. IT departments can be a real help, but there is a lot of important information that resides on desktops and laptops and inside the heads of employees. You might find this a time-consuming activity. Once you're outside of the major information systems, virtually no one knows where everything is. Identify the people who actually get things done. If they are effective, they probably have information as a result of their activities.

Office Politics

Office politics is one of the most poorly used tools available to workers in general and leaders in particular. You're not going to set up elaborate schemes to push rivals out or to acquire unlimited bureaucratic power. Instead, you need to look at what office politics actually can and should be, and then consider how they apply to leadership.

Misunderstood

The problem with office politics starts with how the process is perceived. Listen to people complain about work, and they're likely to mention how unpleasant they find the office politics. This one is trying to take credit for a project, and that one is spreading rumors. None of this is what office politics can be any more than mudslinging is an example of social politics. All such escapades are misplaced grade school machinations.

Such actions are not politics because they essentially do nothing. Oh, perhaps some person still trying to overturn authority figures from adolescence will attempt personal gain, but it's petty and laughable. Peering around corners and scheming is simply not worthy of an adult with a real life.

Real Office Politics

If much that people assume is office politics actually isn't, then what does the term mean? Like the social variety, office politics is the path used to gain support to actually accomplish something worthwhile for the company. You find supporters, build coalitions, create partnerships, and convince others that what you are trying to accomplish is worth the time and effort involved. When you have enough support from others in the company, you work on resources: systems, expertise, and budget.

Does this sound familiar? It should. At its foundation, office politics is a classic application of leadership techniques. The difference between what is often thought of as office politics and the reality is the intent of the practitioner. The negative version always starts in a complete focus on you. The positive version? It starts when you focus on something else.

Shifting Politics

You want to change your view of office politics to a more useful outlook. Leadership is a way of getting people to be willing to do what you want them to do. However, that makes one big assumption: that the goals exist.

But what if they don't—yet? You need to get the goals in place so there is something to accomplish. Even then, an organization will have many potential goals, so it must also recognize relative importance among them. When everyone knows what is more important, the group can start to create priorities among the goals and properly apportion resources of all sorts. Office politics is actually is the use of leadership to focus the group internally and have it voluntarily create the understanding of what it should be doing. Much of what leaders do involves negotiating the political environments of organizations.

Understanding Politics

When applied in this sense, office politics becomes an undertaking that is almost anthropological in nature. You are interested in seeing decisions made and in obtaining support for your team and its goals. One of the best preparations for leading in a corporation (or, frankly, any other organization) is to become intimately aware of the structure of its politics. Some people with power can help get things done, while others generally oppose change and improvement.

You can learn the most about company politics from talking to people with a history in the business at a lower level. Executives who understand office politics are often tied up in their own interests. People who have taken time to learn about the structure to avoid being run over by it are more likely to have the most objective views.

To that end, you have to learn how the organization actually makes choices and determines what it will do—not how an org chart states it should happen, but how the process actually occurs. You start as a researcher would, by paying attention to what is around you. Listen to everyone in the organization and strike up conversations, asking people how they might go about getting support for something specific. Know the power players and political actors in an organization and understand their individual histories and alliances.

Dealing with the Negative

Even if you are trying to use politics to gain agreement and support for undertakings that would be good for the company, not everyone will work this way. The negative approach to office politics is too well entrenched in the world, and you'll never find an organization that is completely free of it. You can't get rid of it, and you don't want to join it, so you must learn to work around people's machinations.

You must first make your intent clear, particularly to yourself. For positive office politics to work, it must be about achieving something for the organization, and not for you, personally. Your gain is in the practice of leadership skills, nothing more. Of course, you probably want to advance in your career, but the most certain way of doing so is to offer ever-increasing amounts of value to the organization. This is similar to how companies do best financially, by continuing to delight and help their customers, while exercising prudent and frugal operations.

The minute you use politics to advance your personal interests is the moment when you turn to the negative type. If you've done so, go back to square one. Consider what the organization is trying to do and how its goals match your aspirations and sense of meaning. The only way to avoid getting caught up in plots is to concentrate on something higher than personal interests—to get above the fray. The more you do this, the more people will cease to perceive you as a competitor and skip the time it would take to oppose your efforts.

ALERT!

Most people have worked at some point for a company that doesn't aspire to anything great. If there is no room for meaning and true vision in the company, move on to find a more worthy employer. Life is too short to hunt for scraps in a dung heap.

Working with Others

As always, leadership is about working with others to achieve a goal. In a company, that becomes particularly true. People have varying duties and responsibilities. To achieve something, you'll need to involve other employees. The more complex and ambitious the goal, the more people, representing a wider aspect of the company, you'll require.

Individuals

You always start on the individual level. Whether someone is in the same part of the company as you or in another division, you face the same underlying challenge of getting her interested in what you're trying to accomplish. There may be a natural affinity between the goal and the person's job responsibilities, in which case your task might be a little easier.

Whatever the situation, you must demonstrate how your goals as a leader connect to other people's responsibilities as employees. If you cannot make that case in a reasonable fashion, then you're effectively asking people to help you and disregard those duties, which is unfair to them and to the company. Assuming that you've picked goals that are in keeping with the company's interests, showing that connection shouldn't be difficult.

Even so, the person may still have actual conflict with other duties. Use power sharing and see if the employee can help work out a possible solution. The more you involve those people in the process, the more buy-in you get, and the greater your chance of getting the help that you need.

Departments

Getting the aid of other employees is easier if you are in a position of authority and they are working for you. It's more difficult if they work for someone else, and it gets even more complicated if the people work in other departments. The person might need to get permission to help, or you might first need to make the case to a supervisor. Even if the person in charge is sympathetic to what you are trying to achieve, the department will have other demands, as well as limited resources.

Work with the supervisor to see if a solution is possible. Emphasize the corporate goals and principles, and also be realistic. You might have to redefine your goal, look at different deadlines, or otherwise change the scale, timetable, or methods to work within unalterable constraints.

Another approach is to go up the chain of command. Find someone higher up whom you might convince of the necessity of this project. That person could then direct a re-evaluation of department goals or even underscore the importance to the first supervisor. There are few things as motivating—at least on the surface—as a memo from someone in higher authority.

One effective way to get help is to create an ad hoc multidepartmental team to address the initiative. You'd need to get permission from your supervisor. Once that is done, you go to the other appropriate people in the organization—now with the support of someone in authority—and lay out the idea. Because of the official backing, this becomes a company undertaking.

People will generally feel an obligation to make someone available, if for no other reason than to prevent themselves from being surprised by something that is to involve them and their departments. Congratulations! You're now leading an official undertaking of the entire corporation.

Working Outside the Company

The company that exists in a vacuum is one that isn't viable. Any business has ties to the rest of the world. There are customers, suppliers, and stockholders, and all three can be powerful allies in your quest to help the company.

Customers as Allies

It is difficult for a company to refuse to even consider significant customer reaction to an idea. Customers, in this case, can be single large sources of business, or they can be collections of customers that are small individually but large when considered together. Customers generally have an incentive to at least hear you out if you are suggesting something that could improve service, provide attractive new offerings, or otherwise positively affect the business relationship.

More significant customers should be approached directly through the team members that most regularly deal with them. Get their support, and you will now have an even warmer reception in your own company because management cannot readily discount them.

QUESTION?

What do I do if there isn't a receptive significant customer?
Smaller customers in aggregate can represent powerful forces. Consider using a survey or other source of appropriate and accurate statistic to show trends and interests of customers on the average. It is a way of representing the customer view without having a specific significant customer buy-in to your goal.

Suppliers

The companies from which you obtain goods and services are another source of support. They include consulting firms, auditors, and legal firms as well as providers of components or ingredients or those who handle shipping and logistics. They have the obvious impact on costs but can also work closely with virtually any number of departments: engineering, purchasing, manufacturing, marketing, accounting, and so on. Get a supplier to buy into an idea, and it can communicate its support and enthusiasm to part of the company that is critical to your undertaking. A supplier can also help create a process or modify a term that might be the difference between success and failure.

Investors and Governors

This, the trickiest category, can be the most powerful as well. Those who own the company—whether directly or through stock ownership—and the board of directors that provides oversight have enormous influence on the thought of upper management. They often directly affect corporate strategy. However, corporate management often takes a dim view of employees contacting them and, essentially, going over the heads of direct supervisors.

Success generally requires a direct connection to one of the people, whether a director, an owner, or an influential investor. There are almost no circumstances under which you'll be able to approach someone on this level whom you don't previously know. Develop these relationships, if possible, before problems occur. That means you need to network and find someone who can make the introduction in a reasonable way, or use happy circumstance—like being asked to present something to some of these people—to listen for questions or requests and find ways of fulfilling them. Do so in a way that allows you to remain in contact.

CHAPTER 19

Learning to Lead

This book is a combination of helpful theory and pointers. But by itself it won't be everything you need to learn how to lead. Leadership is an ever-evolving field. You'll learn what works for you through trial and error, but circumstances will always change and there will always be something new for you to master. As a leader, you need to keep honing your knowledge and skills. Not only do you need to advance your abilities, so does everyone on your team.

How People Learn

People differ in their educational needs. Some are auditory learners, while others are better at absorbing visual information. There are those who respond only to practical applications, while other people like inspiring examples. You need to understand your approaches to learning and the techniques that would work best for you. Furthermore, you must have a sense of what you need to grasp at any given time and the options open to you for further learning. If that isn't enough, remember that change constantly happens, and many times you'll need to learn to help guide your team through it.

FACT

According to the Marketing Executives Networking Group, between 20 and 30 percent of chief marketing officers are surprised by how much relearning they must do, but two-thirds of CEOs think their chief marketing officers lack important skills. When in doubt, assume you have something to learn—someone else probably thinks you do.

Continued learning is imperative for leaders, and you've got to make the learning process work efficiently because you have other things happening in your life. So it's time to review your past. Think about your educational experiences—not just in school, but in any setting at all, formal or informal, where you tried to gain information. That will give you the clues you need to approach learning in the future.

Learning Styles

We all vary in how we process information. Most people fit into one of three major learning styles:

- Visual (learn through seeing)
- Auditory (learn through hearing)
- Kinesthetic (learn through doing)

Even if you've had challenges in the past, it could be that learning techniques new to you can help. For example, instead of just reading a passage, you might consider the material and then take notes, which helps imprint the information on your mind by adding a kinesthetic element. Creating lists of summary points or graphs of data can help you grasp essential points and order them. Try picking up a book on study methods and see what some fresh ideas can do.

Intelligence Types

Educational theorists suggest that there are different types of intelligences, as well:

- **Visual/spatial:** Good at puzzle solving, creating visual metaphors and analogies, understanding graphic information
- **Verbal/linguistic:** Good at speaking, listening, teaching, remembering information
- **Logical/mathematical:** Good at problem solving, numerical analysis, handling long chains of reasoning
- **Bodily/kinesthetic:** Bodily expressing emotions, hands-on tasks, crafts, physical coordination
- **Musical/rhythmic:** Recognizing tonal patterns, understanding musical structure
- **Interpersonal:** Understanding someone else's perspective, empathy, understanding motivations and intentions, creating trust
- **Intrapersonal:** Self-analysis and awareness, internal reasoning, understanding role in relation to others

This is quite the spread—three types of learning styles as they apply to half a dozen (at least) types of intelligence. Knowing more about the way you acquire information and how different types of intelligence might come into play will help you understand how to structure your own learning.

The theory in this case is easy to see. A great athlete demonstrates one type of intelligence in the body. A chess master can anticipate what the board will look like a few moves down the line. A mathematical genius wouldn't necessarily have the intelligence required to write a literary classic. Successful salespeople show an emotional canniness.

Educational Opportunities

When you want to learn, you need to find an approach that matches with your learning style. You must also connect what you learn to the appropriate types of intelligence, and you must do so within your schedule and budget. Sometimes options you'd prefer won't be available, and other times you may have a chance to learn something when you least expected—if you pay enough attention to take the opportunity.

Formal Education

Some people thrive in a formal atmosphere. Formal could mean a seminar, conference, class, or other setting with a teacher. In general, you'll have to show up at a specific place on a given date and time. There may be a combination of in-class work and assignments to complete on your own time. You can't as easily put things off until later, and the additional commitment can help you obtain more from the experience.

On the down side, one problem of seminars is the question of perspective and motivation. Why is an entity sponsoring a particular seminar? Some companies use seminars as a marketing tool. Their foremost intent is to ultimately sell you products or services for their own gain, not to advance your knowledge. A course based completely on the needs of the provider and not on the students is a waste of time.

Free sales seminars intended to showcase someone's expertise can be useful. Try to get a syllabus ahead of time and compare it to those of other courses as well as to tables of contents of books on the subject. If you see a preponderance of "Solving the problem with Acme's widgets," you might think twice about attending.

The very need to show up at specific times can cause problems with your schedule and make it more difficult to spend the necessary time. Courses generally cost money—sometimes a lot—though you may be in a job that will defray at least some expenses if the topic is work-related. Classes also depend significantly on both the subject knowledge and teaching skill of the instructor, and that can be difficult to ascertain in advance. There are certified experts who couldn't reliably explain how to open a door. There is some chance that you could invest the time and money in a course, only to find it disappointing.

Online Courses

Web technology allows you to take courses online. Although not a panacea, distance learning is a powerful alternative to traditional classroom-based instruction. Universities offer courses and even degree programs online.

There is a range of options associated with online courses. Some courses require you to log on at specific times to receive a lecture and to be able to ask questions of an instructor. Other approaches work asynchronously—you point a browser to a specific spot on the Web, where you read material and complete assignments according to your schedule. You can ask questions and get answers electronically, but there's no need for you and your instructor to be online at the same time.

FACT

While the results can be good, online courses do have their downsides. It's easy for many students to take advantage of the flexibility and find themselves hopelessly behind the pace of the class. It takes dedication and responsibility to commit to an online course.

Depending on the structure of the course, you can also interact with other students, which can add to the learning experience. However, an asynchronous format means you can't depend on having anyone getting back to you in a specific amount of time. If you leave questions on an assignment to the last minute, you may not get the answers you need until it's too late. Flexibility requires personal organization. Online courses also cost money and depend even more than traditional instruction on the communication abilities of the instructor.

Self-Instruction

There is a wealth of tools available to help people who want to advance their knowledge on their own time through their own efforts. You can find books, audio and video, Web-based tutorials, and computer-based training. Depending on the subject, you can also try the old-fashioned, get-your-hands-dirty method by actually practicing, making mistakes, and trying again.

It's a romantic notion and a relatively inexpensive and convenient option. But be clear-headed when considering it. Gleaning knowledge from something fixed on the Web or on paper is trickier than working with an instructor in person. If an explanation makes no sense to you, you may not be able to explain your difficulty and ask for a different version. Because learning requires repeated and regular effort, you need sufficient self-discipline to make progress and not offer yourself the procrastinator's excuse that you'll get around to it eventually.

Environmental Instruction

Gathering information from people and situations around you is one of the most common forms of learning. You can benefit from mentoring, the expertise of those in your group and other parts of the organization, and even from being forced to work through events and problems that are new to you.

You'd think the desire to learn and support others with the same objective, is automatic, but it actually isn't. Before taking advantage of an opportunity, you have to recognize that it exists. Defensiveness about mistakes or an unwillingness to share power can keep leaders blind to the people and things around them.

Even when you know that you have an opportunity to learn, you need to treat it appropriately. The best lessons are those in which you try to extract as much general meaning and instruction as possible. Pointers on how to get more cooperation from the warehouse for a project, for instance, aren't just about that goal. You can make general observations and learn how to deal with that part of the organization in the future. You can also pick up on specific cues about how people doing that type of work react to situations and why they do so. When that happens, you have learned something that you can apply to many other organizations and even analogous situations. Now you're learning universal principles that let you plan and act more deeply and effectively.

Education Plan

Understanding your learning style and options is good, but it's only part of what you need to do. Effective education requires a plan: not a document fixed on paper and in time, but a process that keeps your learning on track with what you need. To create the plan, you must decide what you must learn and the most effective way of accomplishing it.

Analyze Changes

When conditions change, so must your strategy and tactics. Some adjustments are within the sphere of your knowledge, but not all are. The fundamental nature of the people and entities your team serves, or the nature of your duties and goals, can transform into something different. When that happens, you're in unfamiliar territory and need to learn. But what is the necessary lesson?

You don't want to make guesses. By the time you start the learning process, it could be too late to alter your direction. Apply the approaches to meeting change that are described in Chapter 13. As you examine the change, look at what specific knowledge, experience, or skills you need to address it. If you recognize any areas in which you are lacking, you have identified a need for learning.

Analyze Your Weaknesses

Even when conditions are not changing appreciably, you should undertake periodic reviews of how well you handle your responsibilities. You might have the knowledge and experience and yet find you fall down in what you should be accomplishing. You can further look for areas in which you feel the need for help, even if you haven't asked for it and are afraid to. To find weaknesses requires developing a self-critical attitude. You won't be looking to tear yourself or others apart. Instead, you want to see where a bit of help could go a long way.

Team Education Planning

Just as you will need to learn during your time as a leader, so will your team, and you'll need a plan for accomplishing your education. To create the plan, you must decide what the team must learn and the most effective way of reaching that goal. The basic process is the same as determining your own education needs, only with a group twist.

Analyze Changes

Changing conditions affect your team as much if not more than they affect you. A team educational strategy will be broader than your own. For example, a factory team might need extensive education in a new manufacturing technique. A social service agency could require a crash course in new legal requirements. Instead of simply considering what each individual needs, you have to look at the collective set of knowledge, experience, and skills the entire team must possess.

A mistake to avoid is providing just enough skills and knowledge within the whole group. To the greatest degree possible, you should have cross-training on your team. If one person is incapacitated or moves on for another opportunity, you don't want to find yourself unable to function.

One of the most natural forms of change in an organization is turnover in people. Do you have an education process for people joining the team, so they can get up and running sooner rather than later?

Analyze Team Weaknesses

You know you need to look at your own weaknesses, and the same sort of psychological issues that can come up in you can arise in any member of your team. However, you must also address the issue of how the team members interact. If these dynamics are off, you can have a group equivalent of an individual's quirks that make success difficult, if not impossible, to achieve.

Also ensure that team members understand the organization. Do people realize what goes on in other areas? Do they even recognize people they should know from other parts of the company? You can invite people from other disciplines to offer presentations to your team.

Determine Team Needs

When you know what you or your team members need to learn, you are ready to determine how they can best learn it. Here are the basic issues you'll have to consider:

- Subject matter break-out
- Appropriate type of instruction
- Location and time of instruction (if applicable)
- Attendees
- Schedule
- Learning goals

There may not be a single answer, even if you determine that more than one person needs to acquire the same knowledge or skills. You might base your choice in part on the learning styles of different team members or on the roles in the process the team must undertake.

Selling Education

When you know what the team needs for learning, you have to sell the idea. Other parts of the organization might have to approve budgets or change operational timelines to accommodate the teaching. As with all other leadership issues, you also need team member buy-in. The better people understand what they are about to do and need to achieve, the more effective the learning process will be.

Valuing Education

Knowing that education is necessary is one thing, but valuing it is something else. You can make all the plans you want, but education requires commitment. Put things into action so everyone knows that the learning is necessary, expected, and even something to anticipate and enjoy.

Make Time for Yourself

To show that you value education, you must publicly continue to educate yourself. If you don't, then your actions are saying to your team members that you are above learning. Essentially, you're giving them excuses not to spend any time expanding their horizons. On one hand, you don't want to make a big show of your own efforts because they will come across as forced and false. But you can show that you are learning by demonstrating new skills and even by letting yourself be seen in a class with team members or spending time reviewing a book at lunch.

A great way to show respect and instill pride in new skills is to get team members to help. You demonstrate teamwork, and at the same time you pay an effective compliment to their hard work and new knowledge.

Team Member Time

If you need to make time for your own education, you must accommodate team members' thirst for knowledge. Don't begrudge the time necessary for an in-house class, and don't indulge in negative body language when someone must leave promptly to attend a session. Schedule activities around education when possible, and not the other way around.

In addition, spend time with team members, talking to them about what they are learning. Use the occasion to take stock of how well the educational program is going as well as to show interest in what they do.

Learning by Teaching

The old saying goes, "Those who can, do; those who can't, teach." Nonsense. In an effective team, not only is everyone constantly learning, but they are all teaching as well. It saves time and money and actually helps people learn more thoroughly.

Teaching Forces Deep Learning

If you've ever had an experience of teaching something, you'll probably recognize that few things better help you understand the topic. In searching for an explanation, you revisit the basics and look at the rationale for approaching things a certain way. That allows you to re-examine what you do and, in the process, notice where your own practice falls short of the ideal. To teach another is to force yourself to become conscious of what you do and to understand why you do it. Also, instead of being satisfied with your own understanding of a subject, teaching forces you to look for new explanations, metaphors, and descriptions, all of which become part of your own learning process.

Importance of Teaching

You want everyone on your team to teach. You get the benefit of deepening the experience of members as they explain topics to others. But that's not the only payoff. Encouraging teaching among team members is a wonderful way to make more efficient use of your intellectual resources and to minimize the impact that continued learning has on your budget.

If you see the need for a training program, consider whether you can send a few people through the sessions and then have them teach others. In one stroke, you increase the impact of the training on the original group and reduce the cost of formal education programs, which charge by the student. Each person on the team can have the task to teach at least one other, expanding the teaching impact. When you get to the last person or two, have them teach people who join the team. That way you establish a continuing chain of teaching.

Implementing learning inside your team isn't only about acquiring new skills and knowledge. It's also about using the ones you already have. Give people an opportunity to share what they know and gain insight from each other.

CHAPTER 20

Ethics of Leading

In recent years, there have been scandals in corporations, in nonprofits, in politics—virtually every arena in which you can practice leadership. Largely as a reaction to public anger, the government and individual organizations have been crafting more regulations to ensure that people are on the up and up. Yet organizations often pressure people to behave in ways that come up to the line of ethics and even law, and sometimes the groups look the other way when people step over. Some reflection, a little knowledge, and a few simple practices can help keep things in the right and you out of trouble.

Leadership and Principles

Some people might argue an amoral stance, leadership being the practice of getting people to help you with your goals, no matter what they are. At first blush that might seem reasonable, but the argument quickly falls apart.

FACT

Some of the biggest villains in history have been effective at getting large numbers of people to do what they wanted them to. Con artists are also good at getting people to follow along. That doesn't make them real leaders.

Something Higher

This goes back to the basic idea of leadership. You try to mobilize people to jointly achieve something greater than yourself. That means there are fundamental principles you must value beyond your own self-interest. If you don't have them, then all your efforts eventually come down to you. Even if you are a celebrity, you'll find it difficult to keep people focused on your needs and wants; they have their own to tend to. It's only with a joint focus on some principle everyone feels is important that a team can harness its energies and achieve something. Starting from yourself requires you to be extraordinarily good at deceiving people or else your efforts will quickly end. Either case is a waste of the limited time you have.

Furthermore, acting in conflict with principles you believe in forces you to find some way to reconcile your actions. If you are like the vast majority of people in the world, you cannot comfortably live with a clash between principle and action. If you don't rectify the situation, you are stuck creating rationalizations and internal lies to maintain a façade of consistency. Involve a group of people, and the deception takes a lot of collective energy. Develop the reputation for acting unethically, and you might find it hard to get cooperation from others.

Some might argue that real perversions of the group goal concept have still been perceived by participants as goals greater than themselves. Talk to a white supremacist, for example, and you'll hear rationalization of how they fight for a principle. However, they don't. Their real motivations include fear and deep-seated insecurity. Any talk about some higher purpose is really self-delusion and rationalization to avoid facing any remnants of conscience they might have.

FACT

There are people who demonstrate no sense of conscience and actually experience almost no range of emotions. The technical term for these people is sociopath. Such persons are capable of doing anything without regret or concern because literally the only thing they care about is themselves.

Means and Ends

Someone who agrees that a greater principle is necessary could still argue that the issue wasn't about the motive force but the method used to attain the higher goal. That becomes an argument for the ends justifying the means.

The minute you operate by means that are incompatible with the principles you seek, you undermine those principles. The very action of trying to attain your goal with an incompatible approach damages it. It might look as though you still got what you wanted. But if you objectively examined what happened, you'd find that in some essential way, the results weren't what you had first envisioned. This is the process by which a group of people can insist that they want basic freedom but in reality deny it to other people.

Taking a Stand

In the famous tome *How to Read a Book*, Mortimer J. Adler and Charles Van Doren argued that when you read a practical volume, if you find yourself agreeing with an author's line of reasoning, then you have the obligation under intellectual honesty to undertake the advice from the author. To ignore the advice is to say that while you thought the writer had an interesting argument, you didn't find it compelling enough to change your mind and, through that, your actions.

Such logic applies to ethics and leadership. If you have convinced yourself of the need to support a set of principles and goals, to take action that would run counter to them should be unacceptable. So take a stand and don't be satisfied with activity that falls short. To maintain your devotion to your principles and to keep your action in accordance with them, you need to learn something about ethics and related concepts and then understand some practical considerations and techniques.

Morality, Ethics, and Legality

Society as a whole doesn't sit back and contemplate philosophical issues of morality and ethics, and legality often becomes nothing more than a series of arbitrary rules. But all three are important to our lives as human beings. Leadership should be part of your greater life, and so should happen in accordance with them. The first two concepts—morality and ethics—get tossed around and treated as virtually identical. They are closely related, but there are some subtle differences that can make a lot of difference.

Morality

Morality refers to the underlying codes of right and wrong, but those are such slippery words. One group says that a given activity or belief is evil and another says there is nothing wrong with it. A sect in a given religion might spend its energy considering one behavior and ignore many others that its own religious books describe as problems.

It is troublesome for someone to decide on a moral code that dismisses the existence or worth of others. It is also one of the best arguments to support objective morality. Even if you ignore the concepts of right and wrong, you can appreciate that certain types of behavior cause social strife.

The difficulty with morality is the concept of relativity. What do you do when people claim the mantle of morality when their focus is inconsistent and slanted toward their personal neuroses? The only practical choice is to find a subset of rules that promotes behavior that doesn't injure others. A great example is the Golden Rule. Regardless of whether you like the formulation of doing unto others as you'd have them do unto you, or the subtly different *not* doing unto others what you'd have them *not* do unto you, it is a simple and largely workable code.

Ethics

Ethics, on the other hand, is the study of the appropriateness of human action in light of morality. Often this will keep you out of the "how many angels dance on this pinhead" discussions and move from theory to practice. Interestingly, you quickly move from strictly philosophical or theological concepts and into issues that can even spill over from specific industries.

One such example is in the journalistic world. Reporters are forbidden from doing anything that would create the appearance of a conflict of interest. Another would be in certain provisions that keep government employees from immediately profiting from moving to the private sector by immediately lobbying their former colleagues. At one time in the United States, lawyers were prohibited from advertising their services, and the restriction was considered part of the profession's ethics.

FACT

A code of ethics can be inspired by morals or simply be the invention of some group. Whatever the case, it's a set of required and proscribed behaviors. In general, people within an organization, industry, or field of endeavor have more uniform codes of ethics than they do moral codes.

Legality

Law takes ethics and goes one step further. Instead of being satisfied with operating under a set of ethical guidelines, a body of laws suggests that society cannot always trust its citizens to act in an acceptable manner. To ensure compliance, people, through their representatives, agree to levy punishments that can run from fines and other sanctions to imprisonment. However, laws can quickly go beyond ethics as those who draft them try to ensure a whole range of behaviors for various reasons. Sometimes the law effectively duplicates others in existence or is a quick reaction by lawmakers to some perceived problem, even though the statute might do little or nothing when viewed objectively.

Working Ethically

As a leader, you may embrace a set of beliefs that your team members may or may not hold. If you disagree with something that people consider fundamental to their identities, you can quickly develop high degrees of enmity and antagonism to your goals. If that happens, you can largely forget about the chance of actually accomplishing anything.

Workable Concept

Instead of looking to morality, as a leader you should focus on ethics. In general, you'll find that people agree more readily on ethics than on underlying morality. The reason why is a mystery. Perhaps it is easier to accept a defined set of actions rather than argue the reasons for them. People are then free to fill in their own reasons and rationales. Whatever the reason, people are far more amenable to adopting ethical frameworks than moral ones.

Need for Ethics

The reasons your team needs to perform ethically are the flip-side of the problems that occur when it ignores ethical issues:

- Undercut principles you espouse, which hurts the organization
- Undermine goals, also hurting the organization
- Spend time and energy justifying actions, wasting resources
- Loss of trust from those whose help you need, making goals harder to reach
- What goes around comes around

Any of these problems can hurt your team's efforts and leave you further from your goals than ever. Short-sighted people may think that circumventing ethical boundaries gets them to their destination more quickly. However, the truth is that if you are trying to be a real leader, the ethical path is the only one that can actually bring you where you need to be.

Ethics Become Vital

In every business, in every position, everyone understands one common concept: the importance of acting in a professional manner.

There is no limit to the areas in which people act professionally, even if they are not in one of the traditionally licensed professions. Waiters, babysitters, corporate employees, nonprofit volunteers, and everyone who takes on responsibilities and duties can act professionally.

Think of your own life for a moment. Which plumber would you rather hire? Which taxi would you use? Which salesperson would you patronize? Doctor? Fundraiser? The answer is most likely the more professional one. When you are ethical—that is, professional—you create trust and confidence and make all manners of people want to cooperate and work with you. This comes right back to the definition and goal of leadership.

Determining Ethics

For whatever reason, people are more far more amenable to adopting ethical frameworks than moral ones, and a dearth of ethics can prevent your team from obtaining the goals it has in sight. To work ethically, though, you and your team members must agree on what that means. You have to determine what set of ethics you must apply.

Need for Standards

It's worthwhile to develop a set of ethical guidelines. Whether you generate them or there is some pre-existing set of rules in your organization or field doesn't matter. But if you have guidelines, then you can properly set expectations among the team members. There are a number of sources you can mine for suggestions:

- Interview those in your field
- Check if your organization has ethics guidelines
- Poll members of your team
- Ask appropriate academics
- Look at books on the subject

There are two approaches you can take. One is to develop an exhaustive list of rules that cover virtually any possible circumstance. But that sounds so . . . exhausting. Instead, use an approach similar to the one the European Union uses to handle many regulatory issues. Come up with governing principles and allow team members to use their judgment in making their actions compliant.

Setting Expectations

If you want people to be ethically compliant, you must make them aware of this. Many organizations go about this the wrong way. They include a note about ethics in an employee or volunteer handbook. In some speeches, executives might note how they greatly value ethical behavior. This is nothing more than window dressing, a hope to answer potential legal actions in the future—and it is completely inadequate.

Ethics are not morality, and sometimes the ethics that cover a given occupation or endeavor are not necessarily obvious. For example, why should it have been unethical at one point for lawyers to advertise? Clearly, they were going to find other ways to market because they needed to bring in business. If you were entering the legal profession at that time, someone would have had to tell you outright that advertising was forbidden.

You need to train your team in ethical behavior, just as you would need to train people in basic operational matters such as how to use intra-office mail. Schedule people in groups, go over the requirements, and create a discussion. Try some role-playing to help team members understand the potential pressures they'll face and the range of options they might perceive. The more people engage with the concepts, the deeper their understanding will run, and the more likely it is that they will choose an appropriate course of action when faced with a choice.

Era of Regulations

Today, laws govern a dizzying amount of life. Not only are there laws for most behaviors, there are laws for organizations of all types. Regulatory bodies oversee financial activities of virtually all companies. Complicated rules govern telecommunications, health care, and the exercise of legal, medical, and engineering professions. Nonprofits have varying requirements, depending on what they do. And you and your team need to understand any obligations you might have.

Range of Regulations

Public companies in the United States have been dealing with the legislation called the Sarbanes-Oxley Act for a number of years now. This body of law, a reaction to the corruption and legal infractions of Enron, World-Com, and others, places exacting demands on companies in regard to how they report their financial results. But Sarbanes-Oxley is just the sizeable tip of an enormous iceberg. There are regulations covering how to handle accounting issues, for maintaining privacy of financial and health information, for disposing of hazardous waste. There are national and state regulations and international requirements.

Regulatory Obligations

Trying to understand the regulations can be a challenge. For example, the U.S. Securities and Exchange Commission has issued regulations on how public companies must provide plain English explanations of executive compensation. That set of regulations alone runs some 500 pages of fairly impenetrable text. In this area, don't rely on good intentions or the explanations of informed laypersons alone. Talk to the organization's lawyers. You want a definitive answer on where danger lies for your team and exactly what you must do and what you must refrain from doing.

FACT

Some regulations, like Sarbanes-Oxley, affect only public companies. But there are some privately held corporations that try to implement the regulations, at least in part, because it can make it easier for them to become acquired by a public company.

Getting straight information is critical. Without it, you might find yourself, someone on your team, or another person in the organization facing investigation, questioning, fines, and even jail time.

Living by Example

Action is the strongest form of expression. When you are a leader, for better or worse, you are constantly talking to the team. They pay close attention to what you do because they want clues as to what they should do. Your actions, and your ethical behavior, become critical.

What You Request

There are understated situations in which your actions can actually request unethical activity, even if it is the last thing that would normally come to your mind. In 1170, four knights murdered Archbishop of Canterbury Thomas Beckett, purportedly because they heard King Henry II exclaim in a moment of extreme vexation with the cleric, "Will no one rid me of this turbulent priest?" He asked and duly received. Given the history between the two men, there are good grounds for assuming that Henry's request was not entirely unconscious, and yet you might see how an unplanned remark or action can lead to many others outside of your control.

To encourage ethical activity, you must become squeaky clean. That means you must consider everything you do in the following manner:

1. Does it advance a goal of the team or organization?
2. Is it acceptable under your ethical code and law?
3. If not acceptable, how will you modify it and keep it effective?

Know the team and organization ethics as well as all legal requirements. Do not advocate anything that would run counter to these, even if you are sure that no one outside the team would ever know. They don't have to know; you will.

Slips by the Team

There may be times that you will face actions that aren't in keeping with your ethical code or with the law. When that happens, you have to take action quickly and decisively. A response could be anything from a private discussion and additional training to dismissing someone from the team. You should take a few factors into account:

- Was the infraction willful and deliberate?
- Was there a strong perception that the action was ordered by someone in authority?
- Was the violation one of ethics or law?
- How serious was the incident?
- Can the team member learn and correct future behavior?

A mandatory draconian solution to problems may seem good until you realize how easily anyone could slip—even you. Better to have someone learn a painful lesson than to lose the person and face the possibility that someone else will have to face the same event.

If you find yourself in an ethical or legal lapse, the situation immediately becomes more serious because you need to be a role model.

Hopefully, you will never face such a crisis, but if so, better to resign your position and learn a lesson than to hang on and be a leader in name only.

If the problem lies with someone else in the organization or someone completely from the outside, decide whether there has been any real injury to anyone. If so, consider whether it was an aberration that deserves the mercy of human understanding or if it seems to be an ingrained pattern or a violation of law. If it is the latter, you must go to an appropriate authority. Support what is most important and help raise the hopes of people around you. When you are a leader, you are an example whether you like it or not.

APPENDIX A

Leadership Assessment Chart

As a leader, you should be interested in understanding your leadership style so that you can use this knowledge to become a more effective leader. The following quiz is designed to help gain some insight into your approach.

Overview

This assessment is designed to provide you with a personal profile of your leadership competencies, attitudes, and behaviors. Since leadership only becomes "good" or "bad" in its execution, this assessment should not be considered in that way.

Give yourself 4 points if you answer "Frequently," 2 points if you answer "Sometimes," and 0 points if you choose "Rarely or Never." Total your score when you finish to determine your leadership rating.

	Frequently	Sometimes	Rarely/Never

Section A ACTIVISM/CHANGE

	Frequently	Sometimes	Rarely/Never
1. When I sense that something is not right at work or in the community, I find a way to make it better.	O	O	O
2. I understand who in my organization can help me or my employer achieve our goals.	O	O	O
3. I have little tolerance when inertia overcomes a project or employee.	O	O	O
4. I respect the past and our company's legacy; however, I do not avoid rethinking "tradition."	O	O	O
5. I am committed to quality.	O	O	O
6. I am driven toward high performance.	O	O	O

	Frequently	Sometimes	Rarely/Never

Section B INTELLIGENCE/LEARNING

	Frequently	Sometimes	Rarely/Never
1. I believe that I have the mental capacity to think through most complex situations.	O	O	O
2. I welcome the challenge of complex issues and problems.	O	O	O
3. I am committed to creating an environment where mistakes become learning experiences.	O	O	O
4. I encourage my staff to disagree with me.	O	O	O
5. I tend to hire people who have talents, knowledge, and skills I don't possess.	O	O	O
6. I believe I am more intelligent than lucky.	O	O	O
7. I am not intimidated by ingenious people.	O	O	O
8. I like being around "smart" people.	O	O	O

	Frequently	Sometimes	Rarely/Never

Section C VISION

1. I look at things around me and I am able to envision how they can and will be better. ◯ ◯ ◯
2. I articulate abstract ideas to others quite easily. ◯ ◯ ◯
3. I have a picture of the future that I am committed to fulfilling. ◯ ◯ ◯
4. The vision I have for the organization incorporates what is strongest about the firm. ◯ ◯ ◯
5. I often utilize symbols and images to motivate my employees. ◯ ◯ ◯
6. I communicate and exemplify high standards of performance. ◯ ◯ ◯

	Frequently	Sometimes	Rarely/Never

Section D ALTRUISM/CARING

1. I generally respect my coworkers. ◯ ◯ ◯
2. I hold general conversations with my employees. ◯ ◯ ◯
3. I genuinely admire and appreciate the people who work with me. ◯ ◯ ◯
4. Knowing about my employees' values is important to me. ◯ ◯ ◯
5. Knowing about my employees' hobbies is important to me. ◯ ◯ ◯
6. I encourage employees to help each other develop to their full potential. ◯ ◯ ◯
7. I communicate often with employees about work. ◯ ◯ ◯
8. I communicate often with my employees about leisure activities. ◯ ◯ ◯
9. I provide personal attention to people who may need it. ◯ ◯ ◯

	Frequently	Sometimes	Rarely/Never

Section E COMMUNICATION

	Frequently	Sometimes	Rarely/Never
1. I am generous in my praise and recognition of my employees who perform quality work.	○	○	○
2. I seek the opinions of my employees.	○	○	○

	Frequently	Sometimes	Rarely/Never

Section F FLEXIBILITY

	Frequently	Sometimes	Rarely/Never
1. If plans go sour, I recover easily and without searching for a scapegoat.	○	○	○
2. I have a high tolerance for ambiguity.	○	○	○
3. When an employee has a "bright idea" I try to find a way to accommodate it.	○	○	○

	Frequently	Sometimes	Rarely/Never

Section G SPIRIT/SOUL

	Frequently	Sometimes	Rarely/Never
1. I have an inner sense of balance that allows me to move through the day with serenity.	○	○	○
2. I know how to relax.	○	○	○
3. I take the time to enjoy the nonwork component of my life.	○	○	○
4. I have an emerging leadership style that is truly my own.	○	○	○
5. I know how to "play."	○	○	○
6. I allow my employees to see and experience all facets of my personality.	○	○	○

	Frequently	Sometimes	Rarely/Never

Section H INTEGRITY/EGO STRENGTH

	Frequently	Sometimes	Rarely/Never
1. I do my own "dirty work."	O	O	O
2. I don't disappear when an employee is in trouble.	O	O	O
3. I don't ask anyone to do something I would not do.	O	O	O
4. If I had to choose I would treat employees better than bosses.	O	O	O
5. I admit or explain when I am wrong.	O	O	O
6. I can and do take the heat.	O	O	O
7. I consider myself a symbol of success	O	O	O
8. I am comfortable with who I am.	O	O	O

	Frequently	Sometimes	Rarely/Never

Section I CREATIVITY/INNOVATION

	Frequently	Sometimes	Rarely/Never
1. Ideas come readily to me.	O	O	O
2. I strive to have employees conceptualize old problems in new ways.	O	O	O
3. I provide new ways of looking at issues that may seem puzzling to employees.	O	O	O

	Frequently	Sometimes	Rarely/Never

Section J RELIABILITY

	Frequently	Sometimes	Rarely/Never
1. I ensure that my employees have the info and resources necessary to do the job.	O	O	O
2. If I say it is so, I make it so.	O	O	O
3. I don't avoid problems or sticky issues.	O	O	O
4. I make sure that there is congruence between what employees are asked to do and what they can expect from me in support of their efforts.	O	O	O

Scoring

Now add up your total score.

Frequently _____

Sometimes _____

Never _____

TOTAL _____

200+ You are well on your way to being a superior leader. The attributes and behaviors you exhibit tend to motivate, enrich, educate, and inspire others. When those abilities are matched with organizational knowledge and personal drive, they become the mettle for solid leadership.

150-199 You are working well toward the development of leadership savvy. By examining the various factors of the assessment, you can see where you need to focus your attention and possibly even reflect on your assumptions about work, the people who work with you, and why you want to be a leader. You may find from this exercise that you will learn how to stimulate more accountability and independence in others by showing more vulnerability within yourself.

110-149 The reasons for attaining the leadership positions you seek may be more self-centered than organizationally based. Trust is an essential component of leadership, and your score indicates that either you believe that the people you work with are not trustworthy or you doubt your own ability to lead effectively. In either case, you may be holding on too closely or not delegating at all. Consequently, those around you may not be confident of your support. Examine each area of this assessment and reflect on why you are so dedicated to "control" and what you really have to lose by guiding rather than forcing.

0-109 The attitudes, behaviors, and talents you are bringing to a position of leadership are unseasoned. You may be holding on to some archaic notions of "boss/subordinate" relationships, or have been too long under the influence of managers who do not, or a climate that does not value individuals' fundamental objective to do well and to be appreciated. Before you accept or seek a higher position of supervision, management, or leadership, you may want to pursue new mentoring relationships within the organization, take some management courses, read some of the newer writings on management, and consider objectively why you want to lead. The goal of leadership is not out of reach; you are just going to have to do a lot of homework to be effective.

Reflective Leadership Evaluation Tool

B

This evaluation will help you obtain feedback to get a better understanding of how effectively you lead. Give a copy of this chart to the people with whom you work to complete. The results will help you become aware of your weaker areas that you need to improve as well as strengths. Knowing both helps you create strategies to lead more effectively.

Although the chart can help indicate specific needs of other team members, getting candid feedback can be difficult, particularly if you are a manager in an organization and the people filling in the charts work for you. They may think their answers could affect their standing and their job. Such fear is common in corporations. In such a case, consider the option of having a trusted third party administer the assessment and then present the anonymous results to you. That improves the possibility that people will speak their minds.

Employee Leadership Evaluation Chart

Have each person rate each question with one of the following answers.

	Frequently	Sometimes	Rarely/Never

Part I COMMUNICATION

	Frequently	Sometimes	Rarely/Never
1. Do you feel that you are kept informed and are not "in the dark" about your job?	◯	◯	◯
a. Are you aware of priorities?	◯	◯	◯
b. Are you clear about expectations?	◯	◯	◯
c. Are you sure of responsibilities?	◯	◯	◯
d. Are you clear about time frame and deadlines?	◯	◯	◯
2. Do you feel that you receive adequate acknowledgement of and recognition for your contributions?	◯	◯	◯

	Frequently	Sometimes	Rarely/Never

Part II COACHING

	Frequently	Sometimes	Rarely/Never
1. When you are having difficulty with a task, do you receive:			
Support?	◯	◯	◯
Direction?	◯	◯	◯
Feedback?	◯	◯	◯
2. When you are given a new responsibility, do you receive:			
Support?	◯	◯	◯
Direction?	◯	◯	◯
Feedback?	◯	◯	◯
3. Are you involved in setting your own performance goals?	◯	◯	◯

	Frequently	Sometimes	Rarely/Never

Part III CONTINUOUS TRAINING

	Frequently	Sometimes	Rarely/Never
1. Do you feel that you have all the necessary skills and competencies to perform your job?	O	O	O
2. When you are given a new task or responsibility, do you receive adequate training?	O	O	O
3. Are you given opportunities to learn, grow, and develop to expand your career options?	O	O	O

	Frequently	Sometimes	Rarely/Never

Part IV CREATIVE PROBLEM SOLVING

	Frequently	Sometimes	Rarely/Never
1. Are you given opportunities to:			
Participate in decision making?	O	O	O
Provide solutions?	O	O	O
2. Are you involved in determining methods and procedures?	O	O	O
3. Do you experience a sense of power and control in your job?	O	O	O

	Frequently	Sometimes	Rarely/Never

Part V CHALLENGE FREQUENTLY

	Frequently	Sometimes	Rarely/Never
1. Do you associate feelings of achievement and satisfaction with your job?	O	O	O
2. Do you feel that your skills and talents are being used to their fullest?	O	O	O
3. Are you comfortable with your level of responsibility?	O	O	O

Scoring

Now add up the number of times you checked each category.

Frequently _____

Sometimes _____

Never _____

Count the number of answers in the Frequently category. If you scored between 23 and 28 on "Frequently," congratulate yourself; you're doing a great job in creating an environment that fosters motivation in employees. However, there is always room for improvement, so look at the areas where you didn't receive such a high rating.

If you scored between 11 and 22 on "Frequently," you're doing a good job but you need to focus on the questions in which you were marked "Sometimes" or "Rarely/Never," because they point to areas where you need to set goals and make changes in your behavior.

If you scored between 0 and 10 on "Frequently," you definitely need to change your leadership style. First, work on the areas where you received the "Rarely/Never" rating. Then, move on to the areas where you received the "Sometimes" rating and determine how you intend to implement these strategies on a more frequent basis.

Index

Standing organizations,
251–52
Status meeting, 218
Strunk, William, 71, 114
Styles of leadership, 15–30
combining models of,
20–23
matching to individual,
26–28
matching to organization,
28–30
matching to self, 24–26
matching to situation, 30
popular models of, 16–20
Suppliers, working with, 275
Synergy, vision and, 48–49

T

Teaching, learning and,
287–88
Team members
mistakes and, 237–38
motivation and, 105–7
taking stock of, 175–76
viewing as individuals,
101
vision and, 47, 58–60
Teams, 129–45
analysis of, 139–40
decision models for,
140–43
dynamics of, 135–37
education and, 284–86
ethics and, 299–300

fitting people into, 137–39
functional needs of,
130–33
impact of loss and
turnover on, 178–80
stages in development of,
143–45
types of, 133–35
Technology, meetings and,
220
Teleconferencing, 220
Tenacity, as personal trait, 41
Thinking, conflict and, 150
Time management
goals and, 89
meetings and, 214, 216
as organizational skill,
11–12
Training, change and, 206
Trait theory of leadership,
17–18. *See also* Personal
traits
Transformational leadership
model, 20
Transactional leadership
model, 19–20
Transactional process, of
motivation, 98–100
Trust, as personal trait, 41
Tuckman, Bruce, 143–45
Turnover. *See* Retention and
recognition

U

U.S. steel industry, 6

V

Van Doren, Charles, 291
Vision, 45–60
as communicated
direction, 50–52
hierarchy and, 55–58
meaning and, 46–47
motivation and, 100–101
nature of, 47–50
new leadership and,
225–26
as personal trait, 13,
36–39
process of, 52
questioning and, 52–55
teams and, 47, 58–60
Voltaire, 73
Volunteer, leading as, 249–62
benefits of, 250–51
in community, 7–8
dismissing other
volunteers, 261–62
leadership levels and,
256–57
officer and board
positions and, 257–60
organization types, 251–52
working with other
volunteers, 253–56,
260–61

THE EVERYTHING SERIES!

BUSINESS & PERSONAL FINANCE

Everything® Accounting Book
Everything® Budgeting Book, 2nd Ed.
Everything® Business Planning Book
Everything® Coaching and Mentoring Book, 2nd Ed.
Everything® Fundraising Book
Everything® Get Out of Debt Book
Everything® Grant Writing Book, 2nd Ed.
Everything® Guide to Buying Foreclosures
Everything® Guide to Mortgages
Everything® Guide to Personal Finance for Single Mothers
Everything® Home-Based Business Book, 2nd Ed.
Everything® Homebuying Book, 2nd Ed.
Everything® Homeselling Book, 2nd Ed.
Everything® Human Resource Management Book
Everything® Improve Your Credit Book
Everything® Investing Book, 2nd Ed.
Everything® Landlording Book
Everything® Leadership Book, 2nd Ed.
Everything® Managing People Book, 2nd Ed.
Everything® Negotiating Book
Everything® Online Auctions Book
Everything® Online Business Book
Everything® Personal Finance Book
Everything® Personal Finance in Your 20s & 30s Book, 2nd Ed.
Everything® Project Management Book, 2nd Ed.
Everything® Real Estate Investing Book
Everything® Retirement Planning Book
Everything® Robert's Rules Book, $7.95
Everything® Selling Book
Everything® Start Your Own Business Book, 2nd Ed.
Everything® Wills & Estate Planning Book

COOKING

Everything® Barbecue Cookbook
Everything® Bartender's Book, 2nd Ed., $9.95
Everything® Calorie Counting Cookbook
Everything® Cheese Book
Everything® Chinese Cookbook
Everything® Classic Recipes Book
Everything® Cocktail Parties & Drinks Book
Everything® College Cookbook
Everything® Cooking for Baby and Toddler Book
Everything® Cooking for Two Cookbook
Everything® Diabetes Cookbook
Everything® Easy Gourmet Cookbook
Everything® Fondue Cookbook
Everything® Fondue Party Book
Everything® Gluten-Free Cookbook
Everything® Glycemic Index Cookbook
Everything® Grilling Cookbook
Everything® Healthy Meals in Minutes Cookbook
Everything® Holiday Cookbook
Everything® Indian Cookbook
Everything® Italian Cookbook

Everything® Lactose-Free Cookbook
Everything® Low-Carb Cookbook
Everything® Low-Cholesterol Cookbook
Everything® Low-Fat High-Flavor Cookbook
Everything® Low-Salt Cookbook
Everything® Meals for a Month Cookbook
Everything® Meals on a Budget Cookbook
Everything® Mediterranean Cookbook
Everything® Mexican Cookbook
Everything® No Trans Fat Cookbook
Everything® One-Pot Cookbook
Everything® Pizza Cookbook
Everything® Quick and Easy 30-Minute,
    5-Ingredient Cookbook
Everything® Quick Meals Cookbook
Everything® Slow Cooker Cookbook
Everything® Slow Cooking for a Crowd Cookbook
Everything® Soup Cookbook
Everything® Stir-Fry Cookbook
Everything® Sugar-Free Cookbook
Everything® Tapas and Small Plates Cookbook
Everything® Tex-Mex Cookbook
Everything® Thai Cookbook
Everything® Vegetarian Cookbook
Everything® Whole-Grain, High-Fiber Cookbook
Everything® Wild Game Cookbook
Everything® Wine Book, 2nd Ed.

GAMES

Everything® 15-Minute Sudoku Book, $9.95
Everything® 30-Minute Sudoku Book, $9.95
Everything® Bible Crosswords Book, $9.95
Everything® Blackjack Strategy Book
Everything® Brain Strain Book, $9.95
Everything® Bridge Book
Everything® Card Games Book
Everything® Card Tricks Book, $9.95
Everything® Casino Gambling Book, 2nd Ed.
Everything® Chess Basics Book
Everything® Craps Strategy Book
Everything® Crossword and Puzzle Book
Everything® Crossword Challenge Book
Everything® Crosswords for the Beach Book, $9.95
Everything® Cryptic Crosswords Book, $9.95
Everything® Cryptograms Book, $9.95
Everything® Easy Crosswords Book
Everything® Easy Kakuro Book, $9.95
Everything® Easy Large-Print Crosswords Book
Everything® Games Book, 2nd Ed.
Everything® Giant Sudoku Book, $9.95
Everything® Giant Word Search Book
Everything® Kakuro Challenge Book, $9.95
Everything® Large-Print Crossword Challenge Book
Everything® Large-Print Crosswords Book
Everything® Lateral Thinking Puzzles Book, $9.95
Everything® Literary Crosswords Book, $9.95
Everything® Mazes Book
Everything® Memory Booster Puzzles Book, $9.95
Everything® Movie Crosswords Book, $9.95

Everything® Music Crosswords Book, $9.95
Everything® Online Poker Book
Everything® Pencil Puzzles Book, $9.95
Everything® Poker Strategy Book
Everything® Pool & Billiards Book
Everything® Puzzles for Commuters Book, $9.95
Everything® Puzzles for Dog Lovers Book, $9.95
Everything® Sports Crosswords Book, $9.95
Everything® Test Your IQ Book, $9.95
Everything® Texas Hold 'Em Book, $9.95
Everything® Travel Crosswords Book, $9.95
Everything® TV Crosswords Book, $9.95
Everything® Word Games Challenge Book
Everything® Word Scramble Book
Everything® Word Search Book

HEALTH

Everything® Alzheimer's Book
Everything® Diabetes Book
Everything® First Aid Book, $9.95
Everything® Health Guide to Adult Bipolar Disorder
Everything® Health Guide to Arthritis
Everything® Health Guide to Controlling Anxiety
Everything® Health Guide to Depression
Everything® Health Guide to Fibromyalgia
Everything® Health Guide to Menopause, 2nd Ed.
Everything® Health Guide to Migraines
Everything® Health Guide to OCD
Everything® Health Guide to PMS
Everything® Health Guide to Postpartum Care
Everything® Health Guide to Thyroid Disease
Everything® Hypnosis Book
Everything® Low Cholesterol Book
Everything® Menopause Book
Everything® Nutrition Book
Everything® Reflexology Book
Everything® Stress Management Book

HISTORY

Everything® American Government Book
Everything® American History Book, 2nd Ed.
Everything® Civil War Book
Everything® Freemasons Book
Everything® Irish History & Heritage Book
Everything® Middle East Book
Everything® World War II Book, 2nd Ed.

HOBBIES

Everything® Candlemaking Book
Everything® Cartooning Book
Everything® Coin Collecting Book
Everything® Digital Photography Book, 2nd Ed.
Everything® Drawing Book
Everything® Family Tree Book, 2nd Ed.
Everything® Knitting Book
Everything® Knots Book
Everything® Photography Book
Everything® Quilting Book

Everything® Sewing Book
Everything® Soapmaking Book, 2nd Ed.
Everything® Woodworking Book

HOME IMPROVEMENT

Everything® Feng Shui Book
Everything® Feng Shui Decluttering Book, $9.95
Everything® Fix-It Book
Everything® Green Living Book
Everything® Home Decorating Book
Everything® Home Storage Solutions Book
Everything® Homebuilding Book
Everything® Organize Your Home Book, 2nd Ed.

KIDS' BOOKS

All titles are $7.95
Everything® Fairy Tales Book, $14.95
Everything® Kids' Animal Puzzle & Activity Book
Everything® Kids' Astronomy Book
Everything® Kids' Baseball Book, 5th Ed.
Everything® Kids' Bible Trivia Book
Everything® Kids' Bugs Book
Everything® Kids' Cars and Trucks Puzzle and Activity Book
Everything® Kids' Christmas Puzzle & Activity Book
**Everything® Kids' Connect the Dots
          Puzzle and Activity Book**
Everything® Kids' Cookbook
Everything® Kids' Crazy Puzzles Book
Everything® Kids' Dinosaurs Book
Everything® Kids' Environment Book
Everything® Kids' Fairies Puzzle and Activity Book
Everything® Kids' First Spanish Puzzle and Activity Book
Everything® Kids' Football Book
Everything® Kids' Gross Cookbook
Everything® Kids' Gross Hidden Pictures Book
Everything® Kids' Gross Jokes Book
Everything® Kids' Gross Mazes Book
Everything® Kids' Gross Puzzle & Activity Book
Everything® Kids' Halloween Puzzle & Activity Book
Everything® Kids' Hidden Pictures Book
Everything® Kids' Horses Book
Everything® Kids' Joke Book
Everything® Kids' Knock Knock Book
Everything® Kids' Learning French Book
Everything® Kids' Learning Spanish Book
Everything® Kids' Magical Science Experiments Book
Everything® Kids' Math Puzzles Book
Everything® Kids' Mazes Book
Everything® Kids' Money Book
Everything® Kids' Nature Book
Everything® Kids' Pirates Puzzle and Activity Book
Everything® Kids' Presidents Book
Everything® Kids' Princess Puzzle and Activity Book
Everything® Kids' Puzzle Book
Everything® Kids' Racecars Puzzle and Activity Book
Everything® Kids' Riddles & Brain Teasers Book
Everything® Kids' Science Experiments Book
Everything® Kids' Sharks Book
Everything® Kids' Soccer Book
Everything® Kids' Spies Puzzle and Activity Book
Everything® Kids' States Book
Everything® Kids' Travel Activity Book
Everything® Kids' Word Search Puzzle and Activity Book

LANGUAGE

Everything® Conversational Japanese Book with CD, $19.95
Everything® French Grammar Book
Everything® French Phrase Book, $9.95
Everything® French Verb Book, $9.95
Everything® German Practice Book with CD, $19.95
Everything® Inglés Book
Everything® Intermediate Spanish Book with CD, $19.95
Everything® Italian Practice Book with CD, $19.95
Everything® Learning Brazilian Portuguese Book with CD,
          $19.95
Everything® Learning French Book with CD, 2nd Ed., $19.95
Everything® Learning German Book
Everything® Learning Italian Book
Everything® Learning Latin Book
Everything® Learning Russian Book with CD, $19.95
Everything® Learning Spanish Book
Everything® Learning Spanish Book with CD, 2nd Ed., $19.95
Everything® Russian Practice Book with CD, $19.95
Everything® Sign Language Book
Everything® Spanish Grammar Book
Everything® Spanish Phrase Book, $9.95
Everything® Spanish Practice Book with CD, $19.95
Everything® Spanish Verb Book, $9.95
Everything® Speaking Mandarin Chinese Book with CD, $19.95

MUSIC

Everything® Bass Guitar Book with CD, $19.95
Everything® Drums Book with CD, $19.95
Everything® Guitar Book with CD, 2nd Ed., $19.95
Everything® Guitar Chords Book with CD, $19.95
Everything® Harmonica Book with CD, $15.95
Everything® Home Recording Book
Everything® Music Theory Book with CD, $19.95
Everything® Reading Music Book with CD, $19.95
Everything® Rock & Blues Guitar Book with CD, $19.95
Everything® Rock & Blues Piano Book with CD, $19.95
Everything® Songwriting Book

NEW AGE

Everything® Astrology Book, 2nd Ed.
Everything® Birthday Personology Book
Everything® Dreams Book, 2nd Ed.
Everything® Love Signs Book, $9.95
Everything® Love Spells Book, $9.95
Everything® Paganism Book
Everything® Palmistry Book
Everything® Psychic Book
Everything® Reiki Book
Everything® Sex Signs Book, $9.95
Everything® Spells & Charms Book, 2nd Ed.
Everything® Tarot Book, 2nd Ed.
Everything® Toltec Wisdom Book
Everything® Wicca & Witchcraft Book, 2nd Ed.

PARENTING

Everything® Baby Names Book, 2nd Ed.
Everything® Baby Shower Book, 2nd Ed.
Everything® Baby Sign Language Book with DVD
Everything® Baby's First Year Book
Everything® Birthing Book

Everything® Breastfeeding Book
Everything® Father-to-Be Book
Everything® Father's First Year Book
Everything® Get Ready for Baby Book, 2nd Ed.
Everything® Get Your Baby to Sleep Book, $9.95
Everything® Getting Pregnant Book
Everything® Guide to Pregnancy Over 35
Everything® Guide to Raising a One-Year-Old
Everything® Guide to Raising a Two-Year-Old
Everything® Guide to Raising Adolescent Boys
Everything® Guide to Raising Adolescent Girls
Everything® Mother's First Year Book
Everything® Parent's Guide to Childhood Illnesses
Everything® Parent's Guide to Children and Divorce
Everything® Parent's Guide to Children with ADD/ADHD
Everything® Parent's Guide to Children with Asperger's
          Syndrome
Everything® Parent's Guide to Children with Asthma
Everything® Parent's Guide to Children with Autism
Everything® Parent's Guide to Children with Bipolar Disorder
Everything® Parent's Guide to Children with Depression
Everything® Parent's Guide to Children with Dyslexia
Everything® Parent's Guide to Children with Juvenile Diabetes
Everything® Parent's Guide to Positive Discipline
Everything® Parent's Guide to Raising a Successful Child
Everything® Parent's Guide to Raising Boys
Everything® Parent's Guide to Raising Girls
Everything® Parent's Guide to Raising Siblings
Everything® Parent's Guide to Sensory Integration Disorder
Everything® Parent's Guide to Tantrums
Everything® Parent's Guide to the Strong-Willed Child
Everything® Parenting a Teenager Book
Everything® Potty Training Book, $9.95
Everything® Pregnancy Book, 3rd Ed.
Everything® Pregnancy Fitness Book
Everything® Pregnancy Nutrition Book
Everything® Pregnancy Organizer, 2nd Ed., $16.95
Everything® Toddler Activities Book
Everything® Toddler Book
Everything® Tween Book
Everything® Twins, Triplets, and More Book

PETS

Everything® Aquarium Book
Everything® Boxer Book
Everything® Cat Book, 2nd Ed.
Everything® Chihuahua Book
Everything® Cooking for Dogs Book
Everything® Dachshund Book
Everything® Dog Book, 2nd Ed.
Everything® Dog Grooming Book
Everything® Dog Health Book
Everything® Dog Obedience Book
Everything® Dog Owner's Organizer, $16.95
Everything® Dog Training and Tricks Book
Everything® German Shepherd Book
Everything® Golden Retriever Book
Everything® Horse Book
Everything® Horse Care Book
Everything® Horseback Riding Book
Everything® Labrador Retriever Book
Everything® Poodle Book
Everything® Pug Book

Everything® Puppy Book
Everything® Rottweiler Book
Everything® Small Dogs Book
Everything® Tropical Fish Book
Everything® Yorkshire Terrier Book

REFERENCE

Everything® American Presidents Book
Everything® Blogging Book
Everything® Build Your Vocabulary Book, $9.95
Everything® Car Care Book
Everything® Classical Mythology Book
Everything® Da Vinci Book
Everything® Divorce Book
Everything® Einstein Book
Everything® Enneagram Book
Everything® Etiquette Book, 2nd Ed.
Everything® Guide to C. S. Lewis & Narnia
Everything® Guide to Edgar Allan Poe
Everything® Guide to Understanding Philosophy
Everything® Inventions and Patents Book
Everything® Jacqueline Kennedy Onassis Book
Everything® John F. Kennedy Book
Everything® Mafia Book
Everything® Martin Luther King Jr. Book
Everything® Philosophy Book
Everything® Pirates Book
Everything® Private Investigation Book
Everything® Psychology Book
Everything® Public Speaking Book, $9.95
Everything® Shakespeare Book, 2nd Ed.

RELIGION

Everything® Angels Book
Everything® Bible Book
Everything® Bible Study Book with CD, $19.95
Everything® Buddhism Book
Everything® Catholicism Book
Everything® Christianity Book
Everything® Gnostic Gospels Book
Everything® History of the Bible Book
Everything® Jesus Book
Everything® Jewish History & Heritage Book
Everything® Judaism Book
Everything® Kabbalah Book
Everything® Koran Book
Everything® Mary Book
Everything® Mary Magdalene Book
Everything® Prayer Book
Everything® Saints Book, 2nd Ed.
Everything® Torah Book
Everything® Understanding Islam Book
Everything® Women of the Bible Book
Everything® World's Religions Book

SCHOOL & CAREERS

Everything® Career Tests Book
Everything® College Major Test Book
Everything® College Survival Book, 2nd Ed.
Everything® Cover Letter Book, 2nd Ed.
Everything® Filmmaking Book
Everything® Get-a-Job Book, 2nd Ed.
Everything® Guide to Being a Paralegal
Everything® Guide to Being a Personal Trainer
Everything® Guide to Being a Real Estate Agent
Everything® Guide to Being a Sales Rep
Everything® Guide to Being an Event Planner
Everything® Guide to Careers in Health Care
Everything® Guide to Careers in Law Enforcement
Everything® Guide to Government Jobs
Everything® Guide to Starting and Running a Catering
    Business
Everything® Guide to Starting and Running a Restaurant
Everything® Job Interview Book, 2nd Ed.
Everything® New Nurse Book
Everything® New Teacher Book
Everything® Paying for College Book
Everything® Practice Interview Book
Everything® Resume Book, 3rd Ed.
Everything® Study Book

SELF-HELP

Everything® Body Language Book
Everything® Dating Book, 2nd Ed.
Everything® Great Sex Book
Everything® Self-Esteem Book
Everything® Tantric Sex Book

SPORTS & FITNESS

Everything® Easy Fitness Book
Everything® Fishing Book
Everything® Krav Maga for Fitness Book
Everything® Running Book, 2nd Ed.

TRAVEL

Everything® Family Guide to Coastal Florida
Everything® Family Guide to Cruise Vacations
Everything® Family Guide to Hawaii
Everything® Family Guide to Las Vegas, 2nd Ed.
Everything® Family Guide to Mexico
Everything® Family Guide to New England, 2nd Ed.
Everything® Family Guide to New York City, 3rd Ed.
Everything® Family Guide to RV Travel & Campgrounds
Everything® Family Guide to the Caribbean
Everything® Family Guide to the Disneyland® Resort, California
    Adventure®, Universal Studios®, and the Anaheim
    Area, 2nd Ed.
Everything® Family Guide to the Walt Disney World Resort®,
    Universal Studios®, and Greater Orlando, 5th Ed.
Everything® Family Guide to Timeshares
Everything® Family Guide to Washington D.C., 2nd Ed.

WEDDINGS

Everything® Bachelorette Party Book, $9.95
Everything® Bridesmaid Book, $9.95
Everything® Destination Wedding Book
Everything® Father of the Bride Book, $9.95
Everything® Groom Book, $9.95
Everything® Mother of the Bride Book, $9.95
Everything® Outdoor Wedding Book
Everything® Wedding Book, 3rd Ed.
Everything® Wedding Checklist, $9.95
Everything® Wedding Etiquette Book, $9.95
Everything® Wedding Organizer, 2nd Ed., $16.95
Everything® Wedding Shower Book, $9.95
Everything® Wedding Vows Book, $9.95
Everything® Wedding Workout Book
Everything® Weddings on a Budget Book, 2nd Ed., $9.95

WRITING

Everything® Creative Writing Book
Everything® Get Published Book, 2nd Ed.
Everything® Grammar and Style Book, 2nd Ed.
Everything® Guide to Magazine Writing
Everything® Guide to Writing a Book Proposal
Everything® Guide to Writing a Novel
Everything® Guide to Writing Children's Books
Everything® Guide to Writing Copy
Everything® Guide to Writing Graphic Novels
Everything® Guide to Writing Research Papers
Everything® Improve Your Writing Book, 2nd Ed.
Everything® Writing Poetry Book

Available wherever books are sold! To order, call 800-258-0929, or visit us at *www.adamsmedia.com*.
Everything® and everything.com® are registered trademarks of F+W Publications, Inc.
Bolded titles are new additions to the series.
All Everything® books are priced at $12.95 or $14.95, unless otherwise stated. Prices subject to change without notice.